More pre-publication
REVIEWS, COMMENTARIES, EVALUATIONS . . .

"This pathbreaking book effectively combines data from the scholarly literature with the work experience of an employee involved in Antarctic tourism. This scientific-pragmatic blend is unique, and provides a solid and useful evaluation of the physical and social impacts induced by seasonal visitors to the lonely continent.

The book clearly belongs in every public as well as university library as a primary resource on land-use of this little-known seventh continent because many of the cited scholarly sources are not readily accessible except in specialized research libraries. The volume is also suitable for the travel-trade market, and should be placed shipboard in libraries and gift shops for the visitors in years to come. The author correctly recognizes that a visit to Antarctica often becomes an educational experience that awakens in tourists a latent ecological awareness, making them advocates of sustainability. The text explains and supports this view.

Bauer is to be commended for his focus on the remote and physically challenging continent, truly the last frontier on earth. Antarctica is certain to host vastly increased numbers of future tourists as Asian economies rebound and Asian tourists extend the expanding cruise activity into adventure cruising in Antarctica."

Valene L. Smith, PhD
Research Professor
of Anthropology,
California State University,
Chico

Tourism in the Antarctic
Opportunities, Constraints, and Future Prospects

Tourism
in the Antarctic
Opportunities, Constraints, and Future Prospects

Thomas G. Bauer, PhD

The Haworth Hospitality Press®
An Imprint of The Haworth Press, Inc.
New York • London • Oxford

Published by

The Haworth Hospitality Press®, an imprint of The Haworth Press, Inc., 10 Alice Street, Binghamton, NY 13904-1580.

Cover design by Jennifer M. Gaska.

Library of Congress Cataloging-in-Publication Data

Bauer, Thomas G.
   Tourism in the Antarctic : opportunities, constraints, and future prospects / Thomas G. Bauer.
     p. cm.
   Includes bibliographical references (p.) and index.
   ISBN 0-7890-1103-4 (hard : alk. paper) — ISBN 0-7890-1104-2 (soft : alk. paper)
   1. Tourism—Antarctica. I. Title.
G155.A54 B38 2000
338.4'79198904—dc21
                                    00-057572

CONTENTS

ABOUT THE AUTHOR

Thomas G. Bauer, PhD, is Assistant Professor in the Department of Hotel and Tourism Management, The Hong Kong Polytechnic University, Hong Kong S.A.R., China. Dr. Bauer has been involved in the hotel and tourism industry since 1971. He has traveled on all continents and has worked in Germany, Australia, the United States, and Hong Kong. He has participated in eight cruises to the Antarctic Peninsula, the sub-Antarctic islands, and the Ross Sea, and has been aboard two overflights of the Antarctic. He is the co-producer and photographer of the *Voyage to Antarctica* CD-ROM and video productions. Dr. Bauer is one of the world's leading experts on Antarctic tourism.

From 1989 to 1999, Dr. Bauer lectured in a variety of tourism subjects at Victoria University in Melbourne, Australia. His achievements earned him an entry into the 1999 *Who's Who in the World.*

Foreword

That tourists can visit Antarctica as easily as India or Patagonia is surprising to many people. For older generations, brought up on stories of Amundsen, Scott, Shackleton, and Byrd, Antarctica remains a continent of hardship and heroes. For a younger generation of scientists it is a laboratory; for diplomats and bureaucrats a proving ground for an international treaty. Who needs Antarctic tourists?

As the author of this book points out, Antarctica is an unusual continent. The tourists who visit are not everyday vacationers. Thomas Cook and others, who, as early as the 1920s, first identified the continent as a venue for tourism, offered cruises but found no takers. The first to make tourism a success was Lars-Eric Lindblad, a Swedish-American entrepreneur who in the 1950s and 1960s specialized in taking small parties of intelligent, wealthy folks to unusual, out-of-the-way places. Chaperoning them with knowledgeable guides, and wielding a strong conservation ethic, Lindblad's pattern worked well for Antarctica. His ten- to fourteen-day cruises to the continent from South America, Australia, and New Zealand proved expensive but popular among those who could afford them. Other tour operators competed and gradually moved down-market: cruises became cheaper, shorter, and more plentiful. Slowly but surely, word got around that the far south is an enchanting, ice-covered world, populated by penguins, seals, and scientists—well worth anyone's time and money to visit.

Equally certain, it was no place for sun worshippers, even less for lager-louts and roustabouts. Antarctica is a cold world, with uncertain and often foul weather. There are more comfortable places to swim, surf, lie in the sun, or get drunk and raise hell. Nor is it right for those who seek sophistication: there are no restaurants, theaters, or art galleries, few museums, and sites of historical interest are thin on the ground.

So what attracts tourists? Scenery, wildlife, and a curious sense of remoteness that tens of thousands of visitors may never have known existed—until they came to Antarctica to enjoy it. On cruise ships in the past few years, I have met thousands of tourists, some on their third and fourth visits. I have yet to meet one who did not find a visit to Antarctica an important and enjoyable event in their lives.

From small beginnings, over four decades, has grown a substantial tourist industry. It is still mainly shipborne, but includes an increasing component of adventure activities ashore, and the recent redevelopment of overflights. This book charts the course, development, and management of Antarctic tourism, and spells out what the author sees as its future. Thomas Bauer, an Australian academic with a background in tourism research, joined forces several years ago with my own Cambridge-based Antarctic study group, to our mutual benefit. His hands-on involvement with the industry and encyclopedic knowledge of its workings are clearly demonstrated in this first-ever major review, covering the past, present, and future of Antarctic tourism.

Dr. Bernard Stonehouse
Polar Ecology and Management Group
Scott Polar Research Institute
University of Cambridge
Cambridge, UK

Acknowledgments

The writing of this book and the PhD dissertation on which it is based was largely a solitary exercise during which the writer faced the screen of the word processor and the loneliness of libraries with millions of books, of which only some are of use for the task at hand. Nevertheless, as in any journey, the hardest part is getting started, and once under way many a helping hand was extended to the weary writer.

I would like to express my great appreciation to the following people and organizations, without whose help this book would not have been completed. My family, Lina, Joey, and Sebastian, for putting up with my endless hours in front of the PC and my many months overseas while conducting research for this work and for giving me the support I needed to carry on with the task. My former colleagues at Victoria University of Technology in Melbourne, in particular Professor Ian Priestly, Associate Professor Leo Jago, Professor Brian King, Dr. Robert Waryszak, Paul Whitelaw, Deidre Giblin, Ari Gamage, and Bronwyn Higgs. Dr. John Heap, Bob Headland, William Mills, Janice Meadows, Dr. Bernard Stonehouse, and Debra Enzenbacher at the Scott Polar Research Institute at the University of Cambridge, where I was privileged to spend several months accessing the world's best polar library. The respondents to my Delphi study for taking the time and interest in responding to my requests for information. The chief librarian, Evelyn Barrett, at the Australian Antarctic Division in Kingston, Tasmania. Staff members at the New Zealand Antarctic Program in Christchurch and Maria Luisa Carvallo at the Instituto Antartico Chileno in Santiago, Chile. Staff at INFUETUR in Ushuaia for providing useful information on visitor movements from Ushuaia to Antarctica. Quark Expeditions, in particular Lars Wikander, for allowing me to travel aboard their cruise ships in Antarctica and to survey passengers. Phil Asker at Croydon Travel for providing me with the opportunity to see Antarctica from above and to survey passengers at the same time. A very big thank you to my supervisors, Associate Professors David Mercer and Jim Peterson in the Department of Geography and Environmental Science at Monash University, for their encouragement and guidance in the preparation of this work. A thank you also to my colleagues in the Department of Hotel and Tourism Management at the Hong Kong Polytechnic University.

Abbreviations and Acronyms

AAD	Australian Antarctic Division
AAT	Australian Antarctic Territory
ACF	Australian Conservation Foundation
ANARE	Australian National Antarctic Research Expeditions
ANI	Adventure Network International
ASOC	Antarctic and Southern Ocean Coalition
ATCM	Antarctic Treaty Consultative Meeting
ATCP	Antarctic Treaty Consultative Party
ATP	Antarctic Treaty Party
ATS	Antarctic Treaty System
BANZARE	British, Australian and New Zealand Antarctic Expedition
BAS	British Antarctic Survey
CCAMLR	Convention on the Conservation of Antarctic Marine Living Resources
CCAS	Convention for the Conservation of Antarctic Seals
CEE	Comprehensive Environmental Evaluation
COMNAP	Council of Managers of National Antarctic Programs
CRAMRA	Convention on the Regulation of Antarctic Mineral Resource Activities

EIS	Environmental Impact Statement
FIT	Free and Independent Tourist
GMMS	Greg Mortimer Mountain Services
IAATO	International Association of Antarctica Tour Operators
IEE	Initial Environmental Evaluation
IGY	International Geophysical Year
INFUETUR	Instituto Fueguino de Turismo
ITB	International Tourism Exchange (Berlin)
IUCN	International Union for Conservation of Nature and Natural Resources (World Conservation Union)
NSF	National Science Foundation (United States)
SPA	Specially Protected Area (now ASPA)
SPRI	Scott Polar Research Institute (UK)
SSSI	Site of Special Scientific Interest (now ASPA)
SSTI	Site of Special Tourist Interest
USARP	United States Antarctic Research Program (also USAP)
WTO	World Tourism Organization
WTTC	World Travel and Tourism Council

Chapter 1

Introduction

Antarctica is the least-visited continent. Until about 1820, no human had seen it and it is doubtful whether anyone landed on it before 1894 or spent a winter ashore before 1899 (Stonehouse 1994:195). Today parts of the continent and several of its offshore islands provide the settings for scientific studies and for some of the world's most remote tourism operations. Between mid-November and early March, when ice conditions are less severe, the region is visited regularly by tourists aboard cruise vessels. Airline passengers view the scenery through the windows of airplanes, which overfly parts of the continent. During the 1990s, the number of voyages increased as tour operators responded to a growing demand for Antarctic tourism.

Opinions with regard to the conduct of tourism and its legitimacy in Antarctica are diverse. In Recommendation VIII-9/1975 the Antarctic Treaty Parties acknowledge that "tourism is a natural development in this Area and that it requires regulation" (Heap 1990:2602). Environmental organizations such as the Antarctic and Southern Ocean Coalition (ASOC) have called for the establishment of Antarctica as a "world park" that would allow controlled tourism activities. In contrast, in Australia the Wilderness Society and the Australian Conservation Foundation (ACF) have policies that would prohibit any tourism from taking place in Antarctica (ACF 1990:3). In a debate with the author (Bauer and Diggins 1994:35), Diggins (writing for the ACF) raised the rather philosophical question of whether humans have the right to travel to all parts of the globe just because it is technically feasible.

Acknowledging that tourism is already well established in Antarctica and that parts of the Antarctic ecosystem may be relatively sensitive to disturbance by tourism activities, this book examines the status and sustainability of commercial tourism operations by investigating current and future trends, opportunities, and constraints.

At the beginning of the new millenium, tourism and its associated social, economic, and environmental impacts are increasingly felt around the globe. During the 1990s the tourism industry developed into one of the world's largest service-based industries. Results produced by the World Tourism Organization (WTO 2000) show that international tourism revenues in 1999 amounted to US$455 billion (excluding airfares).

Technological breakthroughs such as the development of the jet engine during the Second World War and its subsequent incorporation into passenger airliners have had major impacts on the travel behavior and patterns of millions of people. As Smith and Eadington (1992:5) put it: "The first passenger jet service in 1958 is credited with inaugurating modern mass- and charter-tourism, with all its attendant problems of overcrowding and pollution." Since those early days of jet travel, aircraft capacity has increased from 110 passengers aboard a Boeing 707 to over 400 passengers in wide-bodied, long-haul aircraft such as the Boeing 747-400 series. Larger jets such as the Boeing 747-500 or the Airbus A3XX, with a capacity of 500 to 550 passengers, are scheduled for introduction in 2003 (Falvey 1996). Even larger jets, carrying up to 800 passengers, are also on the drawing boards of companies such as Boeing and Airbus Industries. This increase in aircraft capacity, combined with a relative decrease in the cost of air travel and an increase in disposable time and income, have enabled more people than ever before to visit faraway places that had previously been out of their reach. For 1999, the WTO reported 663 million international visitor arrivals (WTO 2000). By comparison, international arrivals in the past were: 1950, 25.3 million; 1960, 69.3 million; 1970, 158.7 million; 1980, 204.8 million; and 1990, 425 million (in addition to hundreds of millions of domestic tourists). In 1998, for example, the most visited country in the world was France, with 70 million international visitor arrivals. By contrast, the tiny island of Kiribati in the South Pacific only received a few thousand international guests.

A visit to tourism industry trade fairs such as World Travel Mart in London or the International Tourism Exchange (ITB), held annually in Berlin, reveals that there are very few countries now that are not involved in international tourism in one form or another. For many, tourism has become an important form of economic development. For better or for worse, nations as far apart and as diverse as Spain, Germany, Costa Rica, Kenya, Fiji, Peru, China, Thailand, India, Australia, and Nepal, to name but a few, are operating in the international marketplace to attract their share of the huge volume of tourism activities. Global tourism continues to expand—the 1999 figure of 663 million international arrivals pales in comparison with the WTO's (2000) forecast of 1.56 billion arrivals by 2020. Poon (1994:91) points out that, coinciding with this growth, "consumers are growing more sophisticated and demanding, have greater environmental awareness and are getting tired of the mass tourism products." She adds that "they are looking for something different and new which often involves natural and authentic experiences" (1994:92). In response to this trend tour operators and tour wholesalers, the developers, organizers, and packagers of travel products, are constantly searching the globe for new, "undiscovered," exciting and unspoiled destinations to satisfy the demands of their clients.

Simultaneously, with the increase in sophistication of the traveling public, the 1980s and 1990s saw a substantial increase in environmental awareness and consciousness among the people of the developed countries. In practical terms this increase in environmental consciousness is, for example, reflected in the many glass, plastic, and newspaper recycling programs that operate in countries such as Australia, Germany, and the United States and in television advertisements which encourage consumers to conserve water and electricity. Environmentally friendly or "green" measures practiced in everyday life by an increasing number of people have also led to an increase in popularity, among the more experienced and sophisticated travelers, of tourist destinations that can offer them a relatively unspoiled and unpolluted environment.

"Sustainability" became one of the catchwords of the 1990s. To maintain (or in some cases to rebuild) their natural and social resources, and hence their competitive edge, tourist destinations have been forced to search for types of tourism developments that have the least negative impacts on the social and natural environments. These "new" more environmentally friendly forms of tourism may in the beginning only generate relatively small numbers of international tourists when compared to "mass tourism." Environmentally and socially conscious tourists have, however, been associated with higher socioeconomic standing and are therefore said to be bigger spenders than their mass-tourism counterparts. In the long term, it is hoped that a "cleaner and greener" image of a tourist destination will therefore also benefit the mass-tourism product of a country or region. Appropriately managed, relatively small-scale, environmentally and socially sensitive tourism can be seen as a form of economic development that offers, in particular, geographically remote, relatively pristine, little-visited and economically underdeveloped regions such as Greenland, Svalbard, Nunavut, Nepal, Tibet, Tierra del Fuego, and the Galapagos Islands the best opportunity for a long-term economically and environmentally sustainable tourism future. In this context, it also holds promise for the southernmost part of the planet, the Antarctic region, the subject of this book.

TOURISM AND THE ENVIRONMENT

Prior to analyzing tourism in Antarctica, it is necessary to take a look at the nexus between tourism and the environment. Tourism depends heavily on the natural resources of the places in which it occurs. National parks, beaches, lakes, rainforests, and mountain ranges are just some of the many natural assets that attract millions of visitors a year to countries around the world. The tourism industry often lays claim to supporting wilderness preservation, maintenance of habitat, and the establishment of national parks. If it were not for tourism, some argue (for example, Lindblad, personal communication 1993) many national parks would never have been established and animal species such as the mountain gorillas of Rwanda would not be protected from exploitation. Likewise, numerous remote and relatively pristine places on the globe would not be protected if it were not for the desire of travelers to visit such sites. De Kadt (1976:339-341), in outlining the policy recommendations adopted by the UNESCO- sponsored seminar on the social and cultural impacts of tourism on developing countries, writes in his conclusion:

> Tourism should capitalize on the unique features of the country in order to make maximum use of local resources, to ensure a marketable product, and to reduce the risk of competition from other destinations. . . . These unique assets include the cultural and natural patrimony of the country. In being partly based on

such cultural and natural attractions, tourism may play a role in preserving and developing them.

Recommendation 4 of the UNESCO seminar is of particular importance to tourism in remote locations (de Kadt 1976:340):

> As a general principle, countries should attempt to develop tourism and tourism projects on a *scale*, at a *rate of growth*, and in *locations*, which are consistent with making maximum use of national and local resources, which do not place undue strain on such resources, and which avoid serious adverse social, cultural, or environmental impacts. . . . In all cases, governments should establish as a matter of course for each tourist area maximum acceptable rates of growth of tourism, and should control construction of hotel rooms (and other accommodation capacity) accordingly. "Tourism carrying capacity" is a useful term to evoke the fact that there can be too much tourism and that it can be developed too rapidly in particular situations. In practice, however, too little is known about precise magnitudes, and this deserves further research.

De Kadt did not state *how* tourism carrying capacity should be measured and whether, for example, Free and Independent Tourists (FITs) had a greater or smaller impact than mass or group tourists. As will be shown in this book, in the Antarctic context there is indeed a lack of baseline data on which to fully evaluate the tourism carrying capacity of tourist sites, and misinformation about tourism's detrimental effects abounds (see Chapter 5).

It was not until the late 1980s that "new" forms of tourism started to emerge which involved significant numbers of tourists. Smith and Eadington (1992:3) speak of "alternative tourism," "broadly defined as forms of tourism that are consistent with natural, social and community values and which allow hosts and guests to enjoy positive and worthwhile interaction and shared experiences." They concede that "to date, however, such reactions have been more notable for their harsh judgements against mass tourism than their positive contributions as to what 'alternative tourism' means" and are of the opinion that "by the 1990s, there is a sense that the public has become 'tired' of the crowds, weary of jet lag, awakened to the evidences of pollution, and in search of something 'new.' " Without clearly defining the term, they stated that the 1990s were shaping up to be the "decade of ecotourism" (Eadington and Smith 1990:8). Boo (1992:ii) sees ecotourism, which she defined as "nature travel that advances conservation and sustainable development efforts," as an idea that emerged when two trends intersected. In the conservation field, she notes that the trend toward the integration of conservation and economic development has been growing in significance. This trend, combined with the recognition that ecotourism can provide a new source of revenue for parks, has intersected with "a tremendous shift in the way people are going on vacation. Demand for adventurous, participatory, and nature-oriented tourism is growing. Like never before, travelers want to be active and educated about the places they visit" (Boo:1992:iv).

Whether the trend is as strong as Boo and other authors perceive it to be is yet to be determined. In a study of sixty-five hotel operators in the Asia-Pacific region, for example, Bauer, Jago, and Wise (1993) could not detect a greater demand from hotel guests for a more environmentally and culturally friendly hotel and tourism product. On the contrary, hotel managers responding to the survey stated that their guests were more interested in bigger rooms that included more creature comforts.

The enthusiasm with which the rhetoric of ecotourism has been embraced by the tourism industry and by governments leads to the questions: What is ecotourism, and does tourism taking place in Antarctica fall into this category? The term itself has two parts: ecology and tourism. The *Hutchinson Encyclopedia* (1995:341) defines *ecology* as: "Greek *oikos* 'house'; study of the relationship among organisms and the environments in which they live, including all living and nonliving components." Many definitions exist for the term *tourism*. One of the most encompassing is used by Mathieson and Wall (1982:1): "tourism is the temporary movement of people to destinations outside their normal places of work and residence, the activities undertaken during their stay in those destinations, and the facilities created to cater to their needs." Orams (1995:3) notes that the argument for the integration of tourism with conservation was first made widespread by Budowski (1976: 27-31) in his article "Tourism and Conservation: Conflict, Coexistence or Symbiosis."

The first use of the term *ecotourism* is attributed to Hector Ceballos-Lascurain, who coined it in 1983. He defined ecotourism as ". . . travelling to relatively undisturbed or uncontaminated areas with the specific object of studying, admiring and enjoying the scenery, its wild plants and animals, as well as any existing cultural manifestations found in these areas" (Richardson 1993:8). Mathieson and Wall (1982) had, however, already used a similar term in 1982 when they referred to tours into the Canadian tundra as "ecotours." Richardson (1993:7) sees ecotourism as falling into the category of special interest tourism that also includes, for example, cultural, sport, and adventure tourism. She observes that ecotourism—traveling to "learn and conserve"—is hardly new and points out that even the "Grand Tours of Europe during the 19th century undertaken by wealthy young Englishmen with their tutors can be seen as one form of ecotourism." Along similar lines, the *National Ecotourism Strategy,* produced by the Commonwealth Department of Tourism in 1994, notes that prior to the emergence of ecotourism, "ecotourism experiences have been offered as educational, outdoor or adventure travel experiences for many years" (p. 15). Noting several subsequent definitions of ecotourism (including those of Valentine 1991; Figgis 1993; and Young 1992 quoted subsequently), the Australian *National Ecotourism Strategy* defines the term as: "nature-based tourism that involves education and interpretation of the natural environment and is managed to be ecologically sustainable" (Commonwealth Department of Tourism 1994:17). Many other definitions of ecotourism have been offered, including the following:

1. Travel to remote or natural areas which aims to enhance understanding and appreciation of the natural environment and cultural heritage while avoiding damage or deterioration of the experience for others (Figgis 1993)
2. Thus ecotourism or tourism to natural areas that fosters environmental understanding, appreciation, and conservation and sustains the culture and well-being of local communities promises both conservation and local community development (Young 1992:55)
3. Ecotourism is nature-based tourism that is ecologically sustainable and is based on relatively undisturbed natural areas; is nondamaging and nondegrading; provides a direct contribution to the continued protection and management of protected areas used; and is subject to an adequate and appropriate management regime (Valentine 1991)

4. Ecologically sustainable tourism that fosters environmental and cultural understanding, appreciation and conservation (Ecotourism Association of Australia, 1992)
5. Environmentally responsible travel and visitation to relatively undisturbed natural areas, in order to enjoy and appreciate nature (and any accompanying cultural features—both past and present) that promotes conservation, has low visitor impacts, and provides for beneficially active socioeconomic involvement of local populations (IUCN's Ecotourism definition quoted in Ceballos-Lascurain 1996:20)

These are but a few of the many attempts to clearly define ecotourism. Although there are some differences with regard to the exact meaning, several underlying concepts make this form of tourism different from mass tourism. Wight (1993:3) sees the acceptance of a number of key principles as fundamental to a sustainable industry. These include: nondegradation of the resources; development that takes place in an environmentally responsible way; the provision of first-hand and participatory experiences for the tourists; a certain level of education; and the provision of long-term benefits for the resource, local community, and the industry.

Wall (1994:5), in reviewing the ecotourism literature, adds that ecotourism is usually defined on the basis of one or more of three criteria: "the characteristics of the destination, the motivation of the participants and the organizational characteristics of the trip." In Australia, a country that sees itself as a leading ecotourism destination, the *National Ecotourism Strategy* is based on three components, or dimensions: "nature-based, environmentally educated, and sustainably managed" (Blamey, 1995:15). Bottrill and Pearce (1995:45) attempted to "operationalize" the concept of ecotourism, that is, to get away from the theories underlying the concept and instead look at ecotourism in practice. Drawing on the literature, they identified three perspectives: "that of the participant, the operator, and the resource manager" (p. 46). The essential elements used by Bottrill and Pearce are motivation (physical activity, education, and participation); sensitive management; and protected environment status [of the location at which ecotourism takes place] (p. 49). When applying these elements to twenty-two nature-based tourism operations in British Columbia, only five could be classified as ecotourism.

In a study of forest tourism in Micronesia, Wylie (1994:9) also summarized what he calls the goals of ecotourism as: "sustainable use, resource conservation, economic development and diversification, life-enhancement and personal growth, maximum potential benefits and minimum costs/impacts, learning about the natural and cultural environment."

Because of the different interpretations attaching to the term, it becomes difficult to define who the ecotourists are and what activities they engage in to be classified as such. Ingram and Durst (1987), quoted by Whelan (1991:5), provide the following profile of ecotourists:

> Most ecotourists are from Europe, North America, and Japan, as they have more money and more leisure time than many of their counterparts in developing countries. The average US ecotourist is a man or woman familiar with the outdoors, a professional or retired, between thirty-one and fifty years of age, who most likely has had previous experience travelling abroad. . . . The most popular activities for ecotourists are trekking/hiking, bird watching, nature photography, wildlife safaris, camping, mountain climbing, fishing, river rafting/canoeing/kayaking, and botanical study. Nepal, Kenya, Tanzania, China, Mexico, Costa Rica, and Puerto Rico are the most popular destinations.

This description can be challenged on a number of grounds. First, what is said with regard to ecotourists from Europe, North America, and Japan holds true for most tourists from these countries, not only for ecotourists. Second, the activities they are interested in are all "soft adventure" activities and as such are probably the dominant form of tourism at the cited destinations. It follows that in reality travelers described by Ingram and Durst as "ecotourists" are travelers described by Plog (1974:13-16) as allocentrics. It should also be noted that it is nearly impossible to be an ecotourist for the full duration of one's annual vacation. Even ecotourists have to reach their, often remote, destinations somehow and, like most tourists, they use the most convenient form of transport such as planes, trains, ships, buses, or motor vehicles. In the process they utilize nonrenewable resources such as fossil fuels. After reaching their destination it is highly unlikely that they can continue to live up to some of the strict definitions of ecotourism twenty-four hours a day for the entire vacation. It is therefore far more likely that ecotourism experiences are "consumed" in small portions of a few hours or a few days at a time and that for the rest of their holidays ecotourists are just people on vacation, or simply tourists. Given that relatively few ecotourism experiences have an overnight component (which would technically qualify them as tourism), it could be argued that much of ecotourism is in reality ecorecreation, an environmentally benign activity carried out in a natural setting with an educational component, for a limited duration.

As Wall (1994:5) puts it: ". . . a strong case can be made for classifying specific trips rather than specific individuals as being examples of ecotourism." Ecotourists are said to be big spenders. Boo (1990), for example, correlates ecotourists in Costa Rica with higher than average incomes. This may well be so, but caution should be taken in assuming that the same will necessarily hold true for other so-called ecotourism destinations. Ecotourism is also seen as being of economic benefit for tourist regions. For example, Boo (1992:vi) lists the benefits of ecotourism as: "increased funding for protected areas and local communities; new jobs created for local residents; and environmental education for visitors" and argues that "positive ecotourism experiences are likely to yield strong advocates for environmental protection." She lists the potential costs of ecotourism as "environmental degradation, economic instability and inequity, and sociocultural changes."

In the Antarctic context, of particular interest are her observations with regard to potential environmental impacts:

> Environmental degradation can happen in many ways. It can be degradation that is easily observed, such as litter, trail erosion, or water pollution. Or degradation can be more subtle, such as alterations in animal behavior or reproduction rates, or alterations in the composition of plant species. The main problem in understanding environmental impacts of tourism is that few scientific tools exist to determine the more subtle changes. The methodology to monitor changes and to establish biological carrying capacity is still unsophisticated. Therefore, we know little about the long-term environmental impacts of tourism on natural resources. (Boo 1992:vi)

In summary, ecotourism is not a radically new concept. The academic debate on what exactly ecotourism is and what its relationships with the broader notion of sustainable development are will continue for some time yet. In the end ecotourism may just be, as Wall (1994:4) put it: "old wine in new bottles." Despite the fact that the term is open to interpretation and abuse, there is little doubt that the emergence of the concept has put the environmental impacts of tourism in the spotlight. Thus, it has forced the industry to be more environmentally conscious and evaluative of its activities. Under the guidance of the United Nations Environment Program (and with the support of the United Nations Educational, Scientific and Cultural Organization and the World Tourism Organization) the *Tour Operators' Initiative for Sustainable Tourism Development* was officially launched during the International Tourism Exchange in Berlin in March 2000. Among the members of the initiative are some of the world's largest tour operators. Members pledge that they will act responsibly toward the physical and cultural environments at the destinations in which they operate (for details on this excellent initiative see <http://www.toinitiative.org>). Other developments include the establishment of the Green Globe program by the World Travel and Tourism Council (WTTC), which aims to make all tourism activities as benign as possible. If ecotourism can contribute to even slightly more benign mass tourism products such as less polluting flights and accommodation operations, the creation of the concept with all its ambiguities has been worthwhile.

BACKGROUND TO ANTARCTIC TOURISM

The history of Antarctic tourism was first investigated by Reich (1979). This early investigation was followed up by Codling (1982b) (see Reich) when she visited the Antarctic Peninsula aboard a cruise ship and reported on her observations of visitor profiles and visitor behavior. Patri (1983), in his work *Les Activités Touristiques en Milieu Polaire: Le Case du Continent Antarctique* also investigated the phenomenon. Other authors who have made Antarctic tourism their field of research include Mussack (1988), Williams (1988), and Christensen (1990). Enzenbacher's (1991) work, which described and assessed the Antarctic tourism industry, established tourist numbers, and described the regulatory framework under which tourism is carried out, is of particular significance.

In addition to the writings of the above authors, two major publications on Antarctic tourism were produced. The first is the collection of Antarctic tourism papers in a special issue of the *Annals of Tourism Research* (Vol. 21, No. 2, 1994), edited by Dr. Valene Smith. This volume provides an excellent insight into a variety of Antarctic tourism issues. The second major publication is the book *Polar Tourism*, edited by Hall and Johnston (1995a), which brings together a number of authors who contribute their knowledge of tourism activities in the Arctic and Antarctic regions.

Antarctica is often referred to as a "fragile" and "unknown" continent. Uncontrolled, large-scale tourism could have destructive impacts on some parts of it, but small-scale, appropriately managed tourism presents an opportunity to utilize what in economic terms is at present a highly underutilized part of the world. Responsible tourism can also contribute to raising the awareness that Antarctica is a place worth preserving and studying, thus lending support to the scientific research efforts being carried out. However, tourists may, by their very presence, add extra pressures on the wildlife and flora of Antarctica, which already exist under some of the most marginal conditions on Earth. Depending on the types of tourism and the way in which activities are carried out, tourism can be a contributing factor to either the preservation or the destruction of parts of the continent.

Taking note of these factors, the aim of this book is to investigate the current state of commercial Antarctic tourism, including its impacts, to identify the most suitable forms of tourism and to explore its likely future directions.

The levels of impact that commercial Antarctic tourism may have on the environment can be seen as being based on several factors:

1. Modes of transport used (e.g., ship, aircraft, and snowmobile)
2. Locations where tourism takes place (e.g., wildlife sites, historic sites, and scientific stations) and during which part of the season the visits occur
3. Types of activities that are undertaken (e.g., sightseeing, photography, hiking, skiing)
4. Length of time spent ashore

5. Number of visitors per season
6. Cumulative numbers of visitors to specific sites

To make tourism a minimal-impact use of Antarctic resources, all tourism infrastructure, practices, products, and behavior must be critically analyzed continuously. Because it is the visitors themselves who may have detrimental effects on the environment, it is important to establish their attitudes toward Antarctica and their expectations of an Antarctic vacation. It is suggested that positive attitudes toward the region, and hence Antarctic conservation, will lead to a minimum of willfully caused environmental damage. It is furthermore necessary to observe the behavior of visitors while they are ashore in order to get a more complete picture of their interaction with the environment.

Unlike most other destinations, where tourism is accepted as a form of economic development for the improvement of the living standards of the local population, there is no such justification in Antarctica. In the absence of a local population, it can be argued that it is only the tourists and the tour operators who benefit directly from this activity. Therefore, there is some debate about whether tourism is a desirable activity.

This book arose out of a strong interest to explore the nature, structure, management, impact, and future directions of tourism in this little-visited, remote, and climatically hostile region. The study is exploratory in nature and its main aim is to contribute to a greater understanding of the tourism phenomenon in the Antarctic by treating the area like any other remote tourist destination. Such an understanding is necessary to ensure that a balanced debate about the advantages and disadvantages of Antarctic tourism can take place. In the process of researching this book several much publicized opinions were challenged. One example of misrepresentation of the impacts of tourism is a cover story in the *Conservation Gazette* (Castellas 1996:1), which under the headline "Tip of the Iceberg" led readers to believe that Antarctica was about to be ruined by passengers who disembarked from flights to various bases, even though the infrastructure for tourists to stay at these bases does not even exist and no runway for civilian air traffic has yet been built.

The book addresses the following questions:

1. What is the status of commercial tourism activities in the Antarctic Treaty area?
2. What are the profiles, attitudes, and images of Antarctica held by those who travel to the region as fare-paying tourists?
3. What are the perceived and observed impacts of commercial Antarctic tourism on the natural and created Antarctic environment?
4. What are the most likely commercial tourism activities in Antarctica in twenty-five years' time?
5. What are the implications of answers to these questions for the management of future tourism activities?

Answers to the second question will assist Antarctic tour operators to better understand the needs and expectations of their clients, thus enabling them to better tailor their products to their clients' needs. The impacts of tourism in Antarctica have been widely debated in the literature. The discussion of these impacts in Chapter 5 contributes to the academic discussion by challenging the notion that at present tourists have a more than transitory impact on the Antarctic environment. Answers to question 4 will provide the Antarctic Treaty Parties with an indication of the medium- to long-term future directions of commercial tourism in the treaty area. This will assist the Treaty Parties in their attempts to manage Antarctic tourism in a proactive way.

To address the above questions, several research techniques were used. These included surveys of Antarctic travelers, a survey of the opinions of Antarctic experts, and personal observations of Antarctic tourism.

LIMITATIONS

Conducting surveys among Antarctic passengers is difficult for two main reasons. First, given the commercial nature of the cruises and overflights, permission and cooperation must be sought from the various tour operators. The granting of permission to survey passengers depends on the researcher asking questions that are seen as "suitable" by the tour operator. Commercially sensitive questions relating to such details as where passengers resided were met with suspicion by one of the operators.

Second, even if questionnaires are placed aboard the ship or aircraft by the operator's head office, there is no certainty that they are actually handed out during the voyage or flight. Even if they are distributed, there is no certainty that passengers actually complete them. As a result, the total number of responses from seaborne passengers was not as high as had been hoped and the results obtained can therefore only reflect the passenger profiles and their motivations during the sampled voyages. Consequently, the author proposes that future surveys of Antarctic passengers be conducted by mail with the assistance of the tour operators, who should send out the questionnaires to their clients when mailing their travel documents. This should increase the response rate considerably.

A study that has as one of its aims the establishment of likely future scenarios is, by its very nature, exploratory. Although the Delphi technique has proven to provide reliable results in other fields (for example, finance and economic diversification), it has not been tested sufficiently to ensure that it is a valuable technique in the tourism context. In common with other Delphi studies, results obtained reflect the opinions and judgments of the carefully selected expert panel that was assembled to tackle the difficult task of exploring future scenarios (see Chapter 7).

DEFINITIONS

For the purposes of this book, *tourism* is defined as the commercial (for profit) transport (including accommodation and catering) of nongovernment travelers to and from Antarctica for the purpose of pleasure. Thus, visits by scientists and their support staff, as well as the visits of government representatives, politicians, and journalists on government-sponsored programs are not included. These trips can be classified as business travel and, as such, they fall outside the focus of this book on pleasure travel. The *Antarctic* is defined as the region governed by the Antarctic Treaty of 1959, which applies "to the area south of 60 degrees South Latitude, including all ice shelves" (Article VI of the Antarctic Treaty, in Heap 1990:xiv). In combination, the two terms mean that for the purposes of this book *Antarctic tourism* is defined as commercial tourism activities carried out in the Antarctic Treaty area.

CHAPTER OUTLINES

Chapter 2 provides an overview of tourism at other remote locations including the Arctic, sub-Antarctic islands, and the Galapagos. These regions were identified as having certain similarities with the study region, and it is clear that the way national tourism regulators manage tourism at these locations can provide examples that could be applied in the Antarctic context.

Chapter 3 introduces the reader to the Antarctic. The chapter first provides an overview of the special circumstances surrounding Antarctica: its discovery, exploration, climatic conditions, fauna, flora, and the exploitation of its resources throughout history. This forms a context for the outline of the unique legal and political status of the region and highlights the framework under which tourism has and will continue to develop.

Chapter 4 outlines the development of tourism from its beginnings until the present. Types of tourism taking place are identified, locations of touristic activities are outlined, and visitor volumes are discussed. The chapter also addresses the management of tourism under the Antarctic Treaty System (ATS) and under self-regulation by tour operators organized within the International Association of Antarctica Tour Operators (IAATO). Because tourism is the only commercial activity taking place on the Antarctic continent, its activities have come under closer scrutiny from a variety of authors and organizations who have at times suggested that the activity has unacceptable impacts on the environment.

Chapter 5 critically evaluates these suggested impacts. Chapter 6 discusses the results of the various passenger surveys carried out by the author. Chapter 7 presents and discusses the results obtained from the study of future directions of Antarctic tourism, which also investigated perceived future impacts. Chapter 8 is based on personal observations of tourism activities aboard overflights and aboard cruise ships in the Antarctic Peninsula region as well as in the Ross Sea, and on observations reported in the literature.

CONCLUDING COMMENTS

As is evident in many issues of *Current Antarctic Literature*, social science research in Antarctica is only in its infancy. The research agendas of national Antarctic programs are dominated by the physical sciences and as a result, physical scientists dominate discussions of Antarctic issues, including tourism. As a social science issue, Antarctic tourism has only relatively recently appeared as a field of serious scientific investigation. When the author first looked at Antarctic tourism in 1991, the most comprehensive study of the topic was over ten years old (Reich 1979), and very little primary Antarctic tourism research had been carried out during the 1980s. Since the 1990-1991 Antarctic season, shipborne visitor numbers to the Antarctic have increased substantially. This increase in interest in the region has resulted in a proliferation of popular media articles and also the publishing of a number of important academic papers on the topic. Several publications were, however, written by authors who had no firsthand experience with tourism operations in Antarctica. This book offers an alternative to this "distance" or "desk study" approach by basing academic research on firsthand observations and tourist opinions as well as on the collective opinions of a panel of Antarctic experts. Antarctic tourism operates under very difficult environmental and political conditions. These have restricted and will continue to restrict the development of tourism in this part of the world.

Chapter 2

Tourism Operations and Management in Remote Areas: The Galapagos Islands, Arctic Region, and Sub-Antarctic Islands

INTRODUCTION

The context for a study of the trends, opportunities, and constraints of commercial tourism in a remote area must include not only the relevant international conventions but also investigate what can be learned from the evolution of wilderness tourism in other remote places. In particular, there is a need to explore how tourism is structured, organized, and managed in other remote regions and to see whether there are lessons to be learned that might be useful in the sustainable management of Antarctic tourism. Price (1996:33) notes that "the three most fragile environments—at least in terms of proportion of the Earth's surface—are deserts, mountains and Arctic areas." With regard to economic impacts, he adds that tourism has been the prime source of foreign exchange earnings for Nepal and Bhutan and points out that tourism is also a key element in the economies of Arctic areas such as Lapland and Alaska. Tourism in these locations is encouraged by the various governments with the potential economic gains for local populations in mind. In the absence of a local population, the economic and social impacts of tourism in Antarctica are of little consequence, leaving only potentially negative environmental impacts as an issue for concern.

This chapter analyzes tourism development in three selected tourist destinations that, because of their remoteness, relatively low visitor numbers, climatic conditions, and wildlife, offer analogies to wilderness tourism in Antarctica. Clearly relevant are the management of tourism in the Galapagos Islands, locations in the Arctic region, and the sub-Antarctic islands of Australia and New Zealand.

GALAPAGOS ISLANDS

Apart from the Antarctic, the Galapagos Islands constitute probably the most environmentally sensitive tourist region in the world. The islands and the Antarctic share a number of attributes:

- Distance from major population centers
- Limited accessibility
- Tame and easily accessible wildlife
- Relatively few endangered species, so that protection in the natural habitat where tourism takes place is still viable
- Wildlife and geological settings are a major attraction
- A "survival of the fittest" ecological context due to natural limitations on food supplies
- Compulsory guiding of visitors while they are ashore

In light of these similarities, it is of interest to examine more closely the management of tourism activities in the Galapagos in order to investigate what could be learned that is applicable to the management of tourism in Antarctica. The Antarctic and the Galapagos Islands are two of the few places where humans and wildlife come in very close contact. Unlike, for example, African wildlife reserves such as the Masai-Mara in Kenya, visitors to the various islands in the Galapagos are not shielded from wildlife by sitting in a minibus or four-wheel-drive vehicle. Galapagos visitors walk among the wildlife and thus have the opportunity to observe at close hand the beauty of wild animals who show little overt fear. In this close encounter between trusting wildlife and tourists rests the beauty and meaning of the touristic experience. At the same time, the possibility for irreparable interference with the life cycles of animals exists. In the extreme, there exists the possible destruction of the "state of innocence" of the wildlife combined with the destruction of their habitat. Craig MacFarland (1991:1), a former president of the Charles Darwin Foundation for the Galapagos Islands, noted in an address to the National Press Club in Washington, DC: "The Galapagos, one of the world's greatest treasures, is still one of the most unspoiled places on earth. In brief, these islands are one-of-a-kind, awe-inspiringly beautiful, and extremely fragile."

The Galapagos Archipelago is located in the Pacific Ocean 960 kilometers to the west of Ecuador, which has sovereignty over the islands. "There are 13 major islands, 6 minor islands and 42 islets that have official names" (White and Epler 1972:12). From 1934 onward, the Ecuadorian government began enacting laws for the protection of several of the islands in the Galapagos Archipelago and declared them a wildlife sanctuary. "On July 4, 1959, all areas not colonized by man were declared a national park" (Constant 1999:260). The park now covers 97 percent of the land area and a 32,000 square mile marine reserve has been established around the islands (MacFarland 1991:1). Also in 1959, the International Charles Darwin Foundation for the Galapagos Islands (CDF) was created in Brussels (Constant 1999:260). In 1960, the Charles Darwin Research Station (CDRS) began operations and formed a close link with the activities of the Galapagos National Park Service. As Rogers (1990:104) puts it: "Together the two institutions have worked to preserve species, protect the environment, control feral animals, and set up a system for management of visitors. It was then that the determination was made to require all tour groups to be accompanied by a trained, licensed park guide, a rule that still exists." Rogers further notes that the Ecuadorian government of the day showed remarkable foresight given that "tourism was a far-off dream rather than a reality, or even a realistic goal . . . and no one could have foreseen the booming interest in environmental issues and conservation that the following decades were to bring" (p. 105).

Of importance in the Antarctic context is the fact that "when it happened and visiting the Galapagos Islands became a goal of nature enthusiasts, Ecuador was ready with a system to accommodate visitors and keep them from causing damage to the wildlife or its habitat" (Rogers 1990:105).

Like Antarctica, the Galapagos Islands are located nearly 1,000 kilometers from the nearest land. This barrier forms a buffer zone, which assists in the protection of the islands. Access to the islands occurs by way of flights and limited cruise vessels. Once in the islands, tourists travel aboard a variety of vessels with accommodations ranging from basic to luxury. These carry between four and ninety passengers and act as floating hotels during their voyages.

More recently, day tours have been introduced, departing regularly from Puerto Ayora on Santa Cruz Island. Medium and larger ships are required to carry one guide for every fifteen passengers. The guides are responsible for their groups while they are ashore, providing interpretation of the wildlife and the environment and ensuring that visitors stay on the premarked tracks. "Forty-eight visitor sites have been designed with marked trails and open areas" (Constant 1999:261). In 1978, the Galapagos Islands were declared a World Heritage site by UNESCO. The following list summarizes the rules that must be observed in the Galapagos National Park (Galapagos National Park Service undated):

- No plants, animals, or remains of such as bones, pieces of wood, or other natural objects should be removed or disturbed;
- Be careful not to transport any live material to the islands, or from island to island;
- Do not take any food to the uninhabited islands;
- Animals may not be touched or handled;
- Animals may not be fed;
- Do not disturb or chase any animal from its resting or nesting spot;
- Litter of all types must be kept off the islands. Disposal at sea must be limited to certain types of garbage, only to be thrown overboard in selected areas;
- Do not buy souvenirs or objects made from plants or animals of the islands with the exception of artifacts made from wood;
- Do not paint names or graffiti on rocks;
- All groups that visit the national park must be accompanied by a qualified guide approved by the national park. Visitors must follow the instructions of the guides;
- The national park is divided into different zones to facilitate its management and administration. There are certain sites where tourist activities are permitted, and others where the public is restricted or prohibited;
- Do not hesitate to show your conservationist attitude. Explain these rules to others and help to enforce them. . . . Your understanding of the islands is important to their conservation. Enjoy yourself fully, but never at the expense of what you came here to see.

Protective regulations in the Galapagos further state that nothing may be taken from the islands and nothing may be left behind. Visitors are also required to be back aboard their respective vessels by sunset.

MacFarland (1991) pointed out that "The single largest and constantly growing threat to the Galapagos, ever since man arrived in the 1500s, has always been the introduction of foreign species" [these include cattle, cats, dogs, donkeys, horses, pigs, and black rats]. In the Galapagos, this is not solely a tourism problem since more and more Ecuadorians have been reported to be migrating to the islands in search of jobs in the booming tourism industry. (For a detailed analysis of tourism in the Galapagos Islands, see also Honey 1999: 101-130.)

In May 1996, the author approached the Charles Darwin Research Institute to obtain an update on the latest developments in Galapagos tourism. In particular there was an interest in finding out which plan the island management was currently using and whether the Global Management Plan for Galapagos Tourism mentioned by MacFarland in 1991 had been finalized and implemented.

The Charles Darwin Station advised the author that several management plans did indeed exist, but that none seemed to be approved or implemented. One such example is the management plan that was developed in 1992 by the Permanent Commission for the Galapagos Island (Comisión Permanente para las Islas Galapagos). Apparently, much squabbling is still occurring over jurisdictions and hence, the plan remains more a set of recommendations with no regulations established on the basis of this document. By late 2000, there was still no comprehensive management plan for tourism in the Galapagos, but a management plan for the marine reserve surrounding the island had been developed and was being enforced. With regard to the impacts of tourists on the islands, the author was advised that management was coping, but barely. Perhaps somewhat surprisingly the biggest issues in the Galapagos were perceived to be internal migration of people from the Ecuadorian mainland by Ecuadorians who sought to participate in the tourism boom and the land-based infrastructure needed to support the tourism industry. The tourists themselves are well controlled by the guides that accompany all their shore excursions during their cruises.

Harris (1984:204) writes that:

> The rapid expansion of tourism in the islands from a few hundred people a year in the mid-1960s to 25,000 visitors per annum in 1981, resulted in the realization that wildlife was a major resource which attracted many people and much money to the islands. Concern in case these developments unduly disturbed the birds in particular resulted in the setting up of studies to monitor the impact of tourism. It is, as yet, too early to be complacent but the indications are that an adequate standard of guiding of the tourists and the extreme tameness of animals have resulted in minimal damage to populations.

Harris's observations, though dated, indicate that provided due care is taken in guiding tourists through wildlife-rich areas, negative impacts can be kept to a minimum. This should bode well for the management of tourism activities in Antarctica.

What can be learned from the Galapagos example with regard to the management of tourism activities in the Antarctic? Several points will be of benefit for the management of Antarctic tourism. By acting early, as the Ecuadorian government did in 1934, it is possible to put in place a system of protection and management that can avoid to a large extent the excesses of modern mass tourism (the fact that the country has sovereignty over the islands and that therefore only a single government was involved in the process clearly facilitated this decision). Once the resource is protected and systems are in place to monitor its well-being, tourism can take place in an orderly and non-destructive way. By using the zoning approach (in the Galapagos the zones are: primitive use, scientific use, colonized, special use, extensive use, and intensive use), which only allows access to certain sites by establishing trails on which tourists must stay during their visits to the islands, and by combining these two measures with the requirement that all passengers must be accompanied by a qualified guide while ashore, the management of the Galapagos National Park has, to date, been able to maintain the resource in as pristine a state as possible. Given that more than eight times as many people (62,809) visited the Galapagos Islands in 1997 than visited Antarctica (7,322) during the 1996-1997 season, this is a great achievement. It is of interest to note that tour operators in the Galapagos Islands are reportedly in the process of establishing an industry association along the lines of the International Association of Antarctica Tour Operators (IAATO). In summary, it seems that the Galapagos model of management can provide some guidance for the management of visitor sites in Antarctica.

ARCTIC REGION

The other remote region that may provide clues for the sustainable management of Antarctic tourism is the vast region which covers the northernmost parts of the globe, the Arctic. This region's sovereign states are Iceland, Norway, Sweden, Finland, Russia, Canada, and the U.S. state of Alaska as well as the Danish dependency of Greenland (Stonehouse, Crosbie, and Girard 1996:23). The number of tourists visiting Arctic lands is far higher than those visiting Antarctica, but tourism takes place, at least in parts, in a similarly hostile climate. There are many tourist destinations in the Arctic region: Alaska, the North Cape, Nunavut, Svalbard, and the geographic North Pole, to mention but a few, but most of them are far more accessible to tourists than Antarctica. Perhaps because of the numerous sovereign countries involved, the region does not have a comprehensive tourism management plan nor, for that matter, an accepted tourist code of behavior. Mason (1994:93) suggested that a visitor code be established that would include the following points: Leave wildlife habitats alone; do not take plants, animals, and samples from nature; keep to marked tracks; limit damage by vehicles; hunting and fishing are under strict national control; accessibility to nature reserves and national parks is regulated by permits; no litter or equipment to be left behind; what was brought in must be taken out; respect indigenous cultures; and be a guest; enjoy yourself. Mason's suggested code is a start, but its implementation depends to a large degree on the willingness of national governments of Arctic countries to accept and implement it and on tourists and tour operators to follow it.

Stonehouse, Crosbie, and Girard (1996) think that Arctic tourism will grow, possibly quickly, and recommend that the governments of the region should take "whatever steps are needed to maintain it [tourism] within sustainable limits" (p. 25). In contrast to Antarctica, tourism management can be legislated by the various sovereign Arctic governments, and Stonehouse and Crosbie (1995:26) state that these governments are advised to take note of "Antarctic tourism's record of successful self-regulation over the past three decades." Thus, despite the existence of national legislation in the Arctic, it appears that Antarctic tourism management can show the way for Arctic tourism management.

Nuttall (1998:129-135) investigated and discussed the implications of tourism for native Arctic communities while Hall and Johnston (1995a) assembled the work of analysts of Antarctic and Arctic tourism issues. Arctic regions covered in their book *Polar Tourism* include northern Canada, the Canadian Arctic, the Yukon Territory, and Svalbard. As outlined by Hall and Johnston (1995b:4), tourism in the Arctic region takes place within the legislative control of sovereign states. Thus, the issues surrounding the management of tourism are similar to the management of tourism activities in more temperate zones of the globe where proactive, comprehensive, and integrated planning are the keys to success. While the Arctic as a whole receives hundreds of thousands of visitors per year, the high Arctic, the region closest to the geographic North Pole and having climatic conditions most similar to the Antarctic, receives only a small number. Johnston (1995:31), drawing on several sources, estimates that, for example, Arctic Alaska received 25,000 visitors during 1989 (compared to a total of 1,049,800 visitors for all of Alaska), the Yukon Territory 177,220 visitors in 1991, and the Arctic region of Canada's Northwest Territories (NWT) 16,100 visitors during 1992. The last figure represents approximately twice the number of tourists that visited the Antarctic during the same year. A comprehensive analysis of all tourism activities in the Arctic is outside the scope of this book, and it is therefore preferable to examine a small number of Arctic regions with environments similar to those in the south.

Alaska

Alaska is the northernmost state of the United States and can, by polar standards, be described as a mainstream tourist destination. Tourism is currently Alaska's major growth industry, generating US$1.4 billion in revenue each year (Nuttall 1998:131). The state offers the traveler several experiences and sights that are comparable to those available in the Antarctic. For example, Glacier Bay, a national park in the south of the state, offers the visitor spectacular glacier scenery. Large cruise ships closely approach Le Conte Glacier, where passengers may witness the breaking off of large chunks of glacier ice. Cruising the Inside Passage along the coast of British Columbia and Alaska affords the traveler many scenic vistas. A *P&O Princess*

Alaska advertisement (*The Age*, January 21, 1995) describes Alaska in the following way:

> Alaska. For a hundred years, the call of this wild land has lured fearless explorers and crazed fortune-hunters to brave its treacherous mountains, rivers of ice and virulent climate. Today, the call is as loud as ever. But now you can surrender to it, far more graciously than ever before, on the modern and beautiful Alaskan fleet of P&O. As you sip champagne and contemplate the choice of caviar or smoked salmon from a lush Alaskan smorgasbord, watch a glacier "calve" a ten-story iceberg while a bald eagle soars above and sea otters frolic among the ice floes.

Alaska, as a cruise destination, is promoted and sold to the upper end of the market. During the 2000 summer season, over 600,000 passengers sailed through southeast Alaska (*South China Morning Post*, 2000). It is of interest to note how the scenic beauty of Alaska seems to play only a secondary role in the written part of this advertisement. By contrast, the visual part of the advertisement depicts stunning mountain and glacier scenery, comparable to certain parts of the island of South Georgia and the Antarctic Peninsula. Interestingly, Crosbie (reported in Stonehouse, Crosbie, and Girard 1996:22), in a survey of cruise ship travelers to the Canadian north, found that a significant percentage of passengers had already been to the Antarctic.

Ellesmere Island National Park Reserve, Nunavut (Canada)

While Alaska is easily accessible, a remote Arctic destination, which is perceived to have many similarities with the Antarctic, is Ellesmere Island National Park Reserve on Ellesmere Island in the new Canadian territory of Nunavut. The park is located at the northern extremity of the Arctic Islands, only 600 kilometers from the geographic North Pole in the Canadian High Arctic. Bruce Rigby, the superintendent for the Eastern Arctic National Parks, outlined the management-planning program in an Ellesmere Island newsletter (Ministry of Environment and Ministry of Supply and Services 1991). The purpose of the newsletter was to give the public the opportunity to have input into the proposed management plan for the Ellesmere Island National Park Reserve. Among all the purposes of the park listed, the most relevant one is this: "The park will provide

opportunities for people to enjoy wilderness recreation in this remarkable part of Canada. But all aspects of use must occur in ways
that leave the area unimpaired for this and future generations. The
management plan will determine the careful balance that must be
struck between protection and use" (p. 2).

With regard to planning issues, the management planning program
poses several questions, the most important one of which is: "What
kind of park will Ellesmere be?" The answer given by the Parks Service:

> The Parks Service has a dual responsibility—to protect park re-
> sources and to provide opportunities for the use and enjoyment
> of those resources. The important question to be answered is
> how much of each is required to keep the right balance. In
> Ellesmere, this decision is complicated by the park's location
> and the unusually fragile nature of its natural and cultural re-
> sources. What is the right concept for the future? Should re-
> source protection be given precedence, and visitor use be tightly
> controlled and confined to a few specific areas? Should the park
> be dedicated to research and scientific discovery? Or should en-
> vironmental education, both for park visitors and Canadians in
> general, be the major focus of the park? After all, many Canadi-
> ans will want to learn more about Ellesmere's resources, history
> and ecology, but may not have the opportunity to actually set
> foot in the park.

The similarities with Antarctica are obvious. If one were to substitute "Antarctica" for "Ellesmere Island" the questions would be the
same. Unlike Ellesmere Island, however, no public consultation process takes place to determine answers to the above questions for
Antarctica. As will be outlined in Chapter 3, decisions on Antarctic
tourism are made at the discretion of the Antarctic Treaty Consultative Parties (ATCPs) in camera and with only limited independent
external advice or guidance. Unlike Ellesmere Island National Park
Reserve, no information brochures are produced by the Treaty Parties
to canvass the opinions of the world community. The main reason for
this is that Antarctica is not in the domain of a single country and thus
can be seen as the largest ungoverned region on earth.

Svalbard

Viken (1995:73-84) provides a case study of tourism experiences in Svalbard. The Svalbard archipelago is located approximately 1,000 kilometers north of Norway, and nearly 70 percent of the islands are permanently covered with ice. Like Antarctica, Svalbard has no indigenous population but, unlike Antarctica, there are three permanent settlements, which depend on mining activities. Although Svalbard is under the sovereignty of Norway, the archipelago is also an international area for industrial and commercial activities, regulated by an international treaty dating back to 1920 (Viken 1995:75).

Svalbard has been visited by tourists since 1871, with cruises from Germany and Norway visiting the islands on a regular basis. In the early days a hotel was established, but it was abandoned after two years, while cruising remained (Viken 1995:73). A new hotel has been built recently.

In 1970, an airstrip was established near the major settlement of Longyearbyen on Spitsbergen, the largest of the islands in the Svalbard archipelago. Exact tourist numbers are somewhat difficult to obtain. Info-Svalbard (1999) provides the following numbers for 1998: guest nights in Longyearbyen in hotels and hostels, 46,201; guest nights in Longyearbyen, camping, 1,098; passengers arrived and departed Svalbard Airport in Longyearbyen, 59,463.

It is important to note that most tourists visit Svalbard aboard cruise ships. They make one or two landings, during which they visit heritage sites related to whaling and explorer activities (Viken 1995:77). These activities show similarities with activities carried out in the Antarctic region, in particular the South Shetland Islands, Ross Island, and the island of South Georgia, where tourists land for the same reasons.

Other tourist activities undertaken by a comparatively small number of visitors to Svalbard include trekking, exploring, and special-interest tourism. Viken (1995:77) concludes that "In general tourism in Svalbard may be characterized as nature tourism or nature-based tourism." Tourism in Polar Regions is not without risk, and the perils of tourism operations in Svalbard are those that apply in all polar environments, including the Antarctic. In this context Christensen (1990:14) mentions the 1989 incident near Svalbard when the cruise vessel *Maksim Gor'kiy,* with 575 passengers and 378 crew, struck an ice floe and was seriously damaged. Parallels can be drawn with several similar incidents involving Antarctic ships.

Viken's case study provides an overview of tourism in this remote location but it does not address the issues of how tourism is regulated and what its impacts are. He suggests, however, that "So far the damage caused by tourism is small" (Viken 1995:82).

The publication *Regulations Relating to Tourism and Other Travel in Svalbard* (Norwegian Ministry of Justice 1993) deals exclusively with the issue of tourism management in Svalbard. The twelve regulations were issued by Royal Decree on October 18, 1991 and have as their purpose ". . . to regulate tourism and travel in Svalbard, particularly in order to protect the archipelago's natural environment and historical remains, ensure compliance with other laws and regulations, provide for the safety of tourists and other travelers" (Norwegian Ministry of Justice 1993:3). The main points of the regulations can be summarized thus:

- Tour operators must issue travel guarantees according to the rules that apply on the Norwegian mainland.
- Tour operators are responsible for the safety of their clients and for seeing that they are acquainted with and comply with relevant laws, in particular as they pertain to the protection of the natural and cultural environment.
- Tour operators must take out insurance cover to cover possible costs for rescue operations.
- Tour operators must give notice of their plans before each season.
- Tourist vessels and individual travelers must give notice before entering national parks or nature reserves.
- Notice to the governor of Svalbard is recommended for all journeys, irrespective of the area to be visited.

Paragraph 11 of the regulations prescribes that: "Deliberate or negligent violation of these Regulations or of prohibitions or orders issued in pursuance of these Regulations is punishable by fines or imprisonment for up to one year" (Norwegian Ministry of Justice 1993:1).

A detailed case study on tourism in Svalbard was released in 1996 by the Arctic Environmental Protection Strategy (AEPS) Task Force on Sustainable Development and Utilization (Kaltenborn and Hindrum 1996). The objective of the case study was "to assess the problems, challenges and opportunities associated with the development of tourism in Svalbard" (p. 8). Much of what Kaltenborn and Hindrum report is of interest with regard to tourism in Antarctica. The following items highlight these points:

- Humans and wildlife are both active in the short summer period (p. 14).
- The natural environment in Svalbard is still relatively intact and characterized by large continuous wilderness areas (p. 15).
- Some populations of marine mammals and seabirds were overharvested and became threatened (pp. 15-16).
- The Arctic environment of Svalbard is robust in the sense that it is able to stand the harsh natural conditions, but it can be very vulnerable to human impact (p. 16).
- Abnormal disturbance to animal life living at the "edge of existence" could lead to serious impact on certain populations (p. 16).
- The historical monuments in Svalbard show the relatively short history of human activity in this archipelago, a history of an activity at the edge of the possible. They are mainly traces left from utilization of the natural resources and scientific expeditions or voyages of discovery (p. 16).
- Svalbard was one of the last no-man's-lands on earth to come under national jurisdiction. In 1920 an international treaty was signed in Versailles by twelve countries, giving Norway sovereign powers over the islands (today there are about forty-two signatory nations) (pp. 16-17).
- Twenty to thirty thousand people come by cruise ship every summer, but they spend very little, if any, time ashore (p.18).
- The total number of tourists visiting Svalbard cannot be estimated with great precision, but the figure is thought to have been approximately 30,000 in 1994. This makes it the most visited place in the Arctic. . . . About 80 percent of visitors are passengers on cruise liners (p. 19).

- All overseas cruise activity is carried out in summer. Its volume has increased more than four times during the last twenty years from about 5,000 in 1975 to 24,000 in 1994. In 1994, reports show 198 landings and 46,105 tourists put ashore . . . (the figure indicates that many passengers are landed two or more times during a cruise).

Kaltenborn and Hindrum (1996) mention that coastal cruises with smaller vessels also operate in Svalbard and that "tourists joining these coastal cruises seem to be people who are relatively concerned about nature, and many of the trips are marketed as ecotourism" (p. 20). Interestingly they also mention that "There have been attempts to start 'panorama' flights around the archipelago, but these have been prohibited by the authorities as they would conflict with the environmental policy for Svalbard" (Ministry of Environment 1995, quoted in Kaltenborn and Hindrum 1996:24). With regard to breaches of environmental regulations, they report that "Over the period 1986 to 1995 only very few violators of environmental regulation have been prosecuted" (number of violations ranged from zero to six per year) and "it probably indicates that the Svalbard tourist has respect for the environment and the environmental regulations" (p. 24). With regard to actual and potential impacts of tourism in Svalbard, they state that "Tourism in Svalbard is still a relatively controlled activity and environmental impacts are few and limited. The main ones are impacts on the tundra and historical monuments, spreading of litter, animal disturbance and interruption of the wilderness experience" (p. 30).

In their study they identified nine types of tourism to Svalbard, several of which are of interest in the context of this book. These are: cruise tourism (travelers who visit Svalbard only briefly, without staying overnight on shore); commercial field tourism (organized trips on foot, skis, snowmobiles, and dogsleds, mainly run by local operators); and research activities (visitors who spend time in Svalbard in association with research activities) (Kaltenborn and Hindrum 1996:26). The inclusion of people who visit Svalbard to conduct research into the tourist category is of interest because in the Antarctic, scientists and their support staff do not see themselves as tourists.

With regard to the attractions of Svalbard for visiting tourists, Kaltenborn and Hindrum report that the natural environment, remoteness, history, and culture are the key elements on which tourism is centered.

In 1994, the tourism industry of Svalbard developed a tourism plan (Kaltenborn and Hindrum 1996:28), which states among other things that:

- The tourist industry must be ecologically sustainable.
- The tourist industry must be a commercially profitable business.
- Knowledge and information must be an element of the tourism product.
- Visitors must be informed about and encouraged to respect the special conditions of the islands.
- Tourism is to be controlled and evaluated.

The authors recognize the potentially conflicting views and needs of nature managers and the tourism industry:

> Management agencies need to limit and control the use of the natural environment, whereas the tourist industry must meet certain requirements in order to operate commercially. . . . In addition to a good product and a market, their most important requirements are predictable management in the sense of clear rules and regulations, stable policies and a good dialogue with decision-makers. Until recently, this has been a considerable problem, causing great difficulties for the tourist industry. (p. 32)

The significance of Svalbard as a tourist destination is highlighted by the fact that it was the only Arctic destination discussed during the August 1996 "Polar Tourism: Environmental Implications and Management" symposium held at the Scott Polar Research Institute in Cambridge.

SUB-ANTARCTIC ISLANDS

South of the subtropical convergence—the northern limit of temperate waters—there are twenty-two major oceanic islands or island groups, containing 800 individual islands (Higham 1991). Climatic conditions and types of wildlife on many of these islands are similar to those that can be found in the more temperate parts of Antarctica (particularly the Antarctic Peninsula region). Unlike Antarctica, these islands are all administered as territories of sovereign countries, and as a result, the management of tourism activities on these islands is essentially not very different from the management of tourism activities in wilderness areas or national parks in the various governing countries. The majority of the sub-Antarctic islands are only rarely visited by commercial tourists. The author therefore decided to concentrate on those islands which, at present, are regularly included in the itineraries of cruise vessels. These include, in particular, Australia's Macquarie Island and New Zealand's sub-Antarctic islands. A discussion of the various approaches to the management of tourism in these locations is presented in the following pages.

Macquarie Island, Australia

Macquarie Island is located to the south of Tasmania and is administered by that state. The island was declared a Wildlife Sanctuary in 1933, a State Reserve in 1972, a Nature Reserve in 1978, and a Biosphere Reserve in 1977. The Tasmanian Department of Primary Industry, Water and Environment (DPINE) is responsible for the management of the reserve in accordance with the Tasmanian National Parks and Wildlife Act of 1970 (Tasmanian Department of Parks, Wildlife and Heritage 1991). The Macquarie Island Nature Reserve Management Plan was developed to manage human activities on the island, which include scientific, logistic, and touristic endeavors. (A review of the management plan was under way in late 2000). Section 3.6 of the management plan deals exclusively with tourist and nonstudy visits and states, "Public awareness of the reserve and its specialized flora and fauna should be encouraged in the form of tourism, media coverage and/or other public presentations in so far as they do not conflict with the objectives of management" (points 2.1 to 2.6). This statement makes it clear that tourism is seen as a legitimate use of Macquarie Island provided it is managed within the guidelines and it meets the objectives listed in the management plan:

> 2.1   to protect and manage the reserve as a natural habitat for its indigenous flora and fauna and in order to achieve ecosystem conservation;

2.2 to seek to protect and preserve the marine habitat adjacent to the reserve in so far as it provided access and/or feeding grounds for the majority of the indigenous fauna;

2.3 to conduct, promote and encourage research and studies in so far as they have no permanent detrimental effects into the natural and cultural aspects of the reserve, the surrounding seas and the region;

2.4 to prevent accidental introductions of alien flora or fauna and as far as possible eradicate or control previously introduced species which affect or endanger native species;

2.5 to record, protect and/or preserve any historic localities, artefacts or relics found in the reserve or adjacent waters;

2.6 to permit tourist visits under strictly controlled conditions which allow visitors to experience the natural values of the island without compromising them;

2.7 to publicize and promote the State's successful management of the island as a Nature Reserve and internationally recognized Biosphere Reserve.

Permission and conditions for visits are provided for under section 3.1, "Access to Reserve," with subheadings, "Restricted Area," "Issue of Entry Permits," and "Closure of Areas." The management plan includes a tourism policy (point 3.6.2), which states that:

- Tourist visits will be ship-based but limited facilities such as walkways, viewing platforms and interpretation material may be provided in selected areas to protect the wildlife, environment, historical and/or scientific values of the reserve.
- A condition of permission to enter the reserve will be that all visitors and/or groups of visitors are self-sufficient while in the reserve.
- There shall be a set of "Guidelines for Tourism Operations" which will be reviewed annually in consultation with the Department of Premier and Cabinet, the Department of Tourism, Sport and Recreation and the Antarctic Division.

Macquarie Island, as well as the Heard and McDonald Islands, was nominated for World Heritage listing by the Australian government in June 1996 (Commonwealth Environment Department 1996:1) and was enshrined on the World Heritage list in 1997. World Heritage listing makes a site even more attractive for tourists because it provides a quality assurance to consumers that a place is worth visiting.

Initially the number of visitors allowed during one season was set at a maximum of 600. This quota was not always reached during the early 1990s. During 1993-1994, for example, only three cruise ships visited Macquarie Island, carrying a total of 123 passengers (Information Officer, Tasmanian Dept. of Wildlife and Resource, personal communication, 1994). During discussions with the policy officer of the Australian Antarctic Division (Hay, personal communication, 1995), it was made clear that the limit of 600 passengers per year was seen as about the maximum number the island could take. This opinion may have led to the subsequent reduction in the number of visitors allowed ashore to 500 per season. World Heritage listing may, however, have put pressure on the Tasmanian government to allow more visitors to the island. (*Antarctic Non-Government Activity News* (31) (Australian Antarctic Division 2000b) reports that the number of visitors allowed to visit Macquarie Island in a season has been increased to 750.)

Although the number of visitors permitted to visit was decreased by 100, the per capita fee for visiting increased from A$100 to A$150, (the charge increased to A$165 in 2000) resulting in an increase in revenue despite a reduction in visitor numbers. According to the Information Officer, the funds collected are used to manage tourism and are not, as is the case in other jurisdictions, channeled into consolidated revenue. Despite a general agreement with the notion of charging visitor fees, the question has to be asked whether it really costs A$75,000 (A$150 x 500 passengers) to administer 500 tourists? During this author's visit to Macquarie Island in February 1997 only one landing was undertaken at Sandy Bay. During their three hours ashore the 120 passengers of the *MS Bremen* were accompanied by four rangers from the Tasmanian Department of Environment and Land Management, who provided information and interpretation of the royal and king penguin rookeries visited and who directed passengers to the two boardwalks provided. The total labor cost can be estimated to be approximately A$1,000 while another A$3,000 can be allocated to the production of the information brochure provided to passengers. Thus 24 percent of annual passengers incurred an estimated total cost of A$4,000. Extrapolating these estimates means that the labor and information cost of administering

500 tourists is around A$20,000. This leaves A$55,000 for the provision of boardwalks at two visitor sites!

It is of interest to note that it is not the Australian Antarctic Division (AAD) which sets the visitor quota, but the Tasmanian Department of Environment and Land Management. The operations of the Australian National Antarctic Research Expeditions (ANARE) on Macquarie Island are thus overseen by the Tasmanian government. It appears that the main concern about levels of tourist visitations was not an environmental one (the boardwalks seem to be coping well with what by any national park standard are minute numbers of visitors) but related to the time spent by staff at the station in "entertaining" and educating the visitors. Given that Australian taxpayers fund ANARE, that Tasmanian taxpayers pay the wages of the rangers on the island, and that Macquarie Island has a low profile among the Australian public, one could argue that ANARE should be happy to "entertain and educate" foreign tourists and Australian taxpayers about its activities on the island. It is of note that no "official" ANARE souvenirs are being sold on Macquarie Island. Rather, it is the base staff who, as a private venture, supply and sell T-shirts, posters, coffee mugs, and port wine to tourists who have been deprived of shopping opportunities during their Antarctic voyage.

New Zealand's Sub-Antarctic Islands

New Zealand has five sub-Antarctic island groups under its jurisdiction. These are: the Antipodes, Auckland, Bounty, Campbell, and Snares. The Antipodes and Snares Island groups as well as the unmodified, or near-pristine, islands in the Auckland and Campbell Island groups are "off limits" to tourist landings (Higham 1991:7). The management plan for the Auckland Islands Nature Reserve (Department of Lands and Survey 1987), for example, provides a statement with regard to a tourism policy on these islands. The policy is: "To permit visits to selected areas of the reserve by tourists but under such controls as are deemed necessary to ensure protection of its natural features, ecosystems and cultural values" (p. 14). In the explanation the management plan states that "the Department recognizes that the Auckland Islands hold tourist appeal and that tourism can have positive benefits in the form of increased awareness and can lead to world wide support and sympathy for conservation of our outlying islands" (p. 14). Interestingly, the management plan points out that "strict adherence to IUCN criteria would require a prohibition on tourist entry." The Auckland Islands and the Campbell Islands are regularly visited by cruises organized by the New Zealand company Southern Heritage Tours and are included as part of an Antarctic cruise by several other tour operators, including Hanseatic Tours and Quark Expeditions. The author visited both Auckland and Campbell Island during a voyage aboard the *MS Bremen* in January and February 1997.

The sub-Antarctic Islands guidebook published by the New Zealand Department of Conservation provides a concise overview of all New Zealand sub-Antarctic islands. The book introduces the history, geology, climate, and wildlife of the islands and provides a visitor code of conduct. The main points of this code of conduct (Higham 1991:67-68) are:

- "All the New Zealand sub-Antarctic island groups are National Nature Reserves and entry is by permit only. Tourist visit entry permits are issued on the condition that the group is accompanied by a Department of Conservation (DOC) representative. The representative's role is to oversee visitors' activities to ensure they have no detrimental effects on the ecology of the islands;"
- "The DOC representative has the right to refuse entry or change the landing site on the island for such reasons as: risk of disturbing breeding animals, poor weather conditions, sensitivity of the environment;"
- "Animal and plant quarantine procedures are strictly enforced to ensure there are no accidental introductions of new pests, plants or pathogens. . . . All footwear and clothing must be thoroughly checked and cleaned before and following each separate island visit. All gear must not be packed until immediately prior to landing and must be sealed against rodent entry;"
- No avian food products are permitted ashore;
- No collecting of specimens or souvenirs is permitted during tourist visits;
- No rubbish to be left on any of the islands;
- The individual space of all wildlife must be respected at all times. Visitors must:
  —give all animals the right of way
  —get no closer than five meters to all wildlife

—not touch any wildlife
—avoid surrounding any animal during viewing
—keep noise to a minimum
—keep to formed tracks and boardwalk where provided
—not smoke while ashore;
- There are no toilets provided on any of the islands.

For the purposes of this book, the significance of the Australian and New Zealand sub-Antarctic islands lies in the fact that, despite being visited by comparatively few people, they do have management plans in place which address pertinent tourism issues, prescribe certain enforceable codes of behavior for visiting tourists, and impose visitor fees.

Much can be learned from the handling of tourism on Australia's and New Zealand's sub-Antarctic islands that could be directly applicable to the sustainable management of Antarctic tourism. Writers such as Sanson (1994), Wouters and Hall (1995a), and Cessford and Dingwall (1994, 1996), provide a comprehensive overview of the management of tourism on New Zealand's sub-Antarctic islands. Hall and Wouters (1994) and Wouters and Hall (1995b) also provide discussions of tourism activities and issues on other sub-Antarctic islands.

CONCLUDING COMMENTS

What can be learned from these locations that is relevant and useful for the management of Antarctic tourism? In summary, it can be said that elements of the Galapagos model of tourism management (for example, small groups ashore and the requirement to carry guides) can be, and to a certain degree already are, applicable in the Antarctic context. In the absence of a national Antarctic government, the Galapagos model could actually perform better because it would not be subject to the same level of political interference that appears to exist in Ecuador. Unlike the Galapagos, no visitor quotas have yet been set for tourist sites in the Antarctic.

At this writing, the management of tourism in the Arctic is still lagging behind Antarctic tourism management, and as a result, information on how to manage tourism in a polar environment flows from south to north.

Without question, the most directly applicable models of tourism management are the ones used on the sub-Antarctic islands of Australia and New Zealand. With some relatively minor local modifications these could be adapted to suit the management of tourism sites in the Antarctic.

Chapter 3

Antarctica:
The Resource and the Industry

INTRODUCTION: THE RESOURCE

Antarctica—"last of lands," "the seventh continent," "the bottom of the world." These are just some of the descriptions found in the literature and on the pages of Antarctic tourism brochures that describe the world's most remote continent. Although these definitions are all worthwhile in their particular contexts, for the purposes of this book it is important to provide a more detailed background for Antarctica, the resource used by the Antarctic tourism industry. This chapter, therefore, provides an overview of the physical aspects of Antarctica and introduces the reader to human endeavors in the Antarctic context ranging from the early days of exploration to the various commercial uses of Antarctic resources. The chapter also addresses the unique territorial and political situation of the continent.

ANTARCTICA DEFINED

Antarctica is centered on the geographic South Pole and covers 13.9 million square kilometers, nearly twice the size of Australia, or approximately the size of the continental United States and Mexico combined. It has the distinction of being the highest, coldest, windiest, driest, and remotest of all the continents, and its ice cover makes up 90 to 95 percent of the world's fresh water reserves. Temperatures can drop as low as −89.6°C as measured in July 1983 at Vostok base in the Australian Antarctic Territory. Wind gusts of over 200 miles an hour are common. The interior is a high altitude polar desert that receives only half the annual precipitation of Australia's driest spot,

Mulka Bore on the edge of the Simpson Desert (Reader's Digest 1992:290). The coastline is an area where wildlife is in abundance during the brief summer months, but the interior is practically devoid of life. In contrast to all other continents, Antarctica lacks an indigenous human population, but it is home to millions of penguins and seals and temporary home to several thousand scientists and their support staff.

Behind such an overview as this lies much information, any part of which may be relevant not only to the operators but also to the tourists, before, during, or after their visit. So popular is the appeal of much of this information that there is a ready market for authoritative yet popular publications (e.g., Reader's Digest's *Antarctica,* which was first published in 1985 but has since been revised and updated twice, the last time in 1990). While the above provides a quick introduction to Antarctica, additional information is needed to ensure that the reader is provided with a sound understanding.

The English word *Antarctic* can be traced back to the Greeks, who called the northernmost parts of the globe *Arktos,* the Bear, which they named after the northern constellation of the Great Bear (Ursa Major). From this evolved the English term *Arctic.* The word *Antarctic* consequently evolved from the Greek *avri,* opposite, and *Arktos,* meaning the opposite to the Arctic, thus the Antarctic. The Antarctic region has been defined in several ways and, depending on which definition is used, the region varies in size. The area of Antarctica itself measures 13.9 million square kilometers, making it the fifth largest continent (Reader's Digest 1990:10). Surrounding the continent is the Southern Ocean, where the summer water temperature is only slightly above freezing (sea water freezes at −1.86°C). The parts of this ocean closest to Antarctica are often carpeted with ice, covering an area of between 2.65 million square kilometers in summer and some 20 million square kilometers in winter (Australian Antarctic Division 1995b:2). This frozen ocean is an integral part of the Antarctic ecosystem since it provides habitat for much of the wildlife including whales, seals, flying seabirds, and penguins. For the purposes of this book the terms *Antarctica* and *Antarctic* will be used interchangeably since tourism takes place on the continent itself and in the maritime region surrounding it.

Another way of defining the Antarctic is to use the polar circle as the boundary. The Antarctic circle is located at 66 degrees 32 minutes

South. Stonehouse (1990b:15) points out that polar circles are only meaningful on maps, that "on Earth's surface they are less convincing, for there is nothing to show for them. There are no sudden changes when we cross them; they do not separate polar from non-polar climates, or one kind of habitat from another." As a result, it is often the "biological" boundary, the Antarctic convergence, which is used to define the outer extent of the Antarctic. Stonehouse (1990b:15) defines it thus: "The *Antarctic Convergence* is a boundary at the ocean surface between two well-defined water masses, Antarctic Water to the south and Subtropical Water to the north. Sometimes visible, always detectable by a sudden change in temperature and salinity, it is the most generally accepted boundary defining the Antarctic region."

The last of the defining boundaries, the one used for the purposes of this book, is 60 degrees southern latitude. The region within this boundary is covered by a unique international instrument, the Antarctic Treaty. The treaty and its associated instruments will be discussed in greater detail in the latter part of this chapter. The reason this definition is the most appropriate one is that it is the unique political situation that makes the management of tourism activities different from any other tourist destination.

THE NATURAL ENVIRONMENT: GEOGRAPHY, WILDLIFE, AND FLORA

Geography

Unlike the region surrounding the geographic North Pole, which consists of frozen sea ice, Antarctica is a continent. In its publication *Looking South*, the Australian Antarctic Division (1995:2) provides a concise summary of the physical characteristics of Antarctica:

> For millions of years snow and ice have built up on the land, so that now all but two percent of the land is buried under a permanent ice sheet. The ice sheet holds 90 percent of the world's ice—30 million cubic kilometers—which is 60 to 70 percent of its fresh water. The thickness of the ice sheet averages 2.4 km (4.7 km at its thickest point). If all the ice were to melt, the level of the world's oceans would rise by 65 to 70 meters, and if the weight of the ice were removed it is estimated that the underlying rock would rise by 700 m to 1000 m. Without the ice we

would see a single mass of East Antarctica and a smaller archipelago of rugged mountain islands—West Antarctica.

The issue of the possible melting of the polar ice caps by way of an increase in the earth's temperature (often referred to as *global warming*) has been discussed by numerous writers (see, for example, The Antarctica Project 1997:3) and is discussed frequently in the popular press. As far as Antarctic tourism is concerned, the possible melting of parts of the South Polar ice cap at some future date is only of significance in the sense that the continued coverage of the matter in the media ensures that more and more people become aware of the existence of Antarctica. It is doubtful whether the possible long-term effects of global warming will have significant implications for Antarctic tourism in the foreseeable future. The collapse of ice shelves such as Larsen A in January 1995 (The Antarctica Project 1997:3) can, however, be seen to be of some relevance (and maybe concern) to the conduct of tourism on the eastern side of the Antarctic Peninsula. The physical features of Antarctica, for example its mountains, glaciers, icebergs, and ice-free areas, are of great significance for tourism. These features provide some of the most important attractions for visitors, and several of them can at times also be seen as barriers to the conduct of commercial tourism activities.

Antarctic Wildlife

The biology of polar habitats is described by Fogg (1998), and Lovering and Prescott (1979:22) provide a summary of the fauna and flora. They state that: "Since Antarctica is the coldest, windiest, and driest continent on the Earth, it is not surprising that very few plants and animals whose life cycles restrict them to the continent alone are found there."

The following section introduces some of the species that are significant for the purposes of this investigation. These are the species that are most likely to come in contact with visiting tourists, and as such they deserve special attention. Creatures such as insects, spiders, ticks, lice, mites, springtails, and the largest native inhabitant of Antarctica, a midge or wingless fly called *Belgica antarctica* that grows to a length of 2.5 to 3.0 millimeters (Lovering and Prescott 1979:25), are fascinating to the specialist, but since they can only rarely be observed, are of very little concern to tourists.

Penguins

Penguins are the hallmark of Antarctica. As Smith (1993) put it: "This close, well-publicized link between the Antarctic and penguins has fostered a popular image based on this one attribute." Penguins can only be found in the Southern Hemisphere, but their distribution ranges from Antarctica as far north as the Galapagos Islands on the equator. Stonehouse (1990b:84) provides a concise introduction to this most easily recognized symbol of Antarctica:

> Penguins are flightless seabirds that walk, swim and dive. . . . Penguins are southern hemisphere birds, mostly of temperate or cool seas, but seven species live in or close to the Antarctic region. Emperor penguins live only on coastal Antarctica. . . . They do not make nests, and only the males incubate, standing with the single egg on their feet for nine weeks during the coldest period of winter. . . . Adélie penguins also breed in Antarctica, but they nest in summer, producing two eggs. Chinstrap penguins breed only on the Antarctic Peninsula and nearby islands. Gentoo and crested macaroni penguins range widely throughout the southern islands, north and south of the pack ice. Rockhopper and king penguins breed only on the warmer islands near the Convergence. Emperor and king penguins, the two largest species, feed on fish and squid at intermediate depths, and also on krill and surface fish. The smaller species feed mainly on surface-living fish and krill.

In this paragraph, Stonehouse introduces all the penguin species that are of relevance to Antarctic tourism. Several books concentrate solely on penguins; see, for example, Gorman (1990), *The Total Penguin,* and Nagle (1990), *Penguins,* for a more detailed discussion.

Flying Seabirds

Watching flying seabirds is a popular activity for Antarctic tourists while cruising the Southern Ocean, including the wandering, royal, grey-headed, black-browed, light mantled sooty, and sooty albatrosses, and such petrels and shearwaters as the Southern giant petrel, southern fulmar, Antarctic petrel, cape petrel, snow petrel, Kerguelen petrel, white-headed, and several others. The largest and arguably most impressive of the petrel family is the wandering albatross, which breeds on several of the sub-Antarctic islands. It can reach a wingspan of 3.5 meters and is known to travel up to 9,000 kilometers in a single foraging trip. A breeding colony of wandering albatrosses can, for example, be found on Albatross Island in South Georgia. Because the island is easily accessible and visitors can get close to these magnificent birds, Albatross Island is a frequently visited site on cruises. During the lengthy times cruise ships spend at sea, bird watching is one of the most popular pastimes. Many passengers can be observed spending their days on the bridge or on deck in an attempt to spot a rare bird. Tour operators such as the U.K.-based Wild Wings organize special bird-watching cruises to the region.

Seals and Whales

Six species of seals live within the Antarctic Convergence: Crabeater, southern elephant, leopard, Ross, southern fur seal, and Weddell seal (Stonehouse 1990b:83-85). Tourists in the Antarctic Peninsula region are most likely to encounter significant numbers of crabeater seals (often traveling on ice floes and who, despite their name, do not eat crabs but instead feed on krill, shrimplike crustaceans), southern elephant and Antarctic fur seals (largely on South Georgia), while sightings of other seal species are comparatively rare.

Whales also frequent Antarctic waters. There are two main types of whales, toothed and baleen (filter feeding) (Laws 1989:147). Baleen whales that can be found in Antarctic waters include blue, fin, humpback, minke, sei, and southern right. Toothed whales, which can on occasion be spotted, include sperm and killer (Orca) whales and the hourglass dolphin (Laws 1989:147). Close-up sightings of whales are not necessarily daily occurrences during an Antarctic voyage. As a result watch is kept, and when a whale surfaces close to a ship it is announced over the ship's public address system, resulting in a rush of passengers to the best vantage points.

Antarctic Flora

Laws (1989:14) states that only approximately 2 percent of Antarctica is ice-free, while Lovering and Prescott (1979:18) are of the opinion that the figure is between 2 and 5 percent. Plant life is therefore limited to those ice-free areas. Only two native vascular plants are able to grow in the Antarctic—a grass, *Deschampsia antarctica*, and a cushion-forming pearlwort, *Colobanthus quitensis* (Fogg 1998:

83). There are also mosses, liverworts, and lichens. Because of the hostile climate these plants are slow growing. Many lichens are estimated to be over 100 years old. Mosses and lichens are the two plants that are of greatest interest to tourists. These plants add some color to an otherwise fairly uniformly white, gray, and black environment and thus they are the subjects of many photographs. Unfortunately, in the process of being photographed these plants occasionally run the risk of being trampled upon, an issue that will be discussed in Chapter 5.

HUMAN INVOLVEMENT IN ANTARCTICA

Discovery and Exploration

The history of Antarctica is described in detail by Laurence Kirwan (1961) in his book *A History of Polar Exploration*. Furthermore, many accounts of individual expeditions have been written. In addition, Headland (1989) provides a full chronology of Antarctic expeditions and related historical events, the Reader's Digest (1990) book *Antarctica* devotes over 200 pages to the exploration of the continent, and there is a home page on the Internet (<http://www.terraquest. com/va/history/history.html>) that provides a chronology of Antarctic discovery and exploration. Table 3.1 summarizes the most significant events.

TABLE 3.1. Significant Antarctic Events

Year	Event
650	Ui-te-rangiora sails south of New Zealand and names the sea Taii-uka-apia (meaning the sea with foam like arrowroot, a common white substance in Polynesia).
1772	Yves Joseph de Kerguelen-Tremarec discovers a group of icebound islands in the southern Indian Ocean now known as Iles Kerguelen.
1773	Captain James Cook and the crew of the *Resolution* and *Adventure* become the first men to cross the Antarctic Circle. They eventually circumnavigate Antarctica, crossing the Antarctic Circle three times.
1820-1821	First sighting of the Antarctic Peninsula by Palmer, Bransfield, and Smith. Bellingshausen sights an icefield at 69 degrees south and lays claim to being the first person to set eyes on the Antarctic continent.

TABLE 3.1 *(continued)*

Year	Event
1837-1840	Dumont D'Urville in the *Astrolabe* and *Zelee* sights Adelie Land.
1874	*HMS Challenger* crosses the Antarctic Circle, the first steamship to do so, on a four-year scientific cruise of the world.
1895	Bull, Borchgrevink, and Kristensen make the first-ever landing on the Antarctic continent at Cape Adare, from their ship *Antarctic.*
1898	The Belgica expedition under Adrien de Gerlache finds itself trapped in the Antarctic Peninsula pack ice and becomes the first party to live through an Antarctic winter.
1902	Robert F. Scott, Edward Wilson, and Ernest Shackleton leave McMurdo Sound to attempt the South Pole. At 82 degrees south they are forced to turn back.
1902	Erich von Drygalski and the members of the official German expedition on the *Gauss* sight a high vertical wall of ice and name it Wilhelm II Land.
1904	Scott's British National Expedition establishes a base on Ross Island from the *Discovery*. Carl Larsen sets up the first shore-based whaling station at Grytviken on South Georgia. W. S. Bruce and the members of the Scottish National Antarctic Expedition aboard the *Scotia* sight the coast of Coats Land and build a base on Laurie Island in the South Orkneys.
1905	The International Geographical Congress decides to make Antarctica the main target of future exploration. This launches an era of government-sponsored national expeditions.
1907-1909	Shackleton establishes the British Antarctic Expedition's base on Ross Island from the *Nimrod*. Farthest south (150 km from South Pole), South Magnetic Pole and summit of Erebus attained.
1908	Ernest Shackleton, Frank Wild, Eric Marshall, and Jameson Adams begin their attempt to reach the South Pole.
1910	Roald Amundsen heads for the South Pole rather than the North as officially announced. Meanwhile, Robert F. Scott's second expedition returns to Ross Island. Scott sets out in the spring once again for the South Pole.
1911	Roald Amundsen—with four companions and 18 dogs—pioneers a new route onto the polar plateau and plants the Norwegian flag on the South Pole. Mawson's Australian Antarctic Expedition departs Hobart aboard the *Aurora* bound for Macquarie Island, where a relay station is established.
1912	Scott, Wilson, Bowers, Evans, and Oates reach the South Pole. All perish on the return journey.
1913	Mawson and six others are forced to spend a second winter at Cape Denison.
1915	Shackleton's *Endurance* expedition to cross Antarctica fails.
1922	Shackleton dies aboard the *Quest* and is buried on South Georgia.
1928	The Australian Hubert Wilkins makes the first powered flight in Antarctica.

Year	Event
1929	Richard Byrd and his crew overfly the geographic South Pole.
1923-1931	Mawson leads voyages of BANZARE. British sovereignty proclaimed at seven locations including Cape Denison (January 5, 1931).
1934	Richard Byrd becomes the first person to winter in the interior of the continent.
1935-1937	John Rymill leads the British Graham Land Expedition aboard the *Penola.*
1940	Little America III established by Richard Byrd at the Bay of Whales.
1947	U.S. Operation Highjump maps large areas of the continent.
1955-1958	Commonwealth Trans-Antarctic Expedition crosses the continent.
1957	The International Geophysical Year (IGY) begins, with Antarctica as the main area of study. During the next 18 months, scientists from 67 countries carry out joint Antarctic research. The U.S. establishes Amundsen-Scott base at the geographic South Pole.
1959	The 12 leading participants in the IGY sign the Antarctic Treaty in Washington.
1966	Lars-Eric Lindblad begins regular annual cruises to the Antarctic Peninsula.
1977	Qantas starts day excursion flights over the continent.
1979	An Air New Zealand DC-10 carrying 257 people crashes into Mount Erebus. There are no survivors.
1991	The Madrid Protocol on Environmental Protection is agreed to after two years of negotiations.
1994	Recommendation XVIII-1 is adopted at the XVIII ATCM in Kyoto.
1996	Twenty countries have ratified the Madrid Protocol.
1997	Only Japan has not yet ratified the Madrid Protocol.
1998	On January 14 the Madrid Protocol enters into force.

Sources: Martin 1996:33; Headland 1989; Headland 1994:270; Australian Antarctic Division 2000.

As a result of its geographic isolation and the difficulties in gaining access to the continent, it can be estimated that only around 200,000 humans—explorers, adventurers, scientists, support staff, and tourists—have ever visited Antarctica. Compared to other parts of the world, the general public knows relatively little about Antarctica and it is therefore surrounded by a certain mystique. Some of this is attributable to the many accounts of discovery and exploration that have been written and published during the last 200 years. Travelers are inspired to visit after being introduced to the continent during their school days by books such as Lennard Bickel's (1977) *This Accursed Land,* Mawson's *The Home of the Blizzard,* Scott's *Scott's Last Expedition,* or Shackleton's *The Heart of the Antarctic.* The historic context adds an extra dimension to the Antarctic tourism product, which is otherwise dominated by natural attractions. Lectures on the various aspects of Antarctic history form an integral component of all cruises. An understanding of the historical background is of particular importance when passengers are visiting the historic huts of Scott, Shackleton, Borchgrevink, or Mawson or when they land on Deception Island, site of an abandoned whaling station and location of the first powered flight in the Antarctic.

The exploration of the heart of the continent began with Robert Falcon Scott's first attempt at the geographic South Pole during the Discovery Expedition of 1901-1904. Scott was followed by Sir Ernest Shackleton, who led the 1908-1909 Nimrod Expedition. On January 6, 1909, Shackleton, Wild, Marshall, and Adams reached latitude 88 degrees 23 minutes south, less than 100 miles from the South Pole and farther south than any humans had ever been.

The "race" to the South Pole during 1911 and 1912 stands out as one of the great adventures in exploration. Amundsen, starting from the Bay of Whales and using dogs, reached the South Pole on December 15, 1911. Captain Robert Falcon Scott and his men, man-hauling their sledges, did not reach the Pole until Wednesday, January 17, 1912. Roland Huntford's book *Scott and Amundsen: The Race to the South Pole* (Huntford 1979) provides a fascinating insight into Amundsen's triumph and highlights, somewhat controversially, Scott's deficiencies in expedition planning, which ultimately led to the death of Scott and his men.

Amundsen and Scott are arguably the best known Antarctic explorers, but there are others whose exploits are no less significant. In particular the explorations of Sir Ernest Shackleton deserve attention. As previously mentioned, in 1909 Shackleton came within a hundred miles of the South Pole. Having failed to reach the Pole, his next goal was to traverse the Antarctic continent from the Weddell Sea to the Ross Sea (the Imperial Transantarctic Expedition). He left England in August 1914 and, after stopping on the island of South Georgia, sailed into the Weddell Sea in December 1914. By January 18, 1915, his ship *Endurance* was firmly locked into the ice. For the next ten months, the ship drifted, stuck fast in the pack ice, and finally sank in

November 1915. Hurley (1956) provides a vivid account of the expedition's struggle to survive after the sinking. They walked across the sea ice dragging their lifeboats behind them for months on end and managed to reach the relative safety of Cape Wild on Elephant Island, just off the northernmost tip of the Antarctic Peninsula. From there Shackleton,Worsley, Crean, McCarthy, McNeish, and Vincent sailed the *James Caird* to South Georgia to bring relief to the marooned sailors on Elephant Island. The account of the Endurance Expedition is arguably the greatest story of human survival in a hostile climate ever told. It is often cited in the lecture programs aboard Antarctic cruise vessels.

In the region that today is part of the Australian Antarctic Territory (AAT), another explorer struggled to survive the hostile Antarctic climate. Dr. Douglas Mawson (later Sir Douglas Mawson) first went to Antarctica as a scientific member of Shackleton's Nimrod expedition in 1907-1909 (Crossley 1995). Unlike Scott, Amundsen, and Shackleton, Mawson was a trained scientist. As Sir Edmund Hillary in the foreword to Bickel's (1977) book *This Accursed Land* puts it:

> From 1911 to 1913—at the same time as the Scott tragedy was coming to its sad conclusion—Mawson led his Australasian Antarctic Expedition into the unknown country west of Cape Adare. It was an expedition that carried out a notable amount of scientific research which earned it a place amongst the great scientific expeditions of its day.

Sailing aboard the *Aurora*, Mawson and his crew established a base on Macquarie Island before sailing for Commonwealth Bay. Here they set up their main base camp in a location that was later named by Mawson "the Home of the Blizzard" thanks to the constant strong katabatic winds blowing down from the polar plateau. After his two companions Mertz and Ninnis died, Mawson struggled back to winter quarters alone, in the process coming close to death on several occasions. Mawson (1996), Bickel (1977), and Laseron (1957) all provide accounts of the expedition.

The Mechanized Age

The heroic age of Antarctic exploration ended with the death of Sir Ernest Shackleton aboard the *Quest* on January 5, 1922. His body

was transferred to South Georgia and he was buried in a small ceme-
tery near Grytviken, the whaling "capital" of South Georgia. Today
his grave is regularly visited by tourists aboard cruise ships who have
the opportunity to pay tribute to "The Boss," as Shackleton's com-
rades fondly named him. His grave has become one of the very few
existing physical reminders of a long-bygone era. Shackleton's spirit
of inquisitive and daring investigation can still be found among
(some) modern Antarctic travelers, many of whom see themselves as
adventurers, exploring the final frontier.

Improvements in technology, particularly in the fields of transport,
communication, and clothing, were the precursors of the next era of
exploration, the mechanized age. Kirwan (1961:339) sees the development of aircraft and their subsequent use in Antarctica as the major
technological development that strongly influenced the course of exploration. The air age began with the first Antarctic flight, by Australian Sir Hubert Wilkins, on Deception Island on November 16, 1928.
The South Pole was first overflown by Richard Evelyn Byrd, making
him the first person to overfly both poles. He describes his flight in
the August 1930 issue of *National Geographic* (Byrd 1930).

During the years between Byrd's South Pole flight and the end of
World War II, several noteworthy and groundbreaking expeditions
took place that further enhanced our knowledge and understanding of
the last unexplored continent in the world. The Reader's Digest
(1990:298) book *Antarctica* provides a chronological listing of the
most significant expeditions and events up to 1946.

Scientific Age: The International Geophysical Year

The year 1957 marked a watershed in the history of Antarctic exploration, for it was then that the International Geophysical Year (IGY)
began (it ran from July 1, 1957 to December 31, 1958). The idea of the
IGY is attributed to the American scientist Dr. Lloyd Berkner, who
suggested it in 1950. The regions the IGY concentrated on were
Antarctica and outer space. The following twelve countries became involved in the IGY Antarctic program: Argentina, Australia, Belgium,
Chile, France, Great Britain, Japan, New Zealand, Norway, South Africa, the United States and the (former) USSR. Over forty stations were
established on the Antarctic mainland and peninsula and a further
twenty on various Antarctic and sub-Antarctic islands where scientists
carried out research programs in fields such as glaciology, meteorol-

ogy, geomagnetism, and upper-air studies (Reader's Digest 1990:273). Prior to the start of the IGY, Admiral Byrd pointed out that close cooperation during the IGY would lead to an increase in goodwill among the people of the participating nations.

ANTARCTICA IN THE CONTEXT OF INTERNATIONAL LAW

Unlike any other major landmass, Antarctica is not owned by any country, company, organization, or individual. Many of the complexities of Antarctic tourism have their origins in its unique legal and political situation. Seven countries have established claims to various parts of Antarctica: Argentina, Australia, Chile, France, New Zealand, Norway, and the United Kingdom. Their claims to territorial sovereignty are not universally recognized. For example, the United States and Russia, two of the major players in the exploration of Antarctica, do not lay or acknowledge any claims to Antarctic territory. To prevent a potentially major international conflict from erupting over the issue of ownership, the twelve countries that had established scientific bases in Antarctica during the IGY negotiated the Antarctic Treaty. Negotiations took place during 1958 and 1959 following the success of the IGY, which had seen unprecedented cooperation in scientific research. The treaty was signed on December 1, 1959, and came into force on June 23, 1961. "A total of 44 countries have become Parties to the Antarctic Treaty. Of these, seven claim territory in Antarctica (claimants), 12 are Original Signatories, and 27 are Consultative Parties" (Australian Antarctic Division 2000). The Antarctic Treaty Consultative Parties (ATCPs) meet on an annual basis to discuss issues and to make recommendations to their governments pertaining to the management of Antarctic affairs. The forty-four Antarctic Treaty Parties represent an estimated 80 percent of the world's population. The linchpin of the treaty is Article IV which, in effect, recognizes that the question of territorial sovereignty is insoluble (May 1988). It states that the treaty does not recognize, dispute, or establish territorial claims and that no new claims shall be asserted while the treaty is in force. A summary of treaty provisions that cover the most salient points is listed in Table 3.2.

TABLE 3.2. Antarctic Treaty Summary Provisions

Article I
Antarctica shall be used for peaceful purposes only. All military measures, including weapons testing, are prohibited. Military personnel and equipment may be used, however, for scientific purposes.

Article II
Freedom of scientific investigation in Antarctica and co-operation towards that end, as applied during the International Geophysical Year, shall continue, subject to the provisions of the present Treaty.

Article III
1. To the extent feasible and practical:
   (a) information regarding plans for scientific programs in Antarctica shall be exchanged;
   (b) scientific personnel shall be exchanged in Antarctica between expeditions and stations;
   (c) scientific observations and results from Antarctica shall be exchanged and made freely available;
2. Co-operation with Specialized Agencies of the United Nations and other international organizations having a scientific or technical interest in Antarctic is strongly encouraged.

Article IV (full text)
1. Nothing contained in the present Treaty shall be interpreted as:
   (a) a renunciation by any Contracting Party of previously asserted rights of or claims to territorial sovereignty in Antarctica;
   (b) a renunciation or diminution by any Contracting Party of any basis of claim to territorial sovereignty in Antarctica which it may have whether as a result of its activities or those of its nationals in Antarctica, or otherwise;
   (c) prejudicing the position of any Contracting Party as regards its recognition or non-recognition of any other State's rights of or claim or basis of claim to territorial sovereignty in Antarctica.
2. No acts or activities taking place while the present Treaty is in force shall constitute a basis for asserting, supporting or denying a claim to territorial sovereignty in Antarctica or create any rights of sovereignty in Antarctica. No new claim, or enlargement of an existing claim, to territorial sovereignty in Antarctica shall be asserted while the present Treaty is in force.

Article V
Nuclear explosions and disposal of radioactive wastes are prohibited.

Article VI
All land and ice shelves below 60 Degrees South are included, but high seas are covered under international law.

Article VII
Treaty-state observers have free access—including aerial observation—to any area and may inspect all stations, installations, and equipment. Advance notice of all activities and of the introduction of military personnel must be given.

Article VIII
Observers under Article VII and scientific personnel under Article III are under the jurisdiction of their own states.

Article IX
Treaty states shall meet periodically to exchange information and take measures to further treaty objectives, including the preservation and conservation of living resources. These consultative meetings shall be open to contracting parties that conduct substantial scientific research in the area.

Article X
Treaty parties will discourage activities by any country in Antarctica that are contrary to the Treaty.

Article XI
Disputes are to be settled peacefully by the parties concerned or, ultimately, by the International Court of Justice.

Article XII
After the expiration of 30 years from the date the treaty enters into force, any member state may request a conference to review the operation of the treaty. [During 1991 the Treaty parties met but no review of the treaty was requested thus extending the treaty indefinitely.]

Article XIII
The Treaty is subject to ratification by signatory states and is open for accession by any state that is a member of the UN or is invited by all the member states.

Article XIV
The United States is the repository of the treaty and is responsible for providing certified copies to signatories and acceding states.

Source: Heap 1990.

Article VI of the Antarctic Treaty establishes the area covered under the treaty, which is also the area under consideration for the purposes of this book. It states: "The provisions of the present Treaty shall apply to the area south of 60 Degrees South Latitude, including all ice shelves, but nothing in the present Treaty shall prejudice or in any way affect the rights, or the exercise of the rights, of any State under international law with regard to the high seas within that area" (Heap 1990:xiv).

CONVENTIONS, PROTOCOLS, AND RECOMMENDATIONS UNDER THE ANTARCTIC TREATY SYSTEM

Since coming into force in 1961, the Antarctic Treaty has developed from a single instrument into a system of conventions, annexes, and recommendations. Collectively these are known as the Antarctic Treaty System (ATS). The *Handbook of the Antarctic Treaty System* (Heap 1990) provides a comprehensive overview of the ATS. The following recommendations and conventions are seen as relevant in the context of this book.

The Agreed Measures for the Conservation of Antarctic Fauna and Flora

"The Agreed Measures were adopted in 1964 as Recommendation VIII at the Third Antarctic Treaty Consultative Meeting" (NSF 1995b:167). "The measures provide for overall protection of native animals and plants while establishing a system of managed protected areas" (Australian Antarctic Division 1995b:23). The Antarctic Treaty Area was considered a "Special Conservation Area" (Heap 1990: 2402) by the Treaty Parties and to maintain this status the following provisions were made:

  i. Prohibition of the killing, wounding, capturing, or molesting of any native mammal or bird except in accordance with a permit
  ii. such permits to be issued only for certain restrictive purposes
  iii. the designation of Specially Protected Species
  iv. the designation of Specially Protected Areas
  v. regulating the importation into Antarctica of nonindigenous species, parasites, and diseases
  vi. minimizing harmful interference with the normal living conditions of Antarctic mammals and birds
  vii. exchange of information between Consultative Parties as to actions they have permitted (Heap 1990:2402)

Ross seals and fur seals were granted special protection and twenty areas were designated as Specially Protected Areas (SPA), four of which have had their status changed to Sites of Special Scientific Interest (SSSI) (Heap 1990:2402). The Agreed Measures are of great importance for tourism in Antarctica because they greatly influence where tourists can go and how they are required to behave while in Antarctica.

Convention on the Conservation
of Antarctic Marine Living Resources

The negotiations for the Convention on the Conservation of Antarctic Marine Living Resources (CCAMLR) began in Canberra in 1978 and were concluded in 1980 (Heap 1990:4201). CCAMLR "established the world's only fishing agreement which seeks to manage the whole ecosystem rather than just individual commercial species" (Australian Antarctic Division 1995b:23). As Heap (1990:4201) points out, the convention broke new ground in several ways. Although it was negotiated under the Antarctic Treaty, the area covered is larger than the Antarctic Treaty Area in that it extends as far as the Antarctic Convergence, the northern limit of the Antarctic ecosystem. Article I(2) defines Antarctic marine living resources as "populations of fin fish, molluscs, crustaceans and all other species of living organisms, including birds found south of the Antarctic Convergence" and Article I(3) defines the Antarctic marine ecosystem as: "the complex of relationships of Antarctic marine living resources with each other and with their physical environment" (Heap 1990:4209). Article II of the convention sets out the objectives. The two main ones in the present context are:

1. The objective of this Convention is the conservation of Antarctic marine living resources.
2. For the purposes of this Convention, the term "conservation" includes rational use (Heap 1990:4209).

Thus, by affording a certain protection to Antarctic marine living resources, in particular krill, the Treaty Parties provided for the sustained supply of food to most Antarctic marine mammals such as whales and seals, as well as for the various species of seabirds, including penguins. Krill *(Euphausia superba)* is one of the most important animals in the ecology of the Antarctic seas (Stonehouse 1990b:67) and one of the most abundant species in the world. Crossley (1995:47) estimates a population of 600,000 billion. The word "krill" is a Norwegian whaling term meaning "small fry" (May 1988:80). In the tourism context CCAMLR is significant since it ensures the survival of bountiful Antarctic wildlife, which forms one of the main attractions for Antarctic tourists.

Convention for the Conservation of Antarctic Seals

The Convention for the Conservation of Antarctic Seals (CCAS) was accepted in 1972 to provide a means for the regulation of commercial sealing, should it ever be resumed, to fully protect three Antarctic seal species (Ross, elephant, and fur seals), and to establish catch limits for the other three species (crabeater, leopard, and Weddell seals) (Australian Antarctic Division 1995b: 23). The protection of the seals is of relevance to the tourism issue because, like seabirds, seals form an important attraction for visitors and may be worth more as such than as seal meat and pelts.

Convention on the Regulation of Antarctic Mineral Resource Activities

In the late 1970s, it was argued that because no large-scale mineral reserves had been identified in Antarctica and that as a result mining in Antarctica would not be economically viable until at least the next century, there was no need to negotiate a minerals regime (Heap 1990:4301). The Treaty Parties nevertheless noted the possible negative environmental effects of potential mining operations in Antarctica and decided that: "since there would be even greater difficulties in negotiating a minerals regime if it was left until exploitable deposits were found and the necessary technology was available, the better course would be to conclude a framework regime which would cover all stages of prospecting, exploration and development" (Heap 1990: 4301). Throughout the 1980s, the Treaty Parties worked on the difficult task of drafting a minerals regime. During the final session of the Fourth Special Antarctic Treaty Consultative Meeting on Antarctic Mineral Resources held in Wellington, New Zealand from May 2 to June 2, 1988, the Consultative Parties adopted the Convention on the Regulation of Antarctic Mineral Resource Activities (CRAMRA). The convention was opened for signature on November 25, 1988. During 1989, the Australian government decided that it would not ratify CRAMRA but instead seek support from other Antarctic Treaty Parties including France, Italy, and Belgium for full environmental protection for the continent and its surrounding seas (Australian Antarctic Division 1995b:23). Under the Antarctic Treaty all decisions made must be unanimous—thus Australia's refusal to ratify effectively rendered CRAMRA null and void. The Australian action led to arguably the most important addition to the Antarctic Treaty System, the Madrid Protocol.

Protocol on Environmental Protection to the Antarctic Treaty (Madrid Protocol)

The Protocol on Environmental Protection to the Antarctic Treaty was negotiated during two years of special meetings among the Antarctic Treaty Consultative Parties and was signed on October 4, 1991, in Madrid. It consists of twenty-seven articles and a schedule to the protocol consisting of thirteen articles that address the issue of arbitration (National Science Foundation 1995b:187-223). There are also five annexes (for full text of the Madrid Protocol see, for example, National Science Foundation 1995b). The Australian Antarctic Division (1995b:23) summarizes the key provisions of the Madrid Protocol in the following fashion:

> The Protocol places an indefinite ban on mining or mineral resource activity in Antarctica, designating the Antarctic as a natural reserve devoted to peace and science. It provides a multinational, codified set of environmental standards (Antarctica is the only continent for which this applies), and creates a new system of protected areas. The Protocol establishes environmental principles for the conduct of all activities, which must be assessed for their potential environmental impact before they are undertaken, and provides guidelines for conservation of Antarctic flora and fauna, managing and disposing of waste, and preventing marine pollution.

"The Madrid Protocol entered into force on 14 January 1998 following the deposit of instruments of ratification, acceptance, approval or accession by all states which were Consultative Parties on 4 October 1991" (Australian Antarctic Division 2000).

The Madrid Protocol has significant ramifications for the conduct of commercial tourism in Antarctica. Article 3 establishes the environmental principles that are at the core of the Protocol. These are elaborated and operationalized in Articles 1 through 8 in Annex I and describe the requirements for environmental impact assessments (National Science Foundation 1995b:190; 1995b:202-205). Any activity that has more than a "minor or transitory impact" is subject to the completion of an Initial Environmental Evaluation (IEE) and, where appropriate, a Comprehensive Environmental Evaluation (CEE) (Articles 2 and 3, Annex I of the Protocol). One of the first tourism companies to undertake this procedure was Croydon Travel, which had to prove that its series of Antarctic overflights (see Chapter 4) did not have more than a minor or transitory impact on the Antarctic environment. Likewise, GMMS (now Aurora Expeditions), a Sydney-based Antarctic tour operator, had to submit to the process prior to taking groups of passengers climbing and camping in the Antarctic Peninsula (Greg Mortimer, personal communication 1996).

The Madrid Protocol is the single most important instrument regulating present and future Antarctic tourism activities, and as such, future tourism developments will have to be judged against criteria established by the protocol. For example, prior to the ninth NSF/IAATO meeting in Arlington, Virginia, the U.S. Environmental Protection Agency (EPA) held a public scoping meeting to allow interested parties, including tourism operators, to comment on the Interim Final Rule (Environmental Impact Assessment of Nongovernmental Activities in Antarctica), which EPA had drawn up in order to implement the requirements of Article 8 and Annex I of the Protocol.

ANTARCTIC RESOURCE USE

After Captain Cook's reports, following his discoveries in Antarctic waters from 1774 to 1776, of an abundance of seals and whales in places such as South Georgia, it did not take commercial sealers very long to exploit the resources. Likewise, whalers moved into the area and succeeded in nearly eliminating the great whales of the Southern Ocean. In addition, penguins and fish have also been exploited commercially. The following section introduces the most important forms of the economic uses of Antarctic resources since the first recorded human visits to the region were made only a little over 200 years ago (for a more detailed introduction to the economic history of Antarctica, see Wilder 1992).

Marine Living Resources

In his excellent book, *The Island of South Georgia*, Headland (1992a) provides a detailed account of whaling and sealing activities on the island. He notes that the first sealing epoch was from 1786 until 1913 (pp. 32-57), and that whaling began in 1904-1905 (p. 5). He provides detailed statistics on the number of whales and seals taken during the whaling period from 1904 to 1966 (pp. 260-261), which show that a total of 175,250 whales and 260,950 seals were killed during that period. Especially saddening is the fact that 3,689 blue whales, the largest mammal ever to live on the planet, were taken during the 1926-1927 whaling season. In contrast, only one blue whale was caught during 1958-1959, highlighting the ruthless exploitation of marine-living resources in the South.

Today the abandoned whaling stations at Grytviken and Stromness form an important component of the tourism product in South Georgia, and whale watching is an important activity during Antarctic cruises. The South Georgia Whaling Museum in Grytviken, established by the late Nigel Bonner, provides visitors with an insight into the activities of the whaling industry in this remote location.

Commercial fishing, which began in 1969-1970, has concentrated on three main species: *Champsocephalus Gunnari* (Antarctic ice fish), *Notothenia buntheri* (a perchlike fish), and *Notothenia rossii* (Antarctic cod) (Wilder 1992:49). Wilder points out that overfishing has led to a near collapse of the industry. ASOC (1997:2) is concerned that "a huge illegal and unregulated fishery has exploded, threatening to devastate the remaining stocks of Patagonian toothfish." Interest in Antarctic krill began in the mid-1960s, and krill was commercially harvested throughout the 1970s and 1980s. The initial euphoria over krill as a "vast untapped source of protein for the 'starving masses' " (Wilder 1992:53) seems to have evaporated. The high costs of catching and processing krill and the fact that it is not as palatable as first anticipated has led to a decline in the annual catch. This will benefit marine species that depend on the crustacean for food.

Antarctic Ice

The commercial utilization of several other Antarctic resources has been advocated at one time or another. One of the more popular considerations has been the use of icebergs for the water supply of arid countries such as Australia. Wilder (1992:141) provides a "Chronology of Interest in Antarctic Ice Harvesting." In it he gives 1773 as the year in which Captain Cook's expedition used Antarctic ice to obtain fresh water. Wilder states that during the period from 1890 to 1900, small icebergs were towed from Laguna San Rafael,

Chile, to Callao, Peru, a distance of 3,900 kilometers. Lovering and Prescott (1979:56) elaborate on previous studies that considered the towing of icebergs to, for example, Australia and South America. They state that approximately 1,200 cubic kilometers of ice break off Antarctica in the form of icebergs every year. "Even if only 10 percent of this annual production is capable of being delivered to a suitable site it could provide enough water to irrigate 6 to 10 million hectares or satisfy the water demands of an urban population of 500 million" (p. 56). Drawing on previous studies, they state that an iceberg 2,800 meters wide, 11,200 meters long, and 250 meters deep and with an original value of US$1,254 million could be towed at a speed of 0.5 meters per second to a place such as Australia at a delivery cost of US$0.0013 per cubic meter of ice. This, they say, is cheap compared to the US$0.19 per cubic meter of desalinated water. With these figures in mind it seems surprising that Antarctic icebergs have not been commercially harvested as yet. Circumstances may change, however, and Antarctic icebergs may one day provide water for an increasingly thirsty world. In the meanwhile their only commercial use is their attractiveness to tourists, who photograph them extensively.

Mining

Forming a substantial part of the ancient supercontinent of Gondwana, Antarctica was joined to other southern continents, in particular Australia, South America, and the southern regions of Africa. All these areas are rich in resources such as coal, iron ore, diamonds, and gold. Thus it has been assumed, and proven in some instances, that Antarctica may hold some of the last great reserves of hydrocarbon and nonhydrocarbon resources on the planet. Many expeditions have sailed south with instructions to explore the potential of exploiting these resources, but to date no commercial quantities of Antarctic hydrocarbons or nonhydrocarbons have been extracted. As outlined previously, from 1982 through 1988 the Treaty Parties negotiated CRAMRA, which attempted to regulate possible mining activities in Antarctica, but Australia did not ratify the document. With the subsequent signing of the Madrid Protocol in 1991, which in Article 7 states: "Any activity relating to mineral resources, other than scientific research shall be prohibited," the issue of mining has basically been eliminated for at least the next fifty years.

Antarctic Science

Since the early days of exploration, scientific pursuits have played an important motivation for Antarctic activities. In *A History of Antarctic Science,* Fogg (1992) traces its evolution through a period of 300 years, and the publication *Science and Stewardship in the Antarctic* (National Research Council 1993) provides an interesting overview of scientific objectives in Antarctica. The executive summary of the report states: "From the observations and reporting by the first expeditions to the sub-Antarctic regions to the more intricately-planned ventures of the first half of the 20th century, scientific investigations have had a central role in Antarctic activities" (National Research Council 1993:1).

Many countries spend substantial amounts of taxpayers' funds on the conduct of scientific activities in Antarctica. The general public is often unaware what the tangible benefits of the scientific activities are and whether, indeed, there are any such benefits. Several high-profile contributions of Antarctic science, however, do exist. For example, research into Antarctic meteorology is of great importance for the southern states of Australia, which are under the strong influence of Antarctic weather systems. Likewise, the "hole" in the ozone layer was first detected in 1981 by British scientists working at Halley station (Crossley 1995:98). As a consequence the publicity generated by this discovery has had a significant impact on the outdoor clothing habits and outdoor recreation habits of people.

To provide an insight into Antarctic science priorities, the following example from Australia may be used. During 1993, the Australian government reviewed Australia's Antarctic Program and decided on the following key goals for Australia's Antarctic Science Program (Australian Antarctic Division 1995b:5):

- understanding global climate change
- protecting the Antarctic environment (including management marine ecosystem)
- maintaining the Antarctic Treaty System and Australia's influence in it
- obtaining information of practical importance

Six core discipline areas were established: Atmospheric sciences, biological sciences, geo sciences, glaciology, human impacts, and oceanography (pp. 6-7). On March 21-22, 1996, an open forum on Antarctic Science was held at the Australian Academy of Science in Canberra with the objective of providing a forum for Antarctic scientists to present their research priorities for the next ten years. Issues raised included the influence of the global environment on the Antarctic terrestrial ecosystem and the question whether Antarctic ecosystems are changing more rapidly because of human activities. To provide conclusive answers it was decided that long-term monitoring of several environmental variables was required.

SCIENTIFIC STATIONS

Current Antarctic Literature, produced by the COLD Regions Bibliography Project, the Science and Technology Division of the United States Library of Congress, and the Scott Polar Research Institute at the University of Cambridge, breaks scientific activities down into the following fields: biological sciences, cartography, geological sciences, ice and snow, medical sciences, meteorology, oceanography, atmospheric physics, and terrestrial physics. Apart from seasonal field camps, scientific activities are mainly carried out at the permanent research facilities established by the Treaty Parties. In 1996, there were forty national Antarctic stations that operated all year. Half of them were located in the Antarctic Peninsula region (Australian Antarctic Division 1995b:22). Australia maintains three bases, Mawson, Davis, and Casey, as well as a facility on Macquarie Island. Historically the most significant of these is Mawson, which was established in Mac Robertson Land in 1954 by ANARE under the leadership of Dr. Phillip Law. This was the first large-scale scientific base on the continent, and the only one outside the Antarctic Peninsula. The base has operated continuously since and its research output has contributed significantly to our understanding of Antarctica.

The Australian Antarctic Division (1995b:22) estimates that during winter fewer than 1,200 people populate the permanent bases and that approximately 8,340 scientists and support personnel occupied them during the summer of 1989-1990. Using figures provided by May (1988:178-180), it can be calculated that up to 1996 approximately 103,700 scientists and support staff had spent a summer at permanent bases in Antarctica, whereas only 35,500 persons had wintered there. Assuming that winterers also spend the previous or following summer, it can be calculated that to date some 68,000 humans have spent extended periods of time in Antarctica. Bowden (1997:517) gives the number of wintering expeditioners in the AAT from 1947 through 1997 as 2,573.

CONCLUDING COMMENTS

This chapter has provided a background against which Antarctic tourism takes place. With ratification of the Madrid Protocol, all commercial resource exploitation opportunities (such as mining) on the continent (as opposed to the seas surrounding Antarctica) have ceased, at least for the next fifty years. Thus, largely by default, tourism has emerged as the only commercial activity taking place on the continent. However, commercial fishing still occurs in the waters surrounding it. Southern Ocean waters have been exploited, and in many cases overexploited, for some time. With mining off the agenda, the priorities of the Antarctic Treaty Parties and the attention of scientists and environmental protection organizations, as well as the general and academic press, are now focused on the activities of the commercial tourism industry.

Chapter 4

Antarctic Tourism:
Development, Operation, and Management

INTRODUCTION

This chapter outlines the development of Antarctic tourism from its beginnings to the present. It addresses the various issues concerning tourism, including the types and location of tourism and the legal framework within which it takes place, as well as the regulation of tourism under the ATS and by self-regulation. Many of these topics have also been discussed by other writers (e.g., Reich 1979; Mussack 1988; Enzenbacher 1991). An overview of topics addressed by Antarctic tourism authors can be found in Table 4.1.

The most popular topics discussed are the impacts, regulation, and management of tourism. By contrast, relatively little emphasis has been placed on the tourists themselves and on the long-term future of tourism. These issues are analyzed and discussed in Chapters 6 and 7.

TOURISM DEFINITIONS

Prior to discussing Antarctic tourism, it is necessary to establish which group of people should be considered tourists. Mill (1990:17) outlines the various definitions of tourism.

The League of Nations definition of 1937 describes a "foreign tourist" as "any person visiting a country, other than that in which he

TABLE 4.1. Summary of Topics Addressed by Selected Authors on Antarctic Tourism

Topic	Authors
Arctic/Antarctic	Christensen (1990); Grenier (1998); Nuttall (1998)
Aviation	Mahon (1984); Boswall (1986); Swithinbank (1988, 1990); Burke (1994)
Economy	Wilder (1992); White (1994)
Environment	Barnes (1982); Brewster (1982); IUCN (1991)
Future	Law (1977, 1989); Reich (1979); Bauer (1994a); Johnston and Hall (1995); Gray (1990)
Historic sites	Headland (1989); Hughes (1994); Hughes and Davis (1995)
History	Reich (1979, 1980); Headland (1994); Codling (1995)
Impacts	Stonehouse (1965); Reich (1979); Mueller-Schwarze (1984); Headland and Keage (1985); Erize (1987); Christensen (1990); Hall (1992b); Acero and Aguirre (1994); Hall and Johnston (1995b); Stonehouse and Crosbie (1995)
Legal aspects	Auburn (1982); Nicholson (1986); Triggs (1986); Boczek (1988); Heap (1990); House of Representatives Standing Committee on Legal and Constitutional Affairs (1992)
Management	Reich (1979); Hall (1992b); Splettstoesser and Folks (1994); Beck (1994); Enzenbacher (1994b); Hall and Johnston (1995b); Stonehouse, Crosbie, and Girard (1996); Johnston and Hall (1995); House of Representatives Standing Committee on Environment, Recreation and the Arts (1989); Stonehouse (1990a)
Overview	May (1988); Stonehouse (1994, 2000)
Regulation	Beck (1990a, 1994); Enzenbacher (1991, 1995)
Science	Donachie (1994); Smith (1994)
Sub-Antarctic	Cessford and Dingwall (1994); Hall and Wouters (1994); Wouters and Hall (1995a, b); Sanson (1994); Dingwall (1995)
Visitor numbers	Reich (1979); Enzenbacher (1991); INFUETUR (1994, 1995); National Science Foundation (1997a, 1998, 1999, 2000)
Visitor surveys	Codling (1982b); Smith (1994); Marsh (1991); INFUETUR (1994, 1995); Cessford and Dingwall (1996)

Source: Compiled by author.

usually resides for a period of at least 24 hours" (Mill 1990:17). Under this definition, the following individuals are considered tourists:

- Persons traveling for pleasure, family reasons, health, etc.
- Persons traveling to meetings, or in a representative capacity of any kind
- Persons traveling for business reasons
- Persons arriving in the course of a sea cruise, even when they stay less than twenty-four hours

The following individuals are not regarded as tourists:

- Persons arriving with or without a contract to work, to take up an occupation, or to engage in any business activity within that country
- Other persons arriving to establish residence in that country
- Students and other persons in boarding establishments or schools
- Residents in a foreign zone and persons domiciled in one country and working in an adjoining country
- Travelers passing through a country without stopping, even if the journey takes more than twenty-four hours (Mill 1990:18).

In 1950, the International Union of Official Travel Organizations (IUOTO) recommended that "the term 'excursionist' should be given to someone travelling for pleasure in a country in which he or she normally does not reside for a period of less than 24 hours as long as the person was not there to work" (Mill 1990:18). In 1963, the United Nations Rome Conference on International Travel and Tourism recommended that the term "visitor" should include: "Any person who visits a country other than the one in which he or she lives for any purpose other than one which involves pay from the country being visited" (Mill 1990:18-19). Visits could be for leisure, recreation, holiday, sport, health, study, and religion, or for business, family, friends, missions, and meetings. Thus a person staying less than twenty-four hours would be an "excursionist," someone staying over twenty-four hours would be a "tourist," and both of them would be "visitors." A "tourist" was therefore defined as "someone who traveled for business or pleasure as long as the individual did not receive money from the country visited" (Mill 1990:19). This definition is interesting because technically it could mean that shipborne Antarctic "tourists" are really "excursionists," and scientists and support staff at the stations could be classified as business travelers since they are not remunerated from within the country visited and largely stay less than a year.

In 1978, the United Nations Department of Economic and Social Affairs defined "international visitors" as visitors who visit a given country from abroad (inbound tourists) and those who go abroad on visits from a given country (outbound tourists). The time limit up to which a person was still considered a visitor was one year.

ANTARCTIC TOURISTS

Under the provisions of the Antarctic Treaty, territorial claims have been set aside, and therefore no country exercises full territorial rights on the continent. As a consequence, entry does not require tourists to be in possession of a passport or an entry visa and no customs or immigration formalities must be completed prior to going ashore (these, however, must be completed prior to departure and after returning from Antarctica in the countries from which the cruises leave). Because Antarctica is not a single country, the definition of "foreign tourist" used by the League of Nations does not apply. In the absence of an indigenous population, all humans are foreign and domestic visitors at the same time. In the widest sense, the scientists and their support staff at the scientific stations and bases operated by the governments of the Antarctic Treaty Parties could be said to constitute a domestic component of Antarctic tourism. As was previously mentioned, for the purposes of this book the recreational tourism activities of station and base personnel are excluded since they do not meet the criteria of commercial, for-profit tourism activities.

Reich (1979:18) proposed that in the Antarctic context, people engaged in the following activities should be considered tourists: (1) tourist cruises; (2) tourist flights, including those by small aircraft; (3) specialist expeditions, including mountaineering, small craft, and other nongovernmental efforts; (4) goodwill/VIP visits, including those by representatives of the media, photographers, and artists; and (5) off-duty visits by those already working in the Antarctic. This book focuses on commercial tourism, and categories 4 and 5 are not discussed in detail.

Comparing Arctic and Antarctic tourism activities, Stonehouse (1994:196) states that "Tourists discovered the north polar region during the mid-nineteenth century, attracted by sailing, hunting, and huge-scale wilderness," and he points out that Arctic expeditions sometimes "defrayed expenses by carrying a few paying passengers" (p. 197). He writes that Antarctica waited longer for its tourists, that none sailed there casually, and that expedition ships "were traditionally overloaded with men and equipment, with no room for supernumeraries" (p. 197).

Having identified paying customers who participate in Antarctic cruises, flights, and specialist expeditions as Antarctic tourists, the question arises: "Who are these people who venture to Antarctica for the purpose of leisure?" The literature is largely anecdotal, including only a few visitor surveys. Codling (1982b), Smith (1994), and Marsh (1991) provide some insight into visitor profiles, and several other authors variously describe tourists as largely older, affluent people, mainly from North America and Europe. I set out to provide a profile of Antarctic tourists. As a member of the Project Antarctic Conservation Team (PAC), it was possible for me to distribute survey questionnaires aboard cruise ships during the 1994-1995 and 1995-1996 seasons. PAC is a ten-year investigation of Antarctic shipborne tourism based in the Polar Ecology and Management group at the Scott Polar Research Institute, University of Cambridge (Stonehouse and Crosbie 1995). Surveys were also carried out aboard overflights of Antarctica. Results are reported in Chapter 6.

To put Antarctic tourism into perspective, it is of note that the 14,762 shipborne tourists who reached Antarctica during the 1999-2000 season (IAATO 2000) represented only 0.002 percent of the 663 million international visitor arrivals recorded worldwide during 1999.

THE ANTARCTIC TOUR CYCLE

Table 4.2 was developed to conceptualize the decision-making processes that may influence a person to take an Antarctic trip and to describe the various phases an Antarctic tourist goes through during the course of a visit to the continent. Table 4.2 raises a variety of issues, several of which are addressed in this book, while others provide scope for future research.

TABLE 4.2. Antarctic Tourist Expectation Model and Phases of an Antarctic Tour

---

Predeparture Phase

Initial curiosity about Antarctica	Raised by schooling, reading, friends and relatives who have visited Antarctica, TV documentaries, newspaper articles, and magazines.
Availability of tourist information	Is adequate tourism-related material available? Decision to book a trip to Antarctica. How did people find out about travel options? Where do they book? Who do they travel with? Where have they been before deciding on the Antarctic as a destination?

Travel Phase

Type of tourist	Group tour or free, independent traveler. How is the trip organized?
Travel to the port of departure	Which airlines are used? Do passengers fly directly to the port of departure, or do they take their time getting there? Are they visiting the gateway countries in the process?
Length of stay at gateway port	How many nights do passengers stay in Ushuaia, Punta Arenas, Christchurch, Bluff, or Hobart prior to embarkation?
Embarkation/first day aboard	First impressions of ship, crew, and fellow passengers. How important are they with regard to enjoyment of the cruise?
First days at sea	Often unpleasant voyage: seasickness, strong winds, rough seas, sea birds, learning from lectures about Antarctica.
The first icebergs	After crossing the Antarctic Convergence, spotting of first iceberg; excitement builds.
First wildlife observed from ship	Whales, penguins, seals, albatrosses, and other seabirds.
First sighting of land	Admiring the Antarctic lands from the distance.
First landing	Anticipation of shore visit. Zodiac cruises and landings. Safety considerations during Zodiac cruises. Excitement at landing where not many people have landed before. Level of excitement: very high.
First contact with wildlife	Marveling at penguin rookeries and seal colonies. Observing of ATS and IAATO Codes of Conduct.
Subsequent landings	Are all passengers still eager to go ashore? Has the level of excitement decreased substantially? Are passengers happy with their land excursions? Would they like to do other things while ashore?
Return voyage	Memories of Antarctic visit. Often uncomfortable return voyage across the Southern Ocean.
Return travel to hometown	Is any time spent in the countries from which the cruise departed?

Posttour Phase

Slide/video nights for friends	How important are they in shaping the experience and influencing other people to visit the Antarctic?
Planning the next trip	Where do Antarctic passengers travel to after they have seen the world's most remote destination?

Source: Bauer 1996.

TOURIST ATTRACTIONS

What attracts people to venture to Antarctica has been described in the literature, but little primary research has been carried out on the issue of visitor motivation. Previous authors have offered a diversity of reasons for the attractiveness of Antarctica, including the following:

- "We had the whole of Erebus Island [Ross Island] spread out in front of us, and it was a very beautiful sight indeed. One of the thoughts that strikes one oftenest I think is what people at home would give to have a glimpse of such a sight" (Wilson 1966, quoted in Reich 1979:15).
- "While scientific research is the sole reason for the British Antarctic Survey, the work is carried out in one of the most interesting regions on earth and certainly that least affected by man's activities. It also contains some of the most beautiful landscapes and natural forms there are, in terms both of color and structure" (Laws 1977, quoted in Reich 1979:15).
- "The white majesty of the Antarctic continent and its association with the heroic deeds of early explorers holds a deep fascination for many tourists" (Lovering and Prescott 1979:99).

The IUCN (1991:54-55) describes the fascination of Antarctica:

Antarctica holds a special fascination and challenge for people, and tourism has become not only an established part of Antarctic life but also, with fishing, one of the principle commercial activities in the region. The Antarctic is a vast wilderness of great natural beauty, laid out on a grand scale, with its tall mountains, massive glaciers and ice shelves, huge floating icebergs and great profusion of seabirds, penguins and seals. . . . The most favored tourist destinations are wildlife colonies, scientific stations, historic huts from the heroic era and areas of spectacular or physically challenging terrain.

Gunn (1988:107) describes "attractions" as "on-location places in regions that not only provide things for tourists to see and do but also offer the magnetism for travel." He adds that "the attractions of a destination constitute the most powerful component of the supply side of tourism. . . . They provide the 'pull factor' . . . and entice, lure and stimulate interest in travel" (Gunn 1994:57-58). Importantly, Gunn also recognizes that "attractions provide visitor satisfaction, the rewards from travel—the true travel product" (p. 58). He suggests that attractions can be classified by ownership, resource foundation, and the length of time tourists spend at them (p. 59). With regard to ownership, Antarctica is unique because only a very small part of the continent's attractions, the scientific stations, are owned by anyone.

In line with Gunn's classification by resource, tourist attractions can be classified as natural or cultural/created attractions. Using these classifications, it is clear that Antarctica's attractions fall primarily into the natural attractions category.

Natural Attractions

Many tourist brochures state that during a voyage to Antarctica visitors can expect to see whales (minke, sei, fin humpback, and sometimes blue), orcas, porpoises, sea birds including penguins and albatrosses, and seals. It is of note that Antarctica has no reptiles, no amphibians, and no land mammals apart from human visitors. The flora of Antarctica is poor compared to most other parts of the world. Mosses and colorful lichens grow on some of the exposed rocky areas, but the continent has only two kinds of flowering plants. The scenery is spectacular, with towering snow- and ice-covered mountains falling off steeply into the often ice-choked sea. Floating and grounded icebergs the size of large buildings (at times the size of small countries) and glaciers calving into the sea provide the visitor with stunning sights. Highlights of the natural attractions of the Antarctic Peninsula region are included in the video and CD-ROM *Voyage to Antarctica,* produced jointly by the author and the Computer Aided Learning Centre at Victoria University (available directly from the producers at <http://www.calc.com.au/Antarctic.htm>).

Created Attractions

Created attractions in Antarctica include the operating and disused scientific stations, historic sites, monuments, huts, and the remains of abandoned whaling stations.

Scientific Research Stations

Antarctic bases are operated by seventeen nations (Crossley 1995: 43). Many of these, for example Georg von Neumayer (Germany), SANAE (South Africa), and Syowa (Japan), are located in remote areas such as Dronning Maud Land and therefore are practically never visited by tourists. Several of the scientific stations do, however, receive regular visits from tourist ships. In particular, research facilities located on King George Island in the South Shetland group, such as the Polish station Henryk Arctowski and the Chilean base Eduardo Frei, are popular with tourists. Indeed, Arctowski proved so popular that during the 1996-1997 season a tourist facility in the form of a trail and a display was established jointly by the Polish Academy of Science and the Scott Polar Research Institute (Bernard Stonehouse, personal communication 1997).

Palmer Station, the large United States research facility on Anvers Island, also receives regular prearranged visits by cruise ships. Because of their location on the Antarctic continent proper, the Argentinian stations of Almirante Brown and Esperanza are also popular sites for tourist vessels. Setting foot on the Antarctic continent carries prestige in the minds of Antarctic visitors. Visits to scientific stations provide tourists with an opportunity to meet inhabitants who often have spent lengthy periods of time in Antarctica, compared to the "average" tourist's stay of between five and seven days. In the eyes of the tourists, meeting people at stations, irrespective of whether they are scientists or support staff, is meeting the "locals," an experience that is taken for granted in any other tourist destination and forms an important part of the tourist experience.

Historic Sites, Monuments, and Huts

The Antarctic Treaty Parties have identified a total of sixty historic sites and monuments in Antarctica (National Science Foundation 1995b:157). The history of Antarctic exploration has fascinated people since the early part of this century. Events associated with the expeditions of Amundsen, Mawson, Shackleton, and Scott, have led to a substantial interest in the relics left behind by these early explorers. Their endeavors have not only become part of the folklore of the explorers' respective home countries, but they have become part of global human heritage as well. Their adventures highlight what humans are capable of doing if they try hard enough. The stamina, endurance, and determination displayed by early—and some modern—explorers can serve as a model for ordinary people when dealing with problems in their daily lives. The most tangible evidence of this bygone era is the huts the explorers left behind. Today their remains are considered historic sites and as such have become attractions for visiting tourists. The most frequently visited huts include those built by Scott and Shackleton on Ross Island as well as Borchgrevink's huts at Cape Adare. The occasional visit is also made to Mawson's hut at Commonwealth Bay in the Australian Antarctic Territory. The successful management and interpretation of historic sites is one of the challenges facing Antarctic managers. Although visitors do have a right to satisfy their curiosity by visiting these huts, too many visits by too many people may have the potential to damage them, thereby reducing the enjoyment levels of subsequent visitors. In the Ross Sea region, the thirty-three historic huts and sites are managed by the New Zealand Antarctic Heritage Trust. The Trust has developed a code of conduct for visitors to the historic huts, which includes restrictions on the maximum number of people inside the huts. At the time of writing these visitor limits are: eight at Discovery Hut (Hut Point), twelve at Scott's Hut (Cape Evans), eight at Shackleton's Hut (Cape Royds), and four at Borchgrevink's Hut (Cape Adare) (Antarctic Heritage Trust undated). An official observer from Antarctica New Zealand carries the keys to the huts and ensures that the maximum number of people inside the huts is not exceeded. For a more detailed discussion on historic sites and huts see Hughes (1994); Hughes and Davis (1995); and Harrowfield (1988, 1990).

Abandoned Whaling Stations

The historic significance of the huts of the early explorers is widely acknowledged, but with regard to the derelict buildings at the former whaling stations it is unclear whether they should be considered "industrial heritage" or "scrap metal." Whaling has become an unacceptable practice for most people and nations, and the exploitation of these great mammals has nearly come to an end. To this purpose, a Southern Ocean whaling sanctuary was established in 1994. However, despite the negative image of whaling, the remains of earlier whaling operations (which of course are not unique to Antarctic waters but can be found in countries such as Australia, South Africa, and Norway, to mention but a few) are nevertheless a part of the heritage of Antarctica. Landings at abandoned whaling stations at places such as Grytviken or Stromness on South Georgia or at Whalers Bay on Deception Island are included in many cruise itineraries.

The fact that entrepreneurs managed to establish a foothold in such a hostile region, many thousands of kilometers from any support base, highlights the ability of the human species to survive and prosper under the most arduous conditions. The Norwegian Captain Carl Larsen, who established a land-based whaling operation at Grytviken, South Georgia, on November 16, 1904 (Headland 1992a), had to transport everything he needed from Norway and Argentina. The remains of this once-flourishing little town (whaling ceased in South Georgia in 1965 and Grytviken was abandoned in 1971), with its church, cinema, soccer field, and ski jump, as well as the whale processing factory, are of great interest to today's visitors. A few years ago the South Georgia Whaling Museum was established in Grytviken (the South Georgia Museum Trust, which administers the museum, was established by Ordinance No. 1 of 1992 by the Commissioner for South Georgia and the South Sandwich Islands, W. H. Fullerton, CMG). The first project director of the museum, the late Nigel Bonner (1993:1), described the merit of the museum as follows:

> No-one would now support whaling as it was carried out at Grytviken, but we should recall that attitudes were very different a generation ago and whaling was a highly respected profession for many Norwegians. The South Georgia Whaling Museum has been set up to preserve something of this industry which was crucial to the modern history of South Georgia and Norwegian industrial development, and which provided the world with valuable whale oil for 60 years.

Spiritual Attractions

Antarctica also has another, less tangible attraction: its spiritual value as the world's last great wilderness. In the age of the Internet, cable television, and twenty-four-hour news broadcasts, there is something soothing about the thought that there are still some parts of the world left where nature dominates the activities of humans rather than the other way around. Likewise, the inspirational value for modern people of the deprivations suffered by discoverers, explorers, and adventurers, their endurance in achieving the "impossible," and their acceptance of hardship has made Antarctica a symbol of inspiration to the world.

ANTARCTIC TOURIST SITES

To date, tourism activities have taken place in relatively few places: the South Shetland Islands, the Antarctic Peninsula, the Ross Sea area, and, to a very limited degree, the Australian Antarctic Territory. Sub-Antarctic islands such as the Falkland Islands, South Georgia, Macquarie Island, and the Auckland and Campbell Islands have also received visitors. Stonehouse (1994:202) stated that "in the Antarctic Peninsula and Scotia Arc alone ship-borne tourists are currently landed at over 70 sites; a further 20 sites have been identified in the Ross Sea sector." The National Science Foundation lists a total of 159 Antarctic sites that have previously been visited by tourists, many of them only sporadically. Table 4.3 displays detailed figures of passenger visits to Antarctic Peninsula sites, ranking the top five visited sites for three or more of the previous eight seasons.

During the period 1989-1990 to 1996-1997, the top ten sites saw a combined 206,931 visits. A geographical analysis of the most visited locations reveals that only Almirante Brown Station is located on the Antarctic Peninsula and hence, on the continent. The base has only been used as a summer camp since it was destroyed by fire on April 12,1984 (Rubin 1996:306).

The other sites are all on offshore islands, mostly in the South Shetland group. The most visited site, Whalers Bay, is located on Deception Island. Whalers Bay, as the name suggests, was the locale of a whaling station (closed in 1931), and remnants of boilers and fuel tanks can still be found there. A British Antarctic Survey (BAS) (formerly Falkland Islands Dependency Survey or FIDS) facility was also previously located at the site. The location therefore cannot be described as pristine. Its biggest attraction is its human history, in particular as the place from which

TABLE 4.3. Most Visited Sites in the Peninsula, 1994 to 1999 (By Season)

	94-95	95-96	96-97	97-98	98-99	Total
Whalers Bay	**5,241**	5,033	3,012	5,344	5,427	24,057
Port Lockroy	1,769	3,851	3,110	**6,429**	**6,473**	21,632
Cuverville Island	3,367	4,343	**3,714**	4,143	4,087	19,654
Half Moon Island	3,017	**5,221**	2,258	4,382	3,931	18,809
Hannah Point	4,010	3,048	3,480	3,399	3,982	17,919
Pendulum Cove	2,803	3,492	2,725	3,426	4,676	17,122
Petermann Island	3,406	3,504	2,576	3,866	3,305	16,657
Paulet Island	2,819	2,315	2,808	732	3,722	12,396
Almirante Brown	1,307	2,244	2,504	3,991	1,612	11,658
Gonzales Videla	1,559	2,384	1,095	2,998	3,379	11,415

Source: National Science Foundation, 1999.

Note: **Bold** figures indicate most visited site for the season.

the Australian adventurer Sir Hubert Wilkins undertook the first powered flight in the Antarctic on November 16, 1928.

Pendulum Cove, located like Whalers Bay on Deception Island, contains several hot water pools (some of which are classified as SSSIs) associated with volcanic activity (Poncet and Poncet 1991:26). Given that the location is included in SSSI No. 21 (National Science Foundation 1995b:119), the continued use of the site for tourism purposes is somewhat surprising. Half Moon Island is home to an Argentine research station and to several penguin rookeries. It is an easily accessible landing place set against the spectacular mountain scenery of nearby Livingston Island.

Port Lockroy served as a whaling facility and as the base for the United Kingdom's wartime Operation Tabarin. Cleanup operations have recently been completed, and Port Lockroy's original station hut, Bransfield House, has been restored by the U.K. branch of the Antarctic Heritage Trust (Rubin 1996: 304).This has provided an additional reason for visiting the site, and a record 7,804 passengers visited there during the 1999-2000 season (National Science Foundation 2000). Petermann Island is located at the southern end of the Lemaire Channel and houses the southernmost population of gentoo penguins. Personnel from the former British base, Faraday, have in the past used the island for recreational activities including skiing.

When the author visited the Chilean station of Gonzales Videla in December 1994, it was unoccupied but appeared well maintained. Gentoo penguins had reclaimed their territory and were nesting among the buildings and in one of the aircraft hangars. Gonzales Videla is popular because at low tide it is possible for tourists to walk across the short distance of exposed seabed and to set foot on the Antarctic continent. This is an important point for "continent collectors," many of whom consider this the seventh continent. It is clear that several of the most visited places are locations that have seen extensive previous human use and which can therefore no longer be described as pristine.

Table 4.4 provides an example of a typical itinerary for a large ship, the *Marco Polo*. In line with other Antarctic tour itineraries, the Orient Line brochure states that: "Exact itinerary and ports of call depend on ice conditions, weather and wildlife" (Orient Lines 1995).

HISTORY OF ANTARCTIC TOURISM

Compared to tourism in the Arctic, commercial Antarctic tourism is a comparatively recent occurrence but, as Headland (1994:269) points out, ad hoc tourist visits to the Antarctic region began more than a century ago. Table 4.5 provides an overview of some of the most significant events in the history of tourism in the region. Headland (1994:275) traces the beginnings of modern commercial tourism back to 1956 when the first commercial tourist flight by Linea Aerea Nacional (the Chilean national airline) took sixty-six passengers on an overflight of the South Shetland Islands and Trinity Peninsula.

This was followed by a Pan American Airways stratocruiser landing at McMurdo Sound on October 15, 1957, making this the first commercial flight to land in Antarctica. Headland (1994:275) gives the beginnings of shipborne tourism as the two voyages undertaken by the *Les Eclaireurs* during January and February 1958, when this Argentine ship carried 100 tourists per cruise to the South Shetland Islands and the west coast of the Antarctic Peninsula. These voyages were followed by further Argentine and Chilean cruises in 1959 (the *Yapeyu* and *Navarino*).

According to Headland (1994:275), the era of modern ship-based Antarctic tourism began with the voyage organized by Lars Eric Lindblad of Lindblad Travel, New York, in 1966 aboard the Argentine naval vessel *Lapataia*. Since then, ships have provided the main

TABLE 4.4. Sample Itineraries for the *Marco Polo*

Voyage 1	**Expedition Antarctica**
Dec. 15	Buenos Aires
Dec. 16, 17	Cruise South Atlantic Ocean
Dec. 18	Stanley, Falkland Islands 08.00-18.00
Dec. 19	West Point, Falkland Islands 07.00-16.00
Dec. 20	Drake Passage
Dec. 21	Hope Bay
Dec. 22	Half Moon Island and Deception Island
Dec. 23	Paradise Harbor, Neumayer Channel, and Port Lockroy
Dec. 24	Port Lockroy; Lemaire Channel
Dec. 25	Drake Passage
Dec. 26	Cape Horn 03.00 am; Ushuaia 08.00 am
Voyage 2	**Antarctic Peninsula—A Thrilling 10-Day Adventure to the White Continent**
Dec. 27	Ushuaia
Dec. 28	Drake Passage
Dec. 29	Hope Bay
Dec. 30	Half Moon Island and Deception Island
Dec. 31	Paradise Harbor, Neumayer Channel, and Port Lockroy
Jan. 1	Port Lockroy and Lemaire Channel
Jan. 2	Drake Passage
Jan. 3	Cape Horn and Ushuaia
Voyage 3	**Grand Antarctic Circumnavigation**
Jan. 12	Punta Arenas
Jan. 13	Beagle Channel cruising
Jan. 14	Drake Passage
Jan. 15	Hope Bay
Jan. 16	Paradise Harbor, Neumayer Channel, and Port Lockroy
Jan. 17	Port Lockroy, Lemaire Channel, Hovgaard Island
Jan. 18-22	Bellingshausen Sea/Amundsen Sea
Jan. 23	At sea
Jan. 24	Cross International Dateline
Jan. 25	Ross Sea
Jan. 26	McMurdo Station
Jan. 27	McMurdo Station and Cape Evans
Jan. 28	Cape Royds
Jan. 29	Ross Sea
Jan. 30	Cape Hallett and Cape Adare
Jan. 31	Cross the Antarctic Circle
Feb. 1, 2	Cruise the Southern Ocean
Feb. 3	Christchurch, New Zealand

Source: Orient Lines 1995.

TABLE 4.5. Brief Chronology of Antarctic Tourism (Earliest Occurrence of Some Events)

Year	Event
1891	Landings made on Auckland Islands, Campbell Island, Macquarie Island.
1924	Landings made on South Georgia.
1933	Landings made on South Orkney Islands.
1956	Flight made over South Shetland Islands and Antarctic Peninsula without landing.
1957	Landing made on Ross Island from an aircraft.
1958	Landings made on South Shetland Islands and Antarctic Peninsula.
1966	Annual tourist voyages begin.
1968	Passenger ship crosses the Antarctic Circle. Landing made on Balleney Islands; tourists fly over the South Pole.
1970	Landing made on Gough Island; first *Lindblad Explorer* voyage.
1971	National expeditions begin regular carriage of tourists.
1973	Large passenger vessel operates off the Antarctic Peninsula, no landings.
1977	Flights made from Australia and New Zealand over Antarctica, no landings.
1979	Crash of tourist aircraft on Ross Island, 257 killed.
1981	Two tourist ships visit Antarctica.
1982	Landings made on Scott Island and South Sandwich Islands.
1983	Annual visits to the South Shetland Islands by aircraft begin.
1984	"Hotel" established on South Shetland Islands.
1986	Antarctic Airways lands on blue-ice runways.
1988	Tourists flown to the South Pole; six tourist ships visit Antarctica.
1989	Wreck of the *Bahia Paraiso* carrying 81 tourists.
1991	Landing made on Shag Rocks. International Association of Antarctica Tour Operators (IAATO) founded.
1992	Twelve tourist ships visit Antarctica.
1994	Antarctic overflights resume from Australia At the XVIII ATCM in Kyoto, the ATCPs adopt Recommendation XVIII-1, which sets out guidelines for tourists and tour operators.
1997	First cruise ship circumnavigates Antarctica.
2000	Nearly 15,000 passengers visited Antarctica by sea.

Sources: Headland 1994; Croydon Travel 1995; Adventure Associates 1996; National Science Foundation 2000.

form of transport for tourists visiting the Antarctic. Headland (1994) attributes the current relatively large numbers of visitors to "great improvements in transport and a vast increase in interest in the Antarctic" (p. 269).

During the period from 1977 to early 1980, overflights of parts of the Ross Sea region and parts of East Antarctica were also available and popular until an Air New Zealand DC-10 crashed into the slopes of Mount Erebus in 1979, killing all 257 people aboard. As will be discussed later, flights did not resume until 1994. The previously available flights to King George Island (Teniente Rodolfo Marsh Base) by the Chilean Air Force have, at least for the time being, been suspended. The only land-based tourist accommodations in Antarctica are the Hotel Polar Star on King George Island and the camp of Adventure Network International in the interior of the continent.

ANTARCTIC TOURISM PRODUCTS

For the independent traveler, Antarctica is a destination that is almost completely inaccessible. There are no scheduled public transport services, no regular commercial flights, no regular shipping services, and, because the continent is an island, obviously no land connections such as railroads, buses, or private automobiles. The only way travelers can reach the continent on their own is by sailing a private yacht (for example, David Lewis in 1972-1973 aboard *Ice Bird* and again in 1977-1978 aboard *Solo* as well as Roger Wallace and Jay Watson aboard *Parmelia* in 1998 and *Tooluka* in 1999-2000). Thus, the only way to experience Antarctica as a tourist is by joining programs organized by commercial tour operators. These companies have made it their business to make Antarctica accessible to the general public. On the following pages the various types of Antarctic tourism product will be introduced. An understanding of these products is important before discussing possible impacts and before examining possible future tourism scenarios more closely. The following types of commercial Antarctic tourism product are currently available:

- Ship based, using cruise or expedition-type vessels
- Yachts
- Land based with air support
- Overflights without landings

SHIP-BASED TOURISM

Because of its remoteness, access to the Antarctic coastline is dif-ficult. Depending on ice conditions, Australia's Antarctic Territory is approximately seven to nine days by ship from Hobart, Tasmania, and access to New Zealand's Ross Dependency takes approximately five to seven days. Consequently, visitor numbers to these two re-gions only make up a small proportion of the total number of visita-tions (Cessford and Dingwall [1996] cited approximately 800 visitors to the Ross Sea during 1995-1996). During 1998-1999 only 5 percent of all Antarctic passengers went to the Ross Sea.

The easiest access to the continent is from the southern tip of South America, from ports such as Ushuaia and Punta Arenas. From these ports the northwestern part of the Antarctic Peninsula region is only 1,000 kilometers away. Consequently, the Antarctic Peninsula and the South Shetland Islands off the west coast of the peninsula have become the major tourist areas. Figures provided by the Antarctic Unit of the Tourism Board of Tierra del Fuego (Galimberti and Ucha 1995:13) show, for example, that during the 1994-1995 season 89 per-cent of all shipborne Antarctic passengers reached the continent via Ushuaia, the southernmost city in the world and the city closest to Antarctica.

Analyses of Antarctic tour brochures reveal the following typical travel itinerary for cruises to the Antarctic Peninsula region: After flying to South America, passengers embark at Ushuaia, Punta Arenas, or, less frequently, Puerto Williams, and then spend two to three days crossing Drake Passage, one of the roughest stretches of water in the world. Cruises are accompanied by Antarctic experts who educate passengers on aspects of geology, biology, and history during the voyage south. Cruise-based tourism that involves a substantial educa-tional component has been described as the Lindblad pattern of tour-ism (Stonehouse and Crosbie 1995), named after the Antarctic tourism pioneer Lars-Eric Lindblad. Once in the Peninsula region, tourists usually make two to three shore landings at wildlife sites per day. Visits to scientific research stations are also scheduled in the pro-gram. Visits to stations require negotiations with the respective na-tional Antarctic programs and the permission of the base commander.

In total, a ten-day voyage only spends approximately five days in Antarctic waters. Depending on the point of departure, the length of the cruise and the cabin class, 2000-2001 cruise-only prices from

Ushuaia range from US$3,700 to US$7,000 per person (Peregrine Adventures 2000). By comparison, prices for Arctic cruises are significantly cheaper. Prices for cruises from Australia to the Ross Sea start at approximately US$7,200 aboard vessels such as the *Bremen*.

Other cruise options include visits to some of the sub-Antarctic Islands such as the Falkland Islands, South Georgia, and South Orkney. Because of the greater distances involved, these cruises tend to be of longer duration, up to eighteen days, and as a consequence they are also more expensive.

During the 1996-1997 season, thirteen tourist ships operated in the Antarctic Peninsula. Passenger capacity of vessels ranged from 36 to 180 and the number of passengers carried ranged from 23 to 162. As previously mentioned, during 1995-1996 a total of 15 vessels made 113 trips and carried a total of 9,212 passengers. Following is an overview of the different types of vessels operating in Antarctic waters.

Antarctic Tourist Vessels

At present some 195 cruise ships are operating around the world, and a further 24 are on the planning board (Aye, H. personal communication 1997). Only two of these additional vessels will be ice strengthened, thus suitable for Antarctic operations. With the breakup of the former Soviet Union, many vessels, in particular former marine research vessels and icebreakers, have become available for international charter. Super Nova Expeditions Ltd., a single-owner company registered in the Isle of Man (Poles Apart 1994:4), is said to be the major charterer of Russian vessels for the Antarctic tourist trade. It is interesting to note that the company's name does not appear in any of the brochures examined by this author. However, it is known that Quark Expeditions, a company registered in Delaware and one of the major players in Antarctic tourism, with an office in Darien, Connecticut, is the general sales agent for Super Nova Expeditions (Poles Apart 1994:4). Poles Apart (1994:5) describes the process of charters, subcharters, and bookings in the following fashion:

> Ships are chartered for Antarctic and Southern Ocean cruises by Super Nova Expeditions and marketed by Quark Expeditions as the worldwide sales agent. Cruises are sold in three ways: All passengers book through Quark Expeditions which runs the en-

tire cruise; passengers book through Quark Expeditions, which runs the cruise, but block bookings are accepted from other tour operators; an entire ship is subchartered to another tour operator which may accept block bookings from other tour operators.

Small Expedition-Type Vessels

The most popular ships in Antarctica are former Russian marine science vessels that carry between twenty and one hundred passengers. According to the Australian Antarctic Division's Antarctic Tourism Web site (www.antdiv.gov.au/tourism), during the 2000-2001 season these are expected to include the *Akademik Shokalskiy* (46 berths), *Grigory Mikheev* (30 berths), *Professor Multanovskiy* (49 berths), *Sir Hubert Wilkins* (30 berths), *Akademik Shuleykin* (53 berths), and the *Professor Molchanov* (52 berths). Because they were not designed to carry tourists, their recreational facilities, as well as their dining facilities, are relatively basic when compared with the *Explorer* (100 berths), which also falls into the small vessel category. Southern Heritage Expedition (1995), for example, describes their vessel, the *Akademik Shokalskiy*, which operates in the Ross Sea sector, in the following way:

> Our ship is the *Akademik Shokalskiy* built in Finland in 1983 and originally designed as a research vessel. She provides comfortable accommodation for 38 passengers. Measuring 236 foot in length and 42 foot in breadth, the *Akademik Shokalskiy* is a steel built, ice strengthened vessel perfect for cruising the sub-Antarctic and Antarctic. Of Russian registry, she will be manned by an enthusiastic Russian crew of about 30 with extensive experience in ice conditions. . . . Powered by two 1560 horse power diesel engines, she is capable of sea speeds of 12 knots. The *Akademik Shokalskiy* will meet all the requirements under the Protocol on Environmental Protection in Antarctica. The ship is well suited for expedition cruising and has a large well equipped bridge and good open deck viewing areas. She has a full compliment of inflatable landing craft enabling landings and wildlife viewing opportunities in otherwise inaccessible areas. A comfortable dining room serving international cuisine from European chefs also serves as a lecture room with TV/VCR facilities plus slide screen.

The vessel also has a library/card room, bar, sauna, laundry, and its own doctor on board.

These expedition-type vessels are ice-strengthened but do not have the capabilities of icebreakers. Their biggest drawback is that many of them are slow—at a maximum cruise speed of twelve knots, traveling to and from Antarctica takes a long time. For example, during a cruise from Ushuaia to the Antarctic Peninsula aboard the *Professor Khromov,* the author spent over five days crossing and recrossing Drake Passage.

Medium-Sized Cruise Ships

In the category of medium-sized ships fall some of the best equipped and most luxurious vessels operating in Antarctic waters. Ships in this category that are planning to operate in Antarctica during the 2000-2001 season (<www.antdiv.gov.au/tourism>) are expected to include the *Akademik Ioffe* (116 berths), *Caledonian Star* (120 berths), *Clipper Adventurer* (122 berths), *Lyubov Orlova* (128 berths), and *Mariya Yermolova* (128 berths). The most luxurious vessels in this category include the *Hanseatic* (180 berths) and the *Bremen* (164 berths), both operated by Hapag-Lloyd Tours. In contrast to the small expedition-type vessels, the *Bremen's* amenities are more luxurious. "All Standard cabins feature: cabin area of 149 square feet; hair-dryer; bathrobe; individual climate control; satellite telephone; writing desk; seating area; panoramic windows . . . spacious wardrobes; stocked minibar and a closed circuit television/radio which broadcasts movies, documentaries, music and radio news" (Adventure Associates 1996:8).

Very Large Cruise Ships

Several very large (by Antarctic standards) cruise ships also operate occasionally in the region. The only regular visitor is the *Marco Polo* (Orient Lines), which has a tonnage of 20,502 GRT, a length of 175 meters, and a passenger capacity of 850. In the Antarctic, the ship usually carries only about half that number of passengers. The longest of their cruises, billed as a "Grand Antarctic Circumnavigation," is really a semicircumnavigation since it only involves sailing from Punta Arenas along the Antarctic Peninsula, through the Amundsen Sea to the Ross Sea, and on to New Zealand. This particular cruise includes landings in the Antarctic Peninsula and Ross Sea regions. Because Orient Lines is no longer a member of IAATO, it is not known whether the *Marco Polo* abides by these rules. In any case, it takes a very long time to ferry 450 to 500 passengers back and forth between the ship and the landing sites in inflatable boats that seat a maximum of 15 passengers on the same number of voyages, and both vessels landed passengers.

The second type of very large cruise ships includes vessels such as the *Eugenio Costa,* operated by Costa Crociere, which took a total of 918 passengers to the Antarctic Peninsula during January 1995 (Galimberti and Ucha, 1995). Initially the company had planned to land passengers at the Argentine base of Almirante Brown in Paradise Bay, but bad weather prevented them from doing so. In any event it is highly unlikely that a total of 918 passengers could have been landed in a reasonable amount of time, given that the safe operating capacity of Zodiacs is a maximum of ten to twelve passengers. Even with ten Zodiacs operating it would have taken many hours to transport passengers back and forth to the base.

As a part of a voyage around the world, the *MS Rotterdam* (operated by Holland America Lines), a non-ice-strengthened vessel of 62,000 GRT, visited the Antarctic Peninsula for a few days in January 2000 carrying 936 passengers, three staff, and 656 crew (NSF 2000). Initially the company had plans to land passengers at the Argentine station Esperanza, but after consultation with Antarctic experts they fortunately gave up on the idea. Attracted by the "dawn of the new millenium," two other large vessels, the *Aegean I* and the *Ocean Explorer,* also visited the region during the 1999-2000 season. The *Aegean I* carried 912 passengers on two cruises and the *Ocean Explorer* 889 on the same number of voyages.

Icebreakers

The appearance of Russian icebreakers in Antarctic waters during the 1991-1992 Antarctic season signaled the beginning of a new era in Antarctic tourism. Ships such as the *Kapitan Khlebnikov* and *Kapitan Dranitysn* have opened up coastal regions that had never been visited by tourists. During the 1992-1993 season, the first tourist visits to stations in the Australian Antarctic Territory (AAT) were made by the *Kapitan Khlebnikov.* Icebreakers have penetrated the ice-choked Weddell Sea and have undertaken semicircumnavigations of Antarctica, involving a voyage from the Antarctic Peninsula through the Bellingshausen and Amundsen Seas into the Ross Sea and on to Australia or New Zealand. Between November 24, 1996, and January 27, 1997, the *Kapitan Khlebnikov* successfully completed the first-ever circumnavigation of Antarctica for expedition tourism, in the process visiting sixteen research stations (Splettstoesser, Headland, and Todd 1997). They describe the voyage as being only the tenth cruise ever to circumnavigate Antarctica and note that the cruise encompassed some 12,565 nautical miles south of 60 degrees south, and that the vessel spent nearly fifty-nine days south of 60 degrees south. The sixty-six passengers from thirteen nations paid between US$29,900 and US$55,000 for the privilege of being the first tourists to circumnavigate the continent. It is not anticipated that such a cruise will be repeated in the near future.

Yacht-Based Antarctic Tourism Operations

A small number of yachts also participate in Antarctic tourism, but as far as the Antarctic tourism industry is concerned, their activities are relatively minor. Departure points tend to be either Ushuaia or Punta Arenas in South America and, much less frequently, ports in Australia and New Zealand. Many of these voyages have been documented in books, films, or magazines and for the purposes of this book are not seen as commercial tourism activities. Enzenbacher (1993) estimates 135 paying passengers during the 1991-1992 season and Poncet and Poncet (1991) lists sixty-seven yacht visits to Antarctica in the period 1985-1986 to 1990-1991. During the 1999–2000 season, seventeen yachts made twenty-five commercial voyages to Antarctica and carried 237 paying passengers (National Science Foundation 2000). The number of landings made by yachts is not known but, because of their maneuverability and shallow draught, yachts may land passengers in many more places than larger vessels can. Bonner and Walton (1984) are quoted by Poncet and Poncet (1991) in their booklet *Southern Ocean Cruising* as saying, "The proliferation of private yachts in the Southern Ocean has added a new and largely unwelcome element to the tourist problem. The activities of these yachts seem at the moment, to be beyond any general control" (p. 6). Several yacht operators were invited to become members of IAATO, but to date only Pelagic Expeditions and Golden Fleece have joined.

Trends in Seaborne Visitor Numbers

From 1985-1986 (544 visitors) to 1991-1992 (6,317 visitors), the number of tourists to Antarctica increased, on average, by 48.3 percent per year. Data provided in Table 4.6 reveal that over 70 percent of all shipborne tourists visiting the Antarctic did so during the 1990s.

The substantial annual growth rate has, however, slowed significantly, with only modest growth rates of 2.2 percent in 1992-1993, 23.2 percent in 1993-1994, 4 percent in 1994-1995, and 11.3 percent in 1995- 1996. The 1996-1997 season saw 7,322 shipborne visitors, a decrease of 21 percent over the previous season. This decrease can be explained by the absence of the large ship *Marco Polo,* which, during the previous season, carried a total of 1,687 passengers. As a result, total passenger figures have to be treated with some caution because the sporadic activities of large cruise ships distort the figures. During the 1997-1998 season the *Marco Polo* returned for four cruises carrying 2,012 passengers and accounting for over 21 percent of arrivals (NSF 1998).

The number of passengers going ashore in the Antarctic is clearly important because the greater the number of people ashore, the greater the potential for negative environmental impact. In 1997, IAATO forecasted that around 14,000 shipborne passengers per season would travel to the Antarctic during the first three seasons of the new millenium. The organization based its forecast on the assumption that Russian flag vessels would continue to be available to operators at a favorable charter rate, and that the regulatory environment would remain largely unchanged, and that large cruise lines would not enter the market. IAATO warns, however, that these forecasts should be treated with great caution. Tables 4.7 and 4.8 show the number of seaborne tourists, the vessels used, and the operators involved for the 1996-1997 season.

Table 4.8 shows that Marine Expeditions dominated the market during the 1996-1997 season with their relatively inexpensive products. It is of interest to note that Canada, where the company has its head office, is not an ATCP, thus is not involved in the decision-making process.

The 1999-2000 Antarctic season began in early November 1999 and ended in late March 2000. Enticed by spending the turn of the millennium in the most remote part of the world, a record 14,623 cruise pas-

TABLE 4.6. Estimated Shipborne Tourist Arrivals in the Antarctic, 1957-1958 to 1999-2000

Season	Visitors	Variation (%)	Decade
1957-1958	194	Base	
1958-1959	344	77	
1950s	**Subtotal**		**538 (0.5%)**
1965-1966	58		
1966-1967	94	62	
1967-1968	147	56	
1968-1969	1,312	792	
1969-1970	972	-26	
1960s	**Subtotal**		**2,583 (2.2%)**
1970-1971	943	-3	
1971-1972	984	4	
1972-1973	1,175	19	
1973-1974	1,876	60	
1974-1975	3,644	94	
1975-1976	1,890	-48	
1976-1977	1,068	-43	
1977-1978	845	-21	
1978-1979	1,048	24	
1979-1980	855	-18	
1970s	**Subtotal**		**14,328 (12.3%)**
1980-1981	855	—	
1981-1982	1,441	69	
1982-1983	719	-50	
1983-1984	834	16	
1984-1985	544	-35	
1985-1986	631	16	
1986-1987	1,797	185	
1987-1988	2,782	55	
1988-1989	3,146	13	
1989-1990	2,460	-22	
1980s	**Subtotal**		**15,209 (13.0%)**
1990-1991	4,698	91	
1991-1992	6,317	34	
1992-1993	6,577	2	
1993-1994	7,957	23	
1994-1995	8,090	4	
1995-1996	9,212	11	
1996-1997	7,322	-21	
1997-1998	9,473	29	
1998-1999	9,934	5	
1990s	**Subtotal**		**84,203 (72.0%)**
1957-1998	**Grand Total**		**116,861 (100.0%)**

Sources: Raich 1980; Enzenbacher 1992b, 1993, 1994a; INFUETUR, 1995, 1996; IAATO, 2000; NSF 1998, 1999, 2000.

Note: Between 1958-1959 and 1965-1966 no commercial tourism took place.

TABLE 4.7. Seaborne Antarctic Tourism During the 1996-1997 Season

Vessel	Passenger Capacity	Voyages	Passengers Carried	Landings
World Discoverer	138	9	1,017	101
Akademik S. Vavilov	80	13	955	91
Alla Tarasova	120	11	948	98
Akademik Ioffe	80	13	879	95
Hanseatic	180	5	781	44
Explorer	100	9	707	109
Akademik Shuleykin	45	10	383	74
Professor Multanovskiy	45	10	374	75
Professor Molchanov	38	8	332	101
Professor Khromov	38	8	296	67
Bremen	164	2	288	14
Kapitan Khlebnikov	114	3	253	60
Akademik Shokalskiy	36	3	109	17
Total		104	7,322	946

Source: National Science Foundation 1997a (based on information provided by members to the IAATO Secretariat).

TABLE 4.8. Tour Operator Ranking by Passengers Carried During the 1996-1997 Season

Tour Company	Total Passengers	Market Share (%)
Marine Expeditions	2,362	32.25
Quark Expeditions	1,028	14.04
Hanseatic Tours	906	12.37
Society Expeditions	888	12.12
A&K/Explorer Shipping	707	9.66
Aurora Expeditions	305	4.16
Zegrahm Expeditions	217	2.96
Playguide Tours	196	2.68
JES	184	2.51
Mountain Travel Sobek	147	2.00
Marathon Tours	124	1.69
S. Heritage Expeditions	109	1.49
Aventyrsresor	75	1.02
Svalbard Polar Travel	38	0.50
ANI	36	0.50
Total	**7,322**	**100.00**

Source: National Science Foundation, 1997a.

sengers ventured south—approximately the same number that had voyaged to Antarctica during the whole decade of the 1970s. Twenty vessels (excluding yachts) made 129 voyages south. During the season the various vessels carried the following numbers of passengers: *Marco Polo* (2,583), *Hanseatic* (1,008), *Rotterdam* (936), *Lyubov Orlova* (933), *Aegean I* (912), *Ocean Explorer* (889), *Akademik Ioffe* (873), *World Discoverer* (828), *Bremen* (791), *Explorer* (764), *Clipper Adventurer* (750), *Akademik Vavilov* (565), *Caledonian Star* (523), *Professor Molchanov* (485), *Professor Multanovskiy* (390), *Boris Petrov* (366), *Akademik Shuleykin* (350), *Kapitan Khlebnikov* (198), *Grigory Mikheev* (153), and *Akademik Shokalskiy* (89) (National Science Foundation 2000). A closer look at the data reveals that 36.4 percent of all Antarctic cruise passengers traveled on very large vessels. It is expected that the only large ships operating in Antarctica during the 2000-2001 season will be the *Marco Polo* (800 berths) and the *Vista Mar* (280 berths) (IAATO 2000).

The various tour operators carried the following number of passengers: Orient Lines (2,583), Marine Expeditions (1,950), The World Cruise Company (assisted by Marine Expeditions) (1,801), Hapag-Loyd Tours (1,799), Quark Expeditions (1,153), Holland America Lines (936), Society Expeditions (828), A&K/Explorer Shipping (764), New World Ship Management Clipper Cruise Line (663), Lindblad Special Expeditions (523), Aurora Expeditions (484), Peregrine Adventures (366), Mountain Travel-Sobek (206), Oceanwide Expeditions (154), Southern Heritage Expeditions (89 plus one joint charter of the *Professor Multanovskiy* with Quark Expeditions), Zegrahm Expeditions (88 plus one voyage with Society Expeditions), and Pelagic Expeditions (16). Thus, as during the 1996-1997 season reported in Table 4.8, Marine Expeditions again carried the most passengers south. Despite its success in attracting large numbers of customers, Marine Expeditions Inc. went into liquidation on July 28, 2000. A new entity called Marine Expeditions (MEX) acquired some of the assets of the failed company, including its name, and will run a two-ship, nineteen-voyage program during the 2000-2001 season (Australian Antarctic Division 2000c).

Impacts and Landing Procedures

As far as the potential impacts of cruise vessels and passengers on the Antarctic environment are concerned, the size of the vessel and the corresponding passenger numbers are the key factors. However, no conclusive evidence shows which type of vessels have the least cumulative impact. Expedition-style vessels have the advantage of carrying only small numbers of passengers but make longer and more frequent landings. By contrast, large vessels land at fewer sites and the duration of shore visits is shorter.

Landing passengers in Antarctica usually involves the use of inflatable rubber crafts, mainly Zodiacs. The procedure is as follows:

1. The expedition leader decides where the next landing should occur, taking weather and ice conditions as well as other environmental factors into consideration.
2. The captain takes the ship as close as possible to the proposed landing site and drops the anchor or lets the vessel drift.
3. Zodiacs are lowered and the expedition leader, together with the cruise director (on larger vessels), and in the Ross Sea also the official New Zealand observer, approach the beach to locate a suitable landing site, taking current weather and wildlife conditions into consideration.
4. Having identified a suitable landing site, the expedition leader returns to the vessel, and passengers begin boarding the Zodiacs (a maximum of fifteen passengers per boat).
5. Passengers make landings that frequently involve wading the last few steps through the icy water.
6. Passengers are free to explore the close vicinity of the landing site with or without a guide. If an SSSI is nearby, guides are posted to ensure that passengers do not enter the protected site.
7. After their shore visit, which usually lasts between one and three hours, passengers are ferried back to the ship by Zodiacs.

Zodiac cruises and landings are popular with passengers. Zodiac rides are exciting, but they are also arguably the most dangerous part of an Antarctic visit because passengers get in and out of the relatively small vessels in sometimes rough conditions.

The Economics of Seaborne Antarctic Tourism

Like commercial tourism elsewhere, Antarctic tourism is carried out by the participating tour operators as a for-profit exercise. Ship operation is a capital-intensive business in which the number of paying passengers on each cruise and the price they pay are important factors. Baumann (1996:316) points out that in order to be profitable a cruise vessel has to operate 350 days per year. Thus, load factors (or occupancy rates of berths) become a crucial indicator of the financial viability of Antarctic cruising. As an example, Table 4.9 illustrates the point for the 1994-1995 season. The load factors can be seen as a highly satisfactory result from the operator's point of view, indicating that despite an increase in available cruise vessels, demand for Antarctic cruising is still strong.

It is an interesting exercise to estimate the economic impact of Antarctic tourism. Table 4.10 illustrates that although visitor numbers are small, during the 1998-1999 season Antarctic tourism was nevertheless a US$39 million-plus industry. On a per-passenger basis this gross revenue, generated during a four-month season from mid-November to early March, is one of the highest in the world, indicating that Antarctic tourism is indeed "big business." In the absence of a local Antarctic population, the question, "Who benefits from Antarctic tourism activities?" is an interesting one. Commercial confidentiality ensures that no detailed profit figures for tour operators are available, but it can be assumed that since they return to the region

TABLE 4.9. Characteristics of Antarctic Peninsula Voyages 1994-1995

Ship	Maximum Passenger Capacity	Percentage of Average	Total Number of Voyages	Total Passengers
Livonia	36	96	11	382
Prof. Khromov	38	80	7	212
Prof. Molchanov	38	73	6	167
Akad. Vavilov	79	88	10	698
Akad. Ioffe	79	91	12	865
Alla Tarasova	94	75	9	631
Explorer	96	86	9	746
Kap. Dranitsyn	106	87	3	277
W. Discoverer	138	89	4	491
Bremen	164	74	4	485
Hanseatic	188	81	6	918
Vistamar	300	89	2	535
Eugenio Costa	1,300	71	1	918
Total				7,325

Source: INFUETUR, 1995.

TABLE 4.10. Estimate of the Economic Value of Antarctic Tourism (Excluding International Airfares) for the 1998-1999 Season (US$)

Type of Tourism	Passengers	Average Rate per Passenger	Total US$
Shipborne	231	6,000	1,386,000
	436	5,000	2,180,000
	3,493	4,000	13,972,000
	5,788	3,000	17,364,000
Air-supported	89	15,000	1,335,000
Overflights	3,000	1,000	3,000,000
Total			**39,237,000**

Source: Author's estimate based on published prices.

year after year their operations must be profitable. Many of them also operate programs in the Arctic, thus enabling them to utilize their chartered vessels year-round.

With regard to the providers of the vessels, the situation may not be as positive. Anecdotal evidence suggests that the Russian owners of vessels employed in Antarctica may not make great financial gains. One expedition vessel was reported to have sailed from its home port of Vladivostok to Ushuaia on one engine because there was not enough money to buy fuel to run both engines. At the end of the Antarctic season the vessel returned to Russia and, according to information obtained from an Antarctic expedition leader, the owners only just broke even on the venture. It appears that the main aim of the Russian ship owners is to keep their vessels and crews employed and that profit is only of secondary importance. Once the Russian economy stabilizes and as it moves forward to a market-driven economy, one has to wonder how long the period of low-cost availability of Russian vessels will last. Once full-market prices have to be paid for these vessels, shipborne Antarctic tourism will become more expensive, and, as a result, a further significant increase in seaborne visitor numbers would appear unlikely.

As previously mentioned, many of the ships used are of Russian registry and are chartered by tour operators in Europe, North America, and Australia. Table 4.11 provides an indication of how these charters are structured. The involvement of a company registered on

TABLE 4.11. Example of the Structure of Antarctic Ship Charters

Owner of vessel	Murmansk Shipping Company
Charter company	Super Nova Expeditions Ltd., Isle of Man
General Sales Agent	Quark Expeditions
Subcharterers	Adventure Associates, Zegrahm Expeditions, Mountain Travel Sobek

Source: Author, based on Poles Apart, 1993.

the Isle of Man is interesting and can be interpreted as an attempt at minimizing liability should a vessel get into difficulties while operating in Antarctic waters.

AVIATION

Since the early days of exploration, the use of aircraft has played an important role in mapping and opening up the region. The most comprehensive summary of Antarctic aviation is provided in the book *Moments of Terror: The Story of Antarctic Aviation* (Burke 1994). The best-known current commentator on Antarctic aviation is Antarctic veteran Dr. Charles Swithinbank, who regularly contributes updates on aviation matters to *Polar Record* (e.g., Swithinbank 1988, 1994). As will be shown, the Antarctic is presently accessible by air only to a very limited number of people who pay a high price for the privilege of actually landing on the continent by aircraft. It could be argued that the introduction of regular air services to Antarctica at a future time would spoil the uniqueness that is today attached to visiting and that, as a result, it would become a more mainstream destination.

On September 30, 1963, an American air crew flew two U.S. Navy C-130 transport planes from South Africa to McMurdo in the Ross Sea and on to Christchurch in New Zealand (Reedy 1964:459) and found no technical difficulties in operating these flights. Before landing at McMurdo, the crew discussed three other landing options: Hallett Station, Byrd Station, or the South Pole. This indicates that aircraft on skis could find possible landing sites in Antarctica to carry tourists. Reedy (1964:464) sums up the results of the flights:

Antarctica could be a logical stop for air traffic between South Africa and Australia or New Zealand. . . . I have no doubt that the day will come when planes will fly this route across the South Pole, just as today transports routinely fly great circle routes across the top of the world.

Despite the technical feasibility of flights across Antarctica, to date no such commercial routes have been established. The New Zealand journal *Antarctic* (New Zealand Antarctic Society 1970b:500) stated that "New Zealand's international airline Air New Zealand has decided that a commercial air service from New Zealand to the Antarctic is at least two summers away . . . because adequate transit accommodation for passengers at Williams Field [McMurdo station] would not be available before the summer of 1972-73." No such air service was ever established and there are no indications that one will be started in the near future.

The first-ever flight from Australia directly to a landing site in Antarctica was made by Dick Smith and Giles Kershaw on November 5, 1988, from Hobart to Casey Station in the Australian Antarctic Territory, but to date Australia has not yet constructed a landing strip in its territory that would support regular supply flights and that could conceivably be utilized for tourism purposes to defray costs.

Air-Supported Tourism Operations

Unlike most other tourist destinations, Antarctica is very difficult to reach by air. The only airstrips are located next to a handful of research stations such as the United States' McMurdo station, the French base at Dumont d'Urville, and the Chilean station Teniente Rodolfo Marsh, and are not open for nongovernment aircraft. As a result, passengers wishing to travel by air can choose between only two companies. The type of tourism these companies carry out is seen as important because they may well provide a model for future air-supported land-based tourism operations in Antarctica.

The first of these companies is Adventure Network International (ANI). Antarctic tourism programs operated by ANI cater to the needs of mountaineers, adventurers, and very wealthy, intrepid travelers. The company provides these modern "explorers" and adventurous tourists with access to the otherwise inaccessible interior of the continent. ANI's summer base is located in the southern Chilean town of Punta Arenas on the Strait of Magellan. From there the company operates chartered transport aircraft such as the Twin Otter and Hercules C-130 for the six-hour flight to their Patriot Hills base camp. Departures are highly dependent on weather conditions, and company brochures clearly state that delays of two to three days are common and that longer delays are not out of the question. The base camp established by ANI in the interior of Antarctica deserves description because it may one day serve as a model for future land-based Antarctic tourism developments, possibly on a larger scale. The ANI (1992) brochure describes the camp as follows:

> Our camp at Patriot Hills is like no other place on earth. At 80 degrees 20 minutes south, we are 600 nautical miles from the nearest habitation—Amundsen-Scott base at the South Pole. ANI's facility at Patriot Hills is the only private camp operating in Antarctica. Patriot Hills was chosen by ANI as our base seven years ago to take advantage of the first bare ice runway to be used in Antarctica. This, the most southerly runway in the world, is a natural phenomenon. The first wheeled landings in the heart of the continent were done here. All other landings in Antarctica are by ski-equipped aircraft. . . . The camp consists of tents and is supplied by air from Chile.

Operating a tourism facility in the interior is difficult. Access to the Patriot Hills camp is susceptible to the whims of the weather. The problem of landing wheeled aircraft has been solved by landing on a natural blue-ice runway. According to Swithinbank (personal communication 1993) there are many more such "runways" in Antarctica, and they may form the basis of future tourism development. Supplies such as aviation fuel have to be transported to the camp at enormous cost to the company. As a result, clients are charged US$2,500 for an hour of aerial sightseeing in a Cessna C185 at the Patriot Hills camp. By comparison, a one-hour flight in a chartered Cessna 172 in Australia is around US$100! Measured by numbers of passengers carried, ANI-Antarctica is only a minor player in Antarctic tourism, carrying only 139 passengers during the 1999-2000 season (National Science Foundation 2000), but gross revenue generated by these few passengers is nevertheless substantial since tour prices are very high. ANI offers a variety of programs in the interior. Examples include: "South Pole Expedition," "Guided Climbing Expeditions to Mt. Vinson," "Emperor Penguin Photo Safari," "The Heart of Antarctica," and "Ellsworth Mountains Ski Safari" (ANI 1992). A description of the itinerary of the "South Pole Expedition" serves as an example of how these tours/expeditions operate.

> From Punta Arenas, Chile, the first leg of the flight to Patriot Hills takes approximately 8 hours. After settling into camp, you will wait for suitable weather conditions for the culminating leg—your flight to the South Pole. The spectacular scenery around our base camp offers the perfect setting for familiarization with the Antarctic interior. . . . The flight from Patriot Hills to the Pole takes just over five hours and we will land on skis. You will spend a few memorable hours there—for photographs and possibly a tour of the Amundsen/Scott base. A complete camp with food and full emergency equipment is carried aboard the aircraft [a Cessna C185]. On the return flight, the plane may stop for fuel at the Thiel Mountains (85 degrees South).

The other programs mentioned are more expedition oriented in nature. They require greater levels of fitness and experience among those wishing to participate. Beginning during the 1996-1997 season, ANI also started to fly to the Dronning Maud Land from South Africa using Hercules aircraft (Charles Swithinbank, personal communication 1996; Kershaw, A., personal communication 1997). The company makes every effort to minimize the impacts of its operations on the local environment and its policy is that "Everything we take in, we take out even if it is eaten first" (ANI 1992). All garbage produced, including human waste, is returned to Chile for proper disposal. In 1992, ANI became one of the first companies to subject its operations to an environmental evaluation.

Flights to King George Island

In the period 1984-1993, the Chilean government actively encouraged tourists to visit the South Shetland Islands, a region where Argentinian, British, and Chilean claims to sovereignty overlap. In particular, the Chilean government actively marketed trips to King George Island. The two-and-a-half-hour flights from Punta Arenas were aboard Fuerza Aerea Chileno C-130 Hercules transport planes, which landed at the 1,300 meter, Chilean-owned airstrip at Teniente

Rodolfo Marsh base. There, passengers stayed in the only commercial accommodation in Antarctica, the Hotel Estrella Polar, an air force hostel. During their stay, passengers went on day excursions to other scientific stations and to wildlife sites such as the Ardley penguin rookery. They also undertook helicopter and Twin Otter flights around King George Island. The Chilean government thus provided the only regular opportunity to reach Antarctica by air. Sample package prices for a four-night stay in October 1991 (Turismo y Hoteles Cabo de Hornos SA. 1990) were between US$3,900 and US$4,200. In 1992, these flights were suspended by the Chilean air force. According to a source at the Instituto Antartida Chileno in Santiago de Chile (personal communication 1993), no official reason had been given, but it was suspected that fear of losing a plane in adverse weather conditions, as well as pressure from environmental organizations, had prompted the suspension of the flights. A private company, Aerovias DAP, Ltd., operating from Punta Arenas in southern Chile, stepped into the gap and is now offering year-round flights to Marsh base at approximately US$2,200 per person.

Overflights of Antarctica

While visiting Antarctica by sea allows passengers to experience the Antarctic environment, the same cannot be said for the experience gained during an aerial sightseeing trip of parts of the continent. At first glance the notion of spending twelve hours aboard an airborne Boeing 747-400 aircraft without actually landing at a destination would seem strange. It is interesting to ponder the question of whether flying to Antarctica and seeing the continent from above, without landing, constitutes reality or "virtual reality" and whether someone who has flown above Antarctica could be considered as having "been" to Antarctica and whether, as a consequence, passengers aboard overflights should be counted as Antarctic tourists. In a way, counting overflight passengers as visitors to Antarctica would be like count- ing passengers who overfly Greenland on intercontinental flights between Europe and North America as Greenland tourist arrivals (it is noteworthy that neither IAATO nor NSF count overflight passengers as Antarctic tourists). With regard to the experience gained from a flight, skeptics may argue that the same impression could be gained by watching a video. As Clark (1995) notes, writing in the context of the debate about conducting future travel by way of virtual reality, ". . . the possibility arises of accessing and exploring extensive 'natural' landscapes . . . and, although 'actual' ecosystems seem bound to continue their decline in scale and integrity in the immediate future, we can predict a burgeoning of virtual ecologies" (pp. 736-737).

Yet, despite these academic concerns, in 1977 the Australian entrepreneur Dick Smith began a series of charter flights that took passengers from Australia to Antarctica and back in one day without undertaking a landing (Burke 1994). Thus was created what to this day remains arguably the most unusual day excursion in the world, that is, a "visit" to another continent without setting foot on it. The duration of overflights is approximately equal to the time required to fly from New York to Los Angeles, north along the coast of California to San Francisco, and back to New York. It would appear that only a few people would cherish this experience, let alone be willing to part with substantial amounts of money for the privilege.

Sightseeing flights in most regions of the world are of short duration, ranging from forty-five minute ascents in hot air balloons over cities or wine-growing regions in Australia and France to light plane excursions of an hour or less over spectacular natural attractions such as the Grand Canyon in Arizona or the Great Barrier Reef in Australia. Other flights take to the air to obtain a better view of specific landmarks such as the Nazca Lines in Peru, Cape Horn, Victoria Falls, or the Mount Everest region. These flights are often operated on an ad hoc basis using aircraft such as the Cessna 172 and seating only a few people.

Longer trips, such as those offered by the Australian company Aircruising Australia, are carried out in relatively small aircraft such as the nine-seat Titan, seventeen-seat Metro, or the somewhat larger forty-seat F27 Fokker Friendship. Although the company's name would suggest that the tourism experience emphasizes the flight component—air cruising—an analysis of the company's 1992 brochure revealed that the flights are mainly promoted as a convenient mode of transport between visits to Australian highlights such as Kakadu National Park, the Bungle Bungles National Park, Broome, and Uluru (Ayers Rock). However, in its 1995-1996 brochure the company places far greater emphasis on the aerial experience of the trips offered. The brochure states, for example, that "the availability of your private aircraft will . . . provide unsurpassed aerial views of Australia's ever changing scenery . . . Large picture windows provide the perfect opportunity to view the magnificent landscape. . . . Spectacular low aerial sightseeing provides unsurpassed viewing of the [Kakadu National Park] escarpment with its gorges, abrupt cliff faces and waterfalls." This shift in emphasis is interesting.

Croydon Travel, the organizers of the series of Antarctic overflights that began in 1994-1995, also organizes charter aerial tours which are marketed under the name Captain's Choice. These tours fly clients aboard a chartered Qantas 767 to some of the most sought-after destinations around the world. One such excursion, in March 1995, included visits to Beijing, the Taj Mahal, Jerusalem, African game reserves, the Seychelles, Cable Beach in Broome, and overflights of Uluru. These tours emphasize the convenience of traveling in a chartered aircraft, with special emphasis on the business class service provided throughout the flights. To the knowledge of the author, no other nonstop sightseeing flights of twelve hours exist today.

It is interesting to note that the Arctic does not have an equivalent of the Antarctic overflights. Flights across the Arctic region tend to be no more than by-products of scheduled air services between northern continents. Flights from Europe regularly overfly Greenland, the Tokyo-to-Frankfurt route overflies northern Siberia, and in the past Japan Airline flights from Tokyo to Europe even crossed the North Pole. Based on observations during several flights in these regions, the scenery is in parts as beautiful as that seen from the window of an aircraft above Antarctica. Yet, the vast majority of passengers observed preferred to keep their blinds shut and, rather than viewing the grandeur of Greenland's ice cap or the snow-covered expanses of Siberia, opted to relax by watching the in-flight entertainment. On one recent commercial flight from Seattle to Denver, the author flew over the summit of Mt. Rainier on a beautiful, clear day. Hardly any of the other passengers took any notice of the event, and the captain did not bother to point it out to the passengers either.

During summers in the late 1970s, a number of flights took place that transported passengers from Montreal and Toronto to the Arctic for the day. The flights briefly crossed the Arctic Circle and landed in Frobisher Bay (now Iqaluit) on Baffin Island. Passengers were shown around the muddy landscape for a few hours before they returned south. These flights were obviously not a tremendous economic success because they did not continue.

One explanation for the availability of Antarctic, compared to Arctic, overflights may be the fact that the Arctic is accessible by a variety of means of transport such as private motor car, coach, and ship as well as by scheduled and chartered air services. In remote Nunavut, Air Nunavut offers charter flights and air tours that cover Nunavut, western Northwest Territories, northern Quebec, and Greenland. The company operates twin-engine Super King Air 200 and Piper Navajo airplanes (<http://www.arctic-travel.com/chapters/flypage.html>).

No such easy accessibility exists in Antarctica and, deprived of the ease of access taken for granted in most other locations, people may be happy just to catch a glimpse of Antarctica, even if it is just through the window of a plane. The author went on several overflights and surveyed passengers as to their motivations for undertaking such flights. The results are discussed in Chapter 6.

Background to Overflights

The first Antarctic overflight took place on December 22, 1956, when a Douglas DC-6B of Linea Aerea Nacional flew nonstop from South America over the South Shetland Islands and the Trinity Peninsula (*Headland* 1994:275). In October 1957, a Pan American Airways Stratocruiser made a chartered flight (including landing) from Christchurch to McMurdo Sound (New Zealand Antarctic Society, 1977a: 100). The inaugural Qantas sightseeing flights took place on February 13 and March 16, 1977, and overflew Macquarie Island, the South Magnetic Pole, and parts of Victoria Land, Oates Land, and George IV Land. Flights were organized by former *Australian Geographic* publisher Dick Smith, who also provided a background. When asked by a reporter why he had started the flights, Dick Smith replied: "Every Monday morning when I was asked what I did at the week-end I've wanted to be able to reply quite casually: 'I took a trip to the South Pole' " (*Adelaide Advertiser,* 1977, quoted in Reich 1979:33).

The first series of flights terminated on February 16, 1980, when the last Qantas plane returned from Antarctica. Headland (1994:277) estimates that a total of 10,000 passengers were carried on a total of thirty Qantas and ten Air New Zealand flights. The end of the first series of overflights came as a result of the crash of an Air New Zealand flight in Antarctica. The crash claimed the lives of all 237 passengers and 20 crew and was the worst disaster in New Zealand's history (for a full account see New Zealand Antarctic Society 1979 and Mahon 1984).

Resumption

After prolonged negotiations with the Australian carrier Qantas and various government departments, the Melbourne-based travel company Croydon Travel succeeded in operating the first overflights of parts of the Antarctic continent in fifteen years. The series of six charter flights resumed from Australia on New Year's Eve 1994, when 356 passengers celebrated the occasion aboard Qantas flight 2601. The remaining five flights of the first series took place on January 7, January 21, January 26, February 11, and February 18, 1995. Despite the cost of A$1,199 for economy class, A$1,699 for business class, and A$2,099 for first-class seats, bookings exceeded expectations, resulting in a total of 2,134 passenger and 151 crew being carried. The series was continued during 1995-1996, when ten departures were scheduled between November 26 and February 25. With the exception of the flight scheduled for February 25, which was cancelled due to the early withdrawal of U.S. personnel from McMurdo (the tour organizer had arranged for McMurdo to provide search and rescue facilities for the flights), all flights took place as scheduled. Air fares on the second series of flights ranged from A$999 to A$2,799. Ten flights took place during the 1996-1997 season with prices ranging from A$799 to A$2,999 (Croydon Travel 1996). The flights carried 3,301 passengers and 224 crew (Asker, personal communication 1997).

As Table 4.12 shows, a total of 8,393 passengers and 577 crew were carried on the flights, which took place between December 31, 1994, and January 27, 1996. Load factors on the 1994-1995 series of overflights were slightly higher (on average an extra twenty-seven passengers per flight were carried) than during the 1995-1996 series. Given the "novelty value" of flights during the 1994-1995 season this was to be expected. The fact that a record number of passengers flew to Antarctica during the 1996-1997 season is evidence that demand for this type of Antarctic tourism product was still strong. Another ten flights were carried out during the 1997-1998 season, nine flights took place during 1998-1999, nine flights took place during 1999-2000, and six are planned for 2000-2001. To date, fifty-two flights have been conducted, which have carried a total of 19,312 people, a

TABLE 4.12. Crew and Passenger Statistics, 1994 to 1997

Flight	Crew	Passengers	Total
QF2601	25	356	381
QF2602	26	345	371
QF2603	24	351	375
QF2604	24	356	380
QF2605	26	362	388
QF2606	26	364	390
Total 1994-1995	**151**	**2,134**	**2,285**
QF2601	23	285	308
QF2602	23	294	317
QF2603	21	323	344
QF2604	21	363	384
QF2605	22	307	329
QF2606	23	326	349
QF2607	23	371	394
QF2609	22	376	398
QF2610	24	313	337
Total 1995-1996	**202**	**2,958**	**3,160**
Total 1996-1997	**224**	**3,301**	**3,525**
Grand Total	**577**	**8,393**	**8,970**

Sources: Qantas 1995:7, 1996:10; Asker, personal communication 1997.

figure made up of 18,141 passengers and 1,171 crew. The total number of passengers is expected to pass the 20,000 mark during the 2000-2001 season (Australian Antarctic Division 2000). Increasingly, Antarctic overflights will attract passengers from overseas, and in this context they can be seen as enhancing the Australian tourism product.

The flight paths varied (sixteen different routes were programmed into the flight plans) but generally went south over Tasmania, to the South Magnetic Pole and on to the French base of Dumont d'Urville. From there two routes were traveled: one to the east, which variously included Cape Hudson, the Russian base Leningradskaya, Cape Adare, Cape Hallett, and Cape Washington. The other route went west from Dumont d'Urville and included parts of the coastline of Wilkes Land as far east as the Australian base Casey.

The special conditions and conditions of carriage for the Antarctic charter flight on Sunday, December 3, 1978, included a clause which stated that every effort would be made to adhere to the attached flight plan, but that weather conditions would determine the actual route taken by the captain on the day of travel. No assurance was given as to what would be seen from the aircraft. In the event of the view being obscured or the route not adhered to, passengers were not entitled to receive a refund. The latest series of overflights had similar conditions:

> Whilst every endeavor will be made to adhere to the proposed route, weather conditions may determine the actual route, according to the absolute discretion of the Captain of the aircraft. No guarantee can be given of clear viewing conditions and no refund or part refund will be made if the views are obscured. Alternate routes will be selected to give the best viewing if the planned route has unfavorable weather conditions. (Croydon Travel 1995)

These clauses make overflights an even more unusual product. Passengers must be willing to take a chance with regard to the condition of the skies above Antarctica: will they be clear during the flight or not? No guarantee is given that people will actually see anything, but reports to date suggest that passengers have not been disappointed with viewing conditions. During the three to four hours spent over the pack ice and the continent, the Boeing 747-400 aircraft maintains a minimum height above ground of 2,000 feet, or 10,000 feet above sea level. This provides passengers with excellent viewing conditions while at all times ensuring the safety of the aircraft. Two thousand feet above ground is a safe altitude when compared to Air New Zealand's minimum flight altitude of 1,000 feet (Reich 1979:34).

As an example, Table 4.13 shows the altitudes flown and the time spent above Antarctica during the 1994-1995 series of flights. It shows that out of a total air time of some 72 hours, only 15.20 hours were spent over the continent.

Overflights departing from Australia are seen as domestic flights, and therefore no passports are required and no duty-free shopping is available. With a duration of around twelve hours, these flights are the longest nonstop domestic flights in the world. The flights have added to the ways in which Antarctica can be experienced but, as mentioned

TABLE 4.13. Flight Details Showing Time Spent Over Antarctica, 1994-1995

Flight	Date	Altitude Above Sea Level (feet)	Duration (hours)
1	Dec. 31, 1994	10,000	2:49
2	Jan. 7, 1995	10,000	2:04
		18,000	0:35
3	Jan. 21, 1995	10,000	0:26
		19,000	1:00
4	Jan. 26, 1995	10,000	0:33
		18,000	1:07
		20,000	0:20
5	Feb. 11, 1995	18,000	2:54
6	Feb. 18, 1995	10,000	0:58
		16,000	0:36
		18,000	1:58
Total time overflying the continent			15.20

Source: Croydon Travel (personal communication 1995).

Note: In addition, all flights spent approximately one hour flying over the pack ice.

above, whether passengers should be considered Antarctic tourists is a matter of interpretation. Certainly, as far as the environmental impacts of their presence above Antarctica is concerned, overflight passengers are the most benign of visitors to the frozen South. In this context it is of interest that Croydon Travel was the winner of the 1996 Victorian Tourism Award for Environmental Tourism.

LAND-BASED TOURISM

To date, no large-scale tourism facilities have been developed in Antarctica. In the late 1980s "a detailed proposal was submitted to the Australian Government by Helmut Rohde and Partners which proposed the development, operation and environmental monitoring of an airport, visitor education and research center, accommodation, hospital, search and rescue and Antarctic Treaty related organization facilities" (House of Representatives Standing Committee on Environment, Recreation and the Arts, 1989:24). The proposal, known as Project Oasis, was to be located in the Vestfold Hills near Australia's

Davis station. To reach the area, it was proposed that a 2,800 meter runway capable of handling Boeing 747 aircraft be constructed at Davis. Project Oasis was to provide accommodation facilities for 344 visitors, 70 researchers, and 174 staff. Two flights per week were proposed and up to 16,000 people per year were to be able to use the facility (p. 25). The project was rejected by the Australian government of the day despite the fact that Rohde and Partners had suggested that a detailed conservation strategy be developed before any decision on their proposal was made. Today a similar proposal may be more difficult to reject since guidelines for the conduct of all human activities in the Antarctic have been established under the Madrid Protocol. Thus a developer could conceivably meet all environmental requirements, and governments may find it difficult to find a reason for an environmentally sound project not to proceed. The author discussed this with several experts, but at least one, John Heap (personal communication 1993), a former director of the Scott Polar Research Institute, disagreed with this notion.

As it has in other remote island tourist destinations such as the Cook Islands, Tahiti, or Easter Island, readily available, affordable, and large-scale air access to Antarctica would alter the pattern of Antarctic tourism irrevocably. The likelihood of such large-scale air transport will be explored in Chapter 7.

PRIVATE EXPEDITIONS

As Heap (1990:2601) points out, nongovernmental expeditions depend for their success on sponsorship in cash or kind. As a result, recent expeditions such as those carried out by Swan (1986), Steger (1989), Messner (1989), Fiennes (1992 and 1996), Kagge (1993), McIntyre and McIntyre (1995-1996), and Ousland (1997), sought and received substantial media coverage. Many books and newspaper articles have been written that outline the adventures of these expeditions. Television programs and lecture tours also form a part of the commercialization process of these expeditions. By sharing their adventures with the general public, Antarctic adventurers, historic and contemporary, stimulate the interest of the public in Antarctic affairs in general and in tourism in particular. Although many of them may not like to think of themselves as such, they are nevertheless breaking ground for more mainstream tourists to follow in their footsteps, a process that is well documented in many other previously remote regions such as Nepal, Bali, Goa, and Tahiti, to name but a few. Because their activities are private endeavors rather than commercial tourist ventures, they are not explored in detail in this book. There is, however, scope for future research to investigate, for example, the motivations of adventurers such as Ousland, the first person to complete an unsupported crossing of Antarctica.

MANAGEMENT AND REGULATION OF COMMERCIAL ANTARCTIC TOURISM

The issue of management and regulation features prominently in the Antarctic tourism debate. As at other destinations, responsible management is the cornerstone of sustainable tourism development. Whether regulation should be exclusively in the domain of government or private industry or whether both sectors should contribute is a matter of considerable debate in many countries, and it is therefore not surprising that the same debate is now taking place in the Antarctic context.

Regulation of Antarctic Tourism Under the Antarctic Treaty System

Antarctic tourism is governed by the Antarctic Treaty of 1959, and its associated agreements, measures, and recommendations that are collectively referred to as the Antarctic Treaty System (ATS). As outlined in Chapter 3, all human activities, including tourism, are covered under the provisions of the Madrid Protocol, which aims to maintain the pristine nature of Antarctica. Heap (1990:2601) illustrates the main concerns of the Consultative Parties with regard to tourism in the treaty area. These are to ensure that:

a. Information about tourist and nongovernmental expeditions is provided in advance (IV-27[1]).
b. Conditions for visits to stations may be made known (IV-27[2], VI-7[2], and VIII-9[2][a]).
c. Scientific research activities are not prejudiced (IV-27 and VI-7).
d. Visitors to the Antarctic not sponsored by a Consultative Party are aware of the relevant provisions of the Treaty, Recommendations, and accepted practices (VII-4[2], VIII-9 and X-8 Part I).

e. The environmental effects of tourism can be monitored (VII-4[3] and VIII-9[3]).
f. Provision exists to concentrate the impact of tourism if this should be considered environmentally prudent (VII-4[3] and VIII-9[2][b]; see also extracts from reports of the IXth and XIIth ATCM's).
g. Tour operators are encouraged to carry experienced guides (X-8, Part III).
h. Consultative Parties consult each other about nongovernmental expeditions organized in one country and requesting assistance from another (X-8, Part II).
i. Nongovernmental expeditions are encouraged to be self-sufficient and to carry adequate insurance (X-8, Part II).

As indicated earlier, several instruments, including the Agreed Measures and the Madrid Protocol, impact heavily on the conduct of commercial tourism. In addition, at the XVIIIth ATCM in Kyoto (April 1994) the delegates adopted Recommendation XVIII-I, which contains "Guidance for Visitors to the Antarctic" and the "Guidance for Those Organizing and Conducting Tourism and Non-governmental Activities in the Antarctic." "Guidance for Visitors to the Antarctic" (IAATO 1995) contains the following recommendations.

Protect Antarctic Wildlife

Taking or harmful interference with Antarctic wildlife is prohibited except in accordance with a permit issued by a national authority.

1. Do not use aircraft, vessels, small boats, or other means of transport in ways that disturb wildlife, either at sea or on land.
2. Do not feed, touch, or handle birds or seals, or approach or photograph them in ways that cause them to alter their behaviour. Special care is needed when animals are breeding or moulting.
3. Do not damage plants, for example by walking, driving, or landing on extensive moss beds or lichen-covered scree slopes.
4. Do not use guns or explosives. Keep noise to the minimum to avoid frightening wildlife.
5. Do not bring nonnative plants or animals into the Antarctic (such as live poultry, pet dogs and cats, or houseplants).

Several of the five points are highly unlikely to apply to commercial tourists. Point 1 is restricted to nongovernmental expeditions where visitors and tour operators/organizers are the same people. Commercial tourists aboard ships do not have any say in the operation of the crafts they travel on. Thus point 1 should be covered under "Guidance for Operators." Point 2 does apply to tourists, as does point 3. It must, however, be noted that visitors do not drive in Antarctica and that they have no say in where landings take place. It is extremely unlikely that tourists would use guns or explosives as suggested in point 4; thus they should only be encouraged to keep noise to a minimum. The introduction of the nonnative plants or animals listed in point 5 by tourists also seems unlikely.

Respect Protected Areas

1. Know the locations of areas that have been afforded special protection and any restrictions regarding entry and activities that can be carried out in and near them.
2. Observe applicable restrictions.
3. Do not damage, remove or destroy Historic Sites or Monuments, or any artifacts associated with them.

Point 1 should be seen as the responsibility of the tour operator, not the tourists.

Respect Scientific Research

Do not interfere with scientific research, facilities, or equipment.

1. Obtain permission before visiting Antarctic science and logistic support facilities; reconfirm arrangements twenty-four to seventy-two hours before arrival; comply with the rules regarding such visits.
2. Do not interfere with, or remove, scientific equipment or marker posts, and do not disturb experimental study sites, field camps, or supplies.

Point 1 is of no concern to commercial tourists. Visits to stations are arranged between tour operators and the national governments of the countries who operate the stations.

Be Safe

Be prepared for severe and changeable weather. Ensure that your equipment and clothing meet Antarctic standards. Remember that the Antarctic environment is inhospitable, unpredictable, and potentially dangerous.

1. Know your capabilities, the dangers posed by the Antarctic environment, and act accordingly. Plan activities with safety in mind at all times.
2. Keep a safe distance from all wildlife, both on land and at sea.
3. Take note of, and act on, the advice and instructions from your leaders; do not stray from your group.
4. Do not walk onto glaciers or large snow fields without proper equipment and experience; there is a real danger of falling into hidden crevasses.
5. Do not expect rescue service. Self-sufficiency is increased and risks reduced by sound planning, quality equipment, and trained personnel.
6. Do not enter emergency refuges (except in emergencies). If you use equipment or food from a refuge, inform the nearest research station or national authority once the emergency is over.
7. Respect any smoking restrictions, particularly around buildings, and take great care to safeguard against the danger of fire. This is a real hazard in the dry environment of Antarctica.

Several of these points do not apply to tourists. Points 1 and 5 are clearly in the domain of the tour operator or the nongovernmental expeditioner.

Keep Antarctica Pristine

Antarctica remains relatively pristine, and has not yet been subjected to large-scale human perturbations. It is the largest wilderness area on earth. Please keep it that way.

1. Do not dispose of litter or garbage on land. Open burning is prohibited.
2. Do not disturb or pollute lakes or streams. Any material discarded at sea must be disposed of properly.

3. Do not paint or engrave names or graffiti on rocks or buildings.
4. Do not collect or take away biological or geological specimens or man-made artifacts as a souvenir, including rocks, bones, eggs, fossils, and parts or contents of buildings.
5. Do not deface or vandalize buildings, whether occupied, abandoned, or unoccupied, or emergency refuges.

Most points raised with regard to the maintenance of the pristine nature of Antarctica do apply to tourists. "Open burning" and "discarding material at sea properly" are, however, unlikely to be carried out by tourists. In summary, it appears that the Treaty Parties have attempted to cover too many potential visitor groups in their "Guidance for Visitors to the Antarctic." Many of the points only apply to tour operators, while others were obviously written with the independent, nongovernmental expeditioner in mind. A clearer set of guidelines such as those produced by IAATO (discussed in the next section) would be more effective in getting the message across to the vast majority of visitors, who are commercial tourists aboard Antarctic cruise vessels.

Self-Regulation of Tourism Operations

Antarctic tour operators have responded to the need to preserve the Antarctic environment by establishing their own industry association and by developing their own code of conduct rules that attempt to minimize the impact visitors have on the environment. Splettstoesser and Folks (1994) outline the establishment of the International Association of Antarctica Tour Operators in 1991. IAATO, they note, was formed by the six active U.S. ship tour operators (Mountain Travel-Sobek, Paquet/Ocean Cruise Lines, Salen Lindblad Cruising, Society Expeditions, Travel Dynamics, and Zegrahm Expeditions) plus an air/land operator, Adventure Network International. Reasons for the establishment of the organization are given by Splettstoesser and Folks (1994:235): "A means of pooling resources and promoting thoughtful legislation that is compatible with the responsible tourism that tour operators have exhibited in their history." They note that members pledged to abide by the US Antarctic Conservation Act of 1978, or its equivalent in the Protocol on Environmental Protection, and to adhere to the industry-generated Guidelines of Conduct for Antarctic Visitors and Tour Operators.

The IAATO Membership Directory gives the purpose of the organization as: "A member organization founded in 1991 to advocate, promote and practice safe and environmentally responsible private-sector travel to the Antarctic." (For full details on IAATO see http://www.iatto.org.) By 2000, IAATO full membership had expanded to the following companies: Abercrombie and Kent/Explorer Shipping Corporation, Adventure Associates, Aurora Expeditions, Hapag-Lloyd Cruises, Heritage Expeditions, Lindblad Special Expeditions, Marine Expeditions, Mountain Travel-Sobek, New World Ship Management Company LLC/Clipper Cruise Line, Pelagic Expeditions, Peresrine Adventures, Quark Expeditions, Society Expeditions, WildWings, and Zegrahm Expeditions. (Orient Lines was a probationary member but was excluded during 1996 for repeatedly violating the rule that ships should not carry more than 400 passengers (IAATO, personal communication 1996). IAATO has several provisional members: Cheeseman's Ecology Safaris, Golden Fleece Expeditions, Ocean-wide Expeditions, Plantours & Partner GmbH, and Emanuel Nature Tours. In addition, the following companies are associate members: Asteria Travel, Expeditions Inc., Galapagos Travel, La Tour Chile, Life Long Learning, Natural Habitat Adventures, and Tauck World Discovery Tours. IAATO also maintains a Secretariat in Basalt, Colorado (IAATO 2000).

Talmadge (1991) points out that the establishment of an industry association was clearly also designed to counteract some moves by members of the U.S. Congress to legislate restrictions on tour operations in the Antarctic. Because of the remoteness of the continent, the enforcement of any government-imposed regulatory restrictions is difficult. As a result, effective and responsible self-control by operators, combined with the occasional government observer aboard cruise vessels, can be considered the best way to manage Antarctic tourism.

Travelers aboard IAATO member expeditions are reminded of the following regulations developed by the tour operators (IAATO 1992a) prior to recommendation XVIII-1 coming into force:

1. Do not disturb, harass, or interfere with the wildlife.
2. Do not walk on or otherwise damage the fragile plants, i.e., lichens, mosses, and grasses.

3. Leave nothing behind, and take only memories and photographs.
4. Do not interfere with protected areas or scientific research.
5. Historic huts may only be entered when accompanied by a properly authorized escort.
6. Do not smoke during shore excursions.
7. Stay with your group or with one of the ship's leaders when ashore.

In addition, IAATO Guidelines for the Conduct of Antarctica Tour Operators (IAATO 1992b) require that tour operators:

1. Are familiar with the Antarctic Conservation Act of 1978 (U.S. Public Law 95-541) and that they abide by it
2. Are aware that entry to Specially Protected Areas (SPAs) and Sites of Special Scientific Interest (SSSIs) is prohibited unless permits have been obtained in advance
3. Enforce the above-mentioned guidelines for Antarctic visitors in a consistent manner
4. Hire a professional team of expedition leaders, cruise directors, officers, and crew, at least 75 percent of whom should have prior Antarctic experience
5. Hire Zodiac drivers who have experience driving Zodiacs in polar regions
6. Educate and brief the crew on the IAATO Guidelines of Conduct for Antarctic Visitors, the Agreed Measures for the Conservation of Antarctic Fauna and Flora, the Marine Mammal Protection Act of 1972, and the Antarctic Conservation Act of 1978 and make sure they are consistently enforced
7. Ensure that for every twenty to twenty-five passengers there is one qualified naturalist/lecturer guide to conduct and supervise small groups ashore
8. Limit the number of passengers ashore to 100 at any one place at any one time

The implementation and effectiveness of these guidelines or codes of conduct depends on several factors. The first is paying visitors' level of understanding of these guidelines, their level of agreement with them, and their willingness to comply. The other crucial factor is the willingness of the operator to enforce the guidelines. Given that passengers have paid a lot of money for the privilege of visiting the Antarctic, this is not always easy. Accounts to date suggest that tourists and tour operators alike have complied with the set industry guidelines and with the Antarctic Treaty recommendations established by the Treaty Parties to protect the environment. Beginning with Lars-Eric Lindblad and continuing with IAATO members, tour operators have been proactive in their measures to protect the resource on which their businesses depend. As a result of the cooperation between international tourists, tour operators, and Treaty Parties, Antarctic tourism today is the best-managed tourism in the world, and other destinations can learn much from the way it is conducted.

Health and Safety Issues

Antarctica is a remote and climatically hostile place where even minor accidents may quickly lead to major disasters. The nearest rescue services are far away, and the Treaty Parties in Recommendation XVIII-I rightly call on those organizing and conducting tourism in the Antarctic to "ensure self-sufficiency and safe operations." The conduct of commercial tourism would not be possible without close cooperation between the governments of the Antarctic Treaty Parties, tour operators, and the Council of Managers of National Antarctic Programs (COMNAP). As in other tourist destinations, the safety of passengers is of prime importance in the conduct of Antarctic tourism. Health and safety issues will be discussed again in a later chapter.

Accidents involving tourist vessels and aircraft have occurred in the past. Reich (1979:61) mentions the following shipping incidents: *Lapataia,* 1967 (stranding of party on Half Moon Island); *Navarino,* 1968 (steering engine failure); *Magga Dan,* 1968 (grounding of ship); *Aquiles,* 1969 (stranding of passengers ashore); *Lindblad Explorer,* 1972 (grounding of ship); *Libertad,* 1973 (damage of ship). The *Lapataia* incident required twenty-one people to resort to stores at the unoccupied Argentine station on Half Moon Island after the landing craft was pushed up the beach. The *Lindblad Explorer* incident saw tourists and crew take to the lifeboats for four hours after the ship had run aground on rocks in Admiralty Bay, King George Island.

The most-cited marine contingency is the sinking of the *Bahia Paraiso.* Bruchhausen (1996:95-115), a marine scientist with many years of Antarctic experience gained during sixty-two cruises and flights to the region, provides an excellent firsthand account of this incident, which has received substantial coverage in the literature. His description of the worst tourism-related marine emergency in Antarctic waters highlights the perils of ship operations in the Antarctic. The *Bahia Paraiso,* a ship built to supply Argentine bases in the Peninsula region, began taking tourists on cruises in February 1986 "to help defray costs of its Antarctic operations" (Bruchhausen 1996:99). During the 1988-1989 season, the ship made three voyages to the Peninsula prior to the ill-fated fourth cruise. The accident, as described by Bruchhausen, occurred as follows:

> The "Bahia Paraiso" departed from Ushuaia on January 20, 1989, with a full complement of tourists [a maximum of eighty-one]. . . . Again, in response to the wishes of the American tourists on board, the Captain obtained authorization to change the cruise plan and stop at Palmer Station before returning to Ushuaia. The "Bahia Paraiso" anchored in front of Palmer Station at approximately 0400 . . . on January 28, 1989, during a beautiful, calm morning. . . . During our visit to Palmer Station, we were told by the senior scientific personnel that the "Bahia Paraiso" had once again approached the Station through a hazardous navigation zone in spite of additional warnings that this was an extremely dangerous procedure. . . . The ship weighed anchor and left shortly after 1400, amidst glorious, calm weather and bright sunshine. A few minutes later, while dining, at approximately 1430, we heard a tremendous grinding crunch and the ship came to a trembling halt, leaning to starboard with her stern low in the water. . . . A shaky voice, speaking in Spanish over the loudspeaker, informed us that we had to immediately abandon ship. The ship continued to list and one had to assume at that moment that she was sinking fast . . .

Passengers were immediately evacuated to nearby Palmer Station, from where they were later transported aboard several tourist vessels to Teniente Rodolfo Marsh Base on King George Island. From there they were flown to Punta Arenas aboard Chilean Air Force C-130 Hercules transport planes.

Bruchhausen adds, "It is fortunate that the accident occurred during fair weather, that the seas were calm, that it was only a little more than a mile from Palmer Station, and that there were other vessels in close proximity, most of which were willing to render assistance"

(p. 109). Concluding that the accident was based on human error and that the loss of the ship was unnecessary, Bruchhausen makes ten recommendations "which may be useful to those who sail Antarctic waters" (p. 111).

The *Bahia Paraiso* incident, and other marine emergencies, highlight the fact that because of the remoteness of the region and the associated climatic conditions, the conduct of Antarctic tourism is a high-risk business. Only through careful attention to details in the organization and conduct of cruises and full compliance with all regulations can risks be reduced to acceptable levels. Safe conduct of Antarctic tourism also requires close cooperation between private and public sector institutions. In an attempt to strengthen cooperation between Antarctic Treaty parties, tour operators, and representatives of the U.S. National Science Foundation (NSF), these parties have met annually since 1989 to discuss schedules for tour ship visits at U.S. scientific stations in Antarctica and to discuss other matters of mutual interest. During the 11th Antarctic Tour Operators meeting on June 30, 1999, in Hamburg, the author was impressed by the spirit of respect and cooperation that now exists between commercial operators and government representatives. Such cooperation for the common good of the resource is rare at other destinations, and decision makers there are advised to take note of Antarctic cooperation.

CONCLUDING COMMENTS

This chapter offers a comprehensive analysis of the tourism phenomenon in the Antarctic context. It has established that shipborne tourism to the Antarctic Peninsula region has increased substantially during the 1990s. The chapter also discussed the resumption of overflights, which are seen as the most benign form of Antarctic tourism. The regulatory framework of tourism activities that has evolved during the 1990s is a unique mix of self-regulation by the industry and regulations, guidelines, and recommendations developed under the ATs. It is hoped that this combination will continue even now that the Madrid Protocol on Environmental Protection has come into force.

Most regulatory efforts are aimed at minimizing the impacts of human activities on the Antarctic environment, and it is therefore necessary to investigate more closely what these potential impacts are. Chapter 5 discusses this issue.

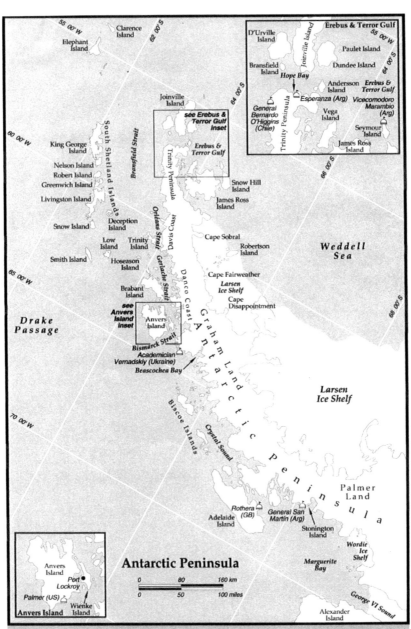

Erebus & Terror Gulf

Clarence Island
Elephant Island
55 00' W
62 00' S

D'Urville Island
Joinville Island
Bransfield Island
Hope Bay
General Bernardo O'Higgins (Chile)
Esperanza (Arg)
Andersson Island
Vega Island
Trinity Peninsula
Paulet Island
Dundee Island
Erebus & Terror Gulf
Vicecomodoro Marambio (Arg)
Seymour Island
James Ross Island
55 00' W
64 00' S
66 00' S

64 00' S

Joinville Island

see Erebus & Terror Gulf Inset

Erebus & Terror Gulf

Snow Hill Island
James Ross Island

Cape Sobral
Robertson Island

Cape Fairweather
Larsen Ice Shelf
Cape Disappointment

Weddell Sea

60 00' W

King George Island
Nelson Island
Robert Island
Greenwich Island
Livingston Island

South Shetland Islands

Bransfield Strait

Trinity Peninsula

Deception Island
Snow Island
Low Island
Trinity Island
Hoseason Island

Orleans Strait

Davis Coast

Gerlache Strait

Brabant Island

see Anvers Island inset

Anvers Island

Danco Coast

Graham Land

Smith Island

65 00' W

Drake Passage

Bismarck Strait
Academician Vernadskiy (Ukraine)
Beascochea Bay

66 00' S

70 00' W

Biscoe Islands

Crystal Sound

Antarctic Peninsula

Larsen Ice Shelf

Palmer Land

Rothera (GB)
Adelaide Island
General San Martín (Arg)
Stonington Island
Wordie Ice Shelf

Marguerite Bay

George VI Sound

Alexander Island

Anvers Island
Port Lockroy
Palmer (US)
Wienke Island
Anvers Island

Antarctic Peninsula

| 0 | 80 | 160 km |
| 0 | 50 | 100 miles |

PHOTO 1. Ushuaia, the southernmost town in the world, has become the major gateway to the Antarctic Peninsula.

PHOTO 2. Ships such as the *World Discoverer* and the *Akademik Boris Petrov* make the majority of voyages to Antarctica.

PHOTO 3. Passengers aboard the *Akademik Boris Petrov* are eagerly awaiting a landing as the ship approaches the Antarctic Peninsula.

PHOTO 4. An Antarctic cruise ship is dwarfed by the sheer size of the snow- and ice-covered mountains on Rongé Island in the Antarctic Peninsula.

PHOTO 5. The stillness of Neko Harbor reflects the unspoiled beauty of Antarctica.

PHOTO 6. A glacier at sea level and a rocky peak in the Antarctic Peninsula. Only 2 percent of Antarctica is not covered by snow or ice.

PHOTO 7. Boats such as this one at Whalers Bay on Deception Island were used by whalers to transport fresh water to their ships.

PHOTO 8. The author in front of boilers and storage tanks at the Hektor whaling station on Deception Island, which operated from 1911 to 1936.

PHOTO 9. Approaching Cape Horn from the south.

PHOTO 10. The author rounding Cape Horn.

Chapter 5

The Impacts
of Commercial Antarctic Tourism

The impacts of tourism are felt in many destinations around the globe. Inskeep (1991) divides them into environmental and socioeconomic categories. He sees the environment as comprising "all the natural and cultural surroundings of people" (p. 339) and recognizes that "Tourism development and tourist use of an area generate environmental impacts" (ibid.). With regard to the scale of potential impacts, Inskeep writes: "The type and extent of environmental impacts as well as socioeconomic impacts also relate closely to the type and intensity of tourism development that is undertaken" (p. 340). He adds that "Tourism can generate either positive or negative environmental impacts, or no appreciable impact, depending on how its development is planned and managed" (ibid.). Of relevance in the Antarctic context are the positive impacts listed by Inskeep (1991:342-344), which include conservation of important natural areas and archeological and historic sites; improvement of environmental quality; enhancement of the environment; and increasing environmental awareness. The major negative environmental impacts include pollution (water, air, noise, and visual); waste disposal; ecological disruption; environmental hazards; damage to historic sites; and land use problems (pp. 344-347). A conceptual framework of tourism and its impacts, for example, was developed by Mathieson and Wall (1982:15).

Much has been written and said about the alleged impacts of tourists on the Antarctic environment, and tourism has frequently been portrayed in the popular media as an activity that is threatening the relatively pristine nature of Antarctica. Several authors describe the perceived negative environmental impacts that tourism may have. Potential negative impacts are often highlighted in the literature, but very little substantiation of arguments is provided. It seems that since the demise of mining as a major issue in Antarctica, tourists and their activities have taken over as the group of people who are seen as most likely to destroy the "pristine wilderness" of Antarctica. In the process of discussing Antarctic tourism activities a certain lack of balance has developed with regard to the actual scale of impacts attributed to tourism activities.

It is the aim of this chapter to explore the theme of environmental impact of Antarctic tourism by reviewing the literature with regard to cited impacts. Responses received from a panel of Antarctic experts with regard to environmental impacts of tourism are reported in Chapter 7, and firsthand observations of Antarctic tourism activities by various observers, including the author, are discussed in Chapter 8.

ANTARCTIC TOURISM ACTIVITIES
IN PERSPECTIVE

Many writers foresee a gloomy future for the environment of the continent if tourism is allowed to continue to grow, but as early as 1989 Dr. Phillip Law, Australia's Antarctic pioneer, noted that he had become increasingly concerned about writers who jumped on the conservation bandwagon without a real understanding of Antarctica. Often some basic facts are overlooked in the excitement of discussing negative tourist impacts. For example, the size of the Antarctic continent, 14.2 million square kilometers or nearly twice the size of Australia, is rarely mentioned in such discussions. According to calculations, human activities use less than 0.005 percent of the total area of the continent (based on forty permanent bases, thirty-one summer stations, and seventy regularly visited tourist sites of approximately 5 square kilometers per site, for a total of 705 square kilometers). As previously stated, only approximately 2 percent of the continent is ice free during summer, and some of these areas provide habitat for penguins, seals, and seabirds. The total ice-free area can be calculated as 284,000 square kilometers, approximately the combined land areas of Victoria and Tasmania. Using these calculations, humans utilize only 0.25 percent of the total ice-free area. Headland (1994:279) puts Antarctic tourism activities into perspective when he states that "the effect of the tourist industry on the Antarctic may be estimated as 0.52 percent of the total human impact," the rest being attributed to scientists and their support staff. It is frequently overlooked that Antarctic tourism is highly concentrated at sites in the Antarctic Peninsula region and that, as a result, most parts of Antarctica are never visited by tourists. This concentration of activities may be cause for concern, but to infer from this that all of Antarctica is under threat from tourists would be wrong.

The profusion of many species of Antarctic wildlife is also often ignored. Chester (1993) quotes the Scientific Committee on Antarctic Research (SCAR 1990) as estimating the populations of Antarctic penguins as follows: 1.07 million pairs of breeding king penguins *(Aptenodytes patagonicus);* 2.47 million pairs of Adélie penguins *(Pygoscelis adeliae);* 7.49 million pairs of chinstrap penguins *(Pygoscelis antarctica);* 314,000 pairs of gentoo penguins *(Pygoscelis papua);* 3.68 million pairs of rockhopper penguins *(Eudyptes crestatus),* nesting mainly in the sub-Antarctic; 11.8 million pairs of macaroni penguins *(Eudyptes chrysolophus);* and 195,000 pairs of emperor penguins *(Aptenodytes forsteri)* nesting on the sea ice. The same source estimates the number of seals as follows: 250,000-800,000 Weddell seals *(Leptonychotes Weddelli);* 200,000 Ross seals *(Ommatophoca rossii);* 30 to 70 million crabeater seals *(Lobodon carcinophagus)* (half the world's pinniped population); 200,000-440,000 leopard seals *(Hydrurga leptonyx);* 600,000 Southern elephant seals *(Mirounga leonina);* and over 2 million Antarctic fur seals *(Arctocephalus gazella)* (largely on South Georgia). These figures indicate that unlike, for example, those of the Galapagos Islands, Antarctic wildlife populations are substantial. This fact has to be kept in mind when the impacts of tourists on the wildlife are discussed.

ENVIRONMENTAL IMPACTS OF ANTARCTIC TOURISM IN THE ACADEMIC LITERATURE

A variety of possible impacts have been reported in the literature. As previously outlined, Reich (1979) was the first to investigate the tourism phenomenon in Antarctica in any depth. She traced the nature of tourism, established its historical background, and elaborated on the planning aspects and the regulatory background of tourism. She also included some discussions on the impact of tourism. Reich (1979:55) states that prior to the seventh SCAR meeting (held in South Africa in 1963), the Working Group on Biology studied and classified the consequences of human influence on the Antarctic environment. They came to the conclusion that the principal causes of impacts were as follows:

1. General pollution by sewage, waste, oil, fuels, and noise
2. Introduction of nonnative, unsterilized soils, microbes, plants, and animals
3. Travel on foot or by vehicle and aircraft, both by scientists and nonscientists
4. Disturbance of local bird or seal breeding colonies
5. Changes in the chemical balance of natural waters, including the intentional or accidental introduction of radioisotopes
6. Uncontrolled dumping of solid and liquid waste in inshore waters
7. The use of explosives
8. Scientific sampling and experiments
9. Nonscientific collecting
10. Animals and eggs taken for food

Reich (1979) rightly concluded that "items 5, 7, 8, and 10 may be omitted, as they almost certainly would not result from tourist activities." She proceeded to evaluate the remaining points with respect to tourism activities. In summary she argued that items 1 and 6 can apply to "any visitor to the Antarctic, whether scientist or tourists" (p. 55). With regard to item 2, Reich found that "no accusations specifically against tourists have been found, but with visitors coming from many countries of the world, the problem must be recognized as very real." She points out that there is a risk of introducing illnesses such as influenza into the scientific station, which could interrupt scientific work. Item 3 does apply to tourism activities, and Reich points out that the issues of stepping on lichens as well as possible impacts of overflights on nesting birds and basking seals should be considered. The disturbance of local bird or seal communities received the most extensive coverage in Reich's writings on the impacts of tourism. She cites the often-mentioned Adélie penguin rookery at Cape Royds, which had a relatively constant bird population between its discovery by Scott and Wilson in 1904 and 1956. By 1962, the penguin population was almost halved (Thomson 1977). Stonehouse (1965:275) attributed this decline to the fact that:

> To an observer on the spot one cause was almost certain: from 1956 Shackleton's hut and the small group of Adelie penguins had become star attractions to congressmen, parliamentarians, journalists, diplomats, soldiers, sailors, and scientists visiting Antarctica as guests of the United States and New Zealand. A steady flow of visiting VIPs is one phenomenon which nature discounted in fitting Antarctic penguins for their environment, and the Cape Royds Adelie were unable to cope.

It is of interest to note that none of the people mentioned in Stonehouse's description were actually tourists. Rather, they were all at Cape Royds in the name of science, politics, or public relations. Mueller-Schwarze and Belanger (1978:375) add the following to the discussion on declining penguin numbers:

> It is true that Cape Royds has been subject to many visits by persons from McMurdo and to frequent and sometimes low overflights by airplanes and helicopters. But it is by no means clear that these are the only or main reasons for the decline. The rookery at Cape Royds is comparatively small, is the southernmost penguin rookery in the world, and is often separated from the feeding grounds by several kilometers of fast ice, so that considerable effort is required of the breeding birds to feed their young. These factors may account for fluctuations in numbers independent of human impact.

Read in conjunction with observations made by Fraser, which are outlined later, it becomes clear that humans, irrespective of whether they have paid to get to Antarctica (tourists), or whether they get paid to be there (scientists and support staff), may or may not be major contributors to the decline of penguins in Antarctica. Reich (1979:59) reported that in 1969, the United States and New Zealand agreed to "restrict activities in the area, firstly by controlling numbers and behaviour of visitors and workers, and secondly by the prohibition of helicopter flying over the rookery, or landing nearby." Thereafter the penguin population started to increase steadily.

As far as positive impacts of tourism are concerned, Reich noted that tourists are taxpayers and as such are the funding source of the research that is carried out in Antarctica. She cites Hedgpeth (1970:952) as saying that:

> One of the most important things about Antarctic tourism is that it allows the scientists to show the non-scientists on whom they depend for money how valuable the work they are doing is. Only well-off and potentially influential people are likely at the present time to tour such far distant parts, and I think it is a good plan to give them well-prepared brochures and politeness, and show them rather more than the McMurdo dump.

Referring to point 9, nonscientific collecting, Reich (1979:61) notes that Norris (1974) and Orchard (1970) were both of the opinion that the general impression given is that visitors exhibit a very responsible attitude. In summary, it becomes clear that none of the negative impacts Reich considered are unique to tourists, and few pose any large-scale threat to the Antarctic environment.

Beck (1994:380) points out that "All human activities in Antarctica, whether conducted by scientists, tourists, or others exert environmental impacts. Tourists, attracted by Antarctica's character as the last great wilderness on earth, are depicted paradoxically as a serious threat to the polar environment."

Erize (1987:134) believes Antarctic cruising has only a negligible impact on the environment, other than that of the disposal of the ship's wastes. With regard to landings he notes that if tourists are careless they may easily disturb breeding colonies of birds. This may scare the parent birds, who may temporarily desert their chicks or eggs, thus risking death from exposure. Tourists may also trample on scarce and fragile vegetation but, as he points out, problems associated with tourists in Antarctica are basically similar to those faced by most national park services in the world, which have found ways of coping with them.

Enzenbacher (1992:261), observes that: "The manner in which tours are conducted affects the nature and extent of impacts made in the Antarctic, yet little is known about the effects of tourist activity on the environment." She lists several environmental issues and questions associated with Antarctic tourism, including wildlife tolerance, waste disposal, passenger education, tour operator management, personnel experience, and frequency of visits.

Stonehouse (1993:331), writing about the results of the visitor/ wildlife monitoring program carried out under Project Antarctic Conservation, highlights the fragility of the Antarctic flora:

> Experiments in restricted areas confirmed quantitatively the extreme sensitivity of moss and lichen communities to even low incidence of trampling, indicating the need for strict visitor management in places where vegetation is at risk, and the need for further studies on the nature of trampling damage and possibilities for rehabilitation.

Stonehouse (1994:202) also notes that passengers ashore are well behaved, and he states that he has yet to see one "drop litter, knowingly trample vegetation or interfere seriously with wildlife." Janiskee (1991:4) lists the negative impacts of Antarctic tourism as:

> Problems for communications, search and rescue operations . . . and scientists complaining about wasted time and disrupted research activities when shiploads of tourists visit research stations. Research is also affected by the operation and pollution products of ships, including Zodiacs, and aircraft, and by tourists disturbing wildlife during shore visits.

An increase in the awareness of Antarctica as a wilderness and the resulting realization that the area needs protection are seen by Janiskee as positive aspects of Antarctic tourism. In the *Greenpeace Book of Antarctica,* May (1988:138-139) describes the impacts of tourism in the following way:

> The question of the effects of Antarctic tourism has been addressed several times at meetings of Treaty members. Under the various rulings and guidelines, it is the responsibility of each Consultative Party to ensure that any of its nationals who are part of a tourist or non-governmental expedition abide by the Agreed Measures. However, it is both politically unacceptable and legally difficult for any Consultative Party to prevent any non-governmental expedition from exploring or traversing the frozen continent. . . . ATCPs have expressed worries that tourism raises the possibility of expensive disruptions to personnel at research stations and a hazard to life and, in some instances,

base equipment. . . . Aside from the disruption caused to bases, by an influx of tourists or by distress calls, there is the question of the additional pressure tourists place on the natural environment. Fragile vegetation could easily be destroyed, and nesting and breeding grounds disrupted. Tourists could unwittingly spread bird or plant diseases and introduce new kinds of organisms to the Antarctic. The expansion of tourist facilities may also have a significant impact. At present this is a small problem, but one that is rapidly worsening. Under a World Park regime there would have to be regulation of some sort.

The possibility of tourists unwittingly spreading a newly discovered poultry virus found in young emperor penguins at Mawson was raised at the twenty-first ATCM in Christchurch.

Hall (1992b:5) believes the most serious concerns are focused on the potential impacts of tourism on the fragile Antarctic environment. Hall (1992b:6) identified the environmental impacts of ship-based tourism as "Transient environmental effects, although pressure may be placed on regularly visited attractions; oil spills; disturbance to wildlife; potential introduction of bird and plant diseases; introduction of exotic flora."

Law (1989) points out that environmentally, the dangers of tourism are exaggerated, and that most of Antarctica will always be inaccessible to tourists. He states that he does not see tourism threatening the future of Antarctica as a whole. At the same time, he cautions that in areas where tourism does take place, a careful control of the tourists will be necessary.

A Strategy for Antarctic Conservation, produced by the IUCN (1991:55-56), takes a positive approach to the impacts of tourism on Antarctica. The strategy points out that "Tourism offers both benefits and threats to Antarctic conservation." It lists the benefits as follows:

1. Visitors gain a greatly enhanced appreciation of Antarctica's global importance and of the requirements for its conservation.
2. Visits bring fulfillment to those seeking personal challenge and wilderness adventure.
3. Scientific activities may also benefit, since tourist visits can provide a useful link with the outside world and strengthen political support for Antarctic science.

The IUCN list of potentially undesirable impacts includes the following:

1. Disturbance at wildlife breeding sites
2. Trampling of vegetation
3. Disruption of routines at stations and of scientific programs
4. Environmental hazards of accidents, the resulting time-consuming and costly search and rescue, as well as environmental cleanup operations

The strategy recognizes the dangers of Antarctic tourism (past ship accidents and the Mount Erebus disaster) but nevertheless concludes (IUCN 1991:56), "Experience to date suggests that, in general, tourist operations have been conducted in a responsible manner and undesirable impacts have not been severe, especially compared to environmental impacts of scientific and associated logistical activity." Lipps (1978:361-362) sees the impacts of tourism this way:

> The greatest immediate threat to the Antarctic Peninsular environment comes from increasing tourist interest in the area. Naturally tourists want to see the animal life, but the sometimes large numbers of tourists visiting rookeries and tramping on the thick vegetation may cause permanent disruption of these associations. The pinnipeds and birds may abandon their rookeries altogether if disturbed enough, but they cannot escape the mobile tourists. . . . Irresponsible tourism remains the greatest potential threat to the Antarctic Peninsula.

As identified by several sources including the IUCN, tourists are seen as having the potential to disrupt scientific work and to interrupt the routine of base life. Because of the relatively easy accessibility of King George Island in the South Shetland Islands, several of these stations, in particular Arctowski, Bellingshausen, Comandante Ferraz, Jubany, and Teniente Rodolfo Marsh, are regularly visited by cruise passengers. It is of interest that in the Antarctic Peninsula region the only stations actually located on the Antarctic continent are Esperanza and Almirante Brown (Argentina), General Bernardo O'Higgins (Chile), and Vernadsky (Ukraine). Among these, Esperanza and Almirante Brown are by far the most visited. Also frequently visited is Palmer Station (United States) on Anvers Island. The only other Antarctic stations that receive regular cruise passengers are McMurdo (United

States), Scott Base (New Zealand), and, very occasionally, Dumont d'Urville (France) as well as Mawson, Casey, and Davis (Australia). During the 1995-1996 season, Amundsen-Scott (United States) at the South Pole was visited by fifty-eight tourists who were participants in tours organized by Adventure Network International (IAATO 1996:2). The other scientific stations are hardly ever visited by Antarctic tourists.

In her case study of tourism at Faraday Station, Enzenbacher (1994b:307) lists the perceived disadvantages of tourist visits to scientific research stations: disruption to base life, disruption to scientific projects, further impacts on the environment of the sites visited, and possible requests for search and rescue operations. She is also worried about future science results when she writes, "Over time, disruptions imposed on limited science seasons may threaten the integrity of Antarctic research" (p. 307). That Antarctic stations are quite capable of handling tourists becomes evident from the "Code of Conduct for Tourists and Non-Governmental Expeditions Requesting Permission to Visit British Antarctic Survey Research Stations" (Enzenbacher 1994b:311-312). As in the academic literature, the popular literature suggests that tourists disturb scientific work. Davidson (1989:4), quoting a National Science Foundation report, states that tourists sometimes arrive at scientific stations uninvited, a practice that an NSF report complains "disrupts and inhibits research." Because only previously approved vessels may visit Palmer Station on certain agreed-upon dates, this is no longer a problem.

The Polish Antarctic station Arctowski likewise imposes some, if somewhat more fluid, regulations for visiting tourists. With regard to tourism at Arctowski, Donachie (1994:341) notes that any visitor (official or tourist) has the potential to disrupt base routine, which may distract people from their work.

In response to increasing tourist numbers, the Polish Academy of Science and Scott Polar Research Institute have jointly developed a tourism management system for the site. Stonehouse (personal communication 1997) describes the project in the following way:

> The concept is that Arctowski now has more visitors than it can cope with unmanaged, so for the first time we are introducing management for tourism. We have (a) identified and marked in the boundary between SSSI 8 and station area; (b) established a buffer zone in the skua and penguin colonies close to the bound-

ary where we can detect and monitor changes; (c) established a trail leading along the storm beach to the wallow, and from there around the back of the station area to the living quarters, with about 15 information points and a number of test sites where the effectiveness of the trail can be monitored; (d) identified safe walks for guided parties on the hills behind the station; (e) provided for an information centre where visitors can relax, see displays on the environs and work of the station, and buy books relating to the trail and working on the test sites, where we shall be able to assess the effectiveness of different kinds of trail marking and identification. This is combined with programs of study of (a) elephant seals using the area, and (b) growth of plants, especially the two flowering plants and prominent mosses, in areas that are trampled by seals and humans. We are working in cooperation with expedition leaders, who will be invited to test the trail and walks and suggest improvements. We hope that tourists will spend at least half a day, rather than the usual couple of hours, and that visitors will gain more than the normal fleeting impression of an Antarctic site and a station in action.

Drawing on the author's observations made during a visit to Arctowski in 1995, it should be noted that it is not a pristine site. Apart from SSSI No. 8, Western Shore of Admiralty Bay, King George Island (National Science Foundation 1995b:94), which tourists are instructed not to visit, there is very little ground that has not already been altered by the use of the site for whaling and for the requirements of the Polish research facility. Buildings with paint peeling off, rusting vehicles (one proudly carrying the sign TAXI), and an improvised sign saying BUS STOP set among bleached whalebone can hardly be described as environmentally sensitive items that can be despoiled by visiting tourists.

ENVIRONMENTAL IMPACTS
OF ANTARCTIC TOURISM
IN THE POPULAR PRESS

In contrast to academic authors, many writers in the popular press are prone to exaggeration of the problems associated with Antarctic tourism. Examples include an article by Evans (1989:62) with the catchy headline: "A Chilling Idea: Tide of Tourists at South Pole— Cigarette butts and luggage tags." Evans blows a minor incident completely out of proportion when she describes how, while cross country skiing at the South Pole, she discovered a luggage tag belonging to a tourist that was buried a few inches below the surface of the snow. "Finding it made me feel sad and angry, like discovering the first scratch on a new car, in this case a Rolls Royce," she writes. Does Evans seriously believe that one luggage tag may have a significant impact on the polar plateau or on Antarctica as a whole? It is this sort of exaggeration and attempts at sensationalizing that sometimes cloud the debate about the true impacts of tourism activities in the Antarctic. Evans quotes a scientist at Amundsen-Scott Station as saying that while the scientists and their support staff are by and large environmentally aware, he had noticed carelessly discarded cigarette butts. Even though this statement attributes the cigarette butts to the local South Polar community, Evans still attributes them to the tourists in her headline.

Sometimes environmental problems in Antarctica are attributed to tourists when there is very little likelihood that they have anything to do with them. Davidson (1989:1) quotes Sir Peter Scott: "Adélie penguin eggs have been found with traces of DDT, and plastic rubbish is often washed ashore . . . I believe we should have the wisdom to know when to leave a place alone."

Lipps (1978:378) refutes this statement when he says, "Concentrations of DDT and DDE reported by Tatton and Ruzicka (1967) in populations of Chinstrap penguins, Brown skuas, and Blue-eyed shags far removed from any bases are comparable to previous studies and point to the conclusion that contamination of Antarctica is probably not of local origin." In citing other studies, Lipps attributes higher than normal DDE levels in Wilson's petrels at Palmer Station to the fact that during the Antarctic winter these birds migrated to the Northern hemisphere, where waters are more polluted than in the Southern hemisphere.

In summing up the environmental concerns raised in the literature, it becomes clear that tourism impacts on the Antarctic fauna and flora as well as on Antarctic scientific research stations, the resident scientists, and their programs, dominate the discussion. The impacts suggested by the academic writers are all potentially real but, with few exceptions, they are hypothesized and not backed up by empirical research data. As a result, it is important to take special note of the few accounts of authors who write based on their firsthand experience in Antarctica. Their views are outlined in the next section.

OBSERVATIONS OF THE IMPACTS
OF ANTARCTIC TOURISM ACTIVITIES

Several firsthand observations have been reported in the literature. In a letter to the editor of *The New York Times* (June 17, 1990) R. D. Goodman, a passenger aboard an Antarctic cruise ship, gives his opinions on the impacts of tourists on Antarctica:

> Magazine and newspaper articles plus TV programs have decried the impact of tourism on Antarctica. Having just completed a cruise on the *Illiria* to that area, the following observations are offered to contradict many erroneous allegations. Firstly, it is said that tourists injure the Antarctic ecosystems and interfere with plant and animal life. This is simply not true. Prior to arriving at our destination, we passengers, accompanied and enlightened by seven naturalists, were indoctrinated again and again on preservation of the environment. We were instructed not to step on moss, which may take 200 years to regenerate. We all kept a respectful distance from the thousands of penguins and seals that we saw. Close-up photos were easily obtainable with our telephoto lenses. On the contrary, curious penguins approached closely to us, rather than the reverse. We were advised to "take nothing and leave nothing," an injunction all of us diligently obeyed. . . . Finally, a visit to any of the abandoned stations reveals a mass of left behind garbage, trash, old rusting oil barrels, construction detritus, boat and airplane ruins and other residue that have far worse impact on the Antarctic environment than we tourists could ever make. In fact, all of us came away with a heightened awareness of the earth's environment.

In a written statement to the Committee on Merchant Marine and Fisheries, Dr. William Fraser of the Point Reyes Bird Observatory, who has conducted research on the Antarctic Peninsula and the Weddell and Scotia Seas since 1974, gives one of the best assessments of the impacts of tourism in the Antarctic. Fraser's comments are based on a sound scientific basis and in this author's opinion carry great weight in refuting attempts by the popular press and certain environmental groups to discredit tourists in Antarctica. In response to a question about the environmental damage and human activity caused by tourism, Fraser (undated:1) states:

> In order to correctly assess what effects tourism has had on the Antarctic environment, relatively long-term studies need to be made that compare coincident environmental change at sites being visited by tourists with control sites where tourists are being excluded. To my knowledge, such studies have not been done, which essentially means that we do not yet possess the data needed to differentiate between natural ecosystem variability and tourist-induced changes. As such, a valid assessment of the extent of environmental damage by tourists is difficult to make.

Fraser continues:

> To illustrate, it is known that penguin populations on the Antarctic Peninsula have been in a state of flux, increasing or decreasing, since at least 1945, and that these changes have been species specific; that is, some species, such as Adelie Penguins, have been decreasing while others, such as Chinstrap Penguins have been increasing. This is the natural pattern of variation. Recently, however, certain environmental groups have claimed that decreases in penguin populations have occurred in areas frequented by tourists. Often cited is one of my research areas at Palmer Station where annual tourist visits have increased from approximately 200 in 1974 to about 1500 at present, qualifying Palmer as one of the most frequented sites in Antarctica. According to our long-term data, however, the environmentalist claims cannot be supported, in that changes in the populations of the area's penguins have exactly matched those evident for the Peninsula as a whole. More importantly, because the National Science Foundation took the early initiative of restricting tourists to a single island [Torgersen Island], we are now capable of making the first tourist-visited vs non-visited island comparisons. Our most recent look at these data indicates that decreases in Adelie Penguin populations have actually been

greater at some of the non-visited islands than at the visited islands, where populations have essentially remained stable. Indeed, the greatest decrease has been recorded at a Specially
Protected Area where human disturbance was eliminated years
ago. In short, there is simply no evidence to support a direct
causal link between tourist visits and population changes in
penguins. (p. 2)

Nimon, Schroter, and Stonehouse (1995:415) seem to think that
well-controlled tourists pose only marginal threats to local penguin
populations. After studying visitor-penguin interaction on Cuverville
Island, they state:

> We conclude that the reactions of nesting penguins to visiting
> humans depend on the visitors' behaviour, and the presence of a
> well-behaved visitor changes, only momentarily if at all, the
> awareness of a penguin with no prior, adverse experience of hu-
> mans. Thus, efforts by tour operators, Antarctic Treaty authori-
> ties and others to encourage non-disruptive behaviour in
> visitors are not misplaced.

Observations of Antarctic tour operations and tourists are a useful
way of establishing their likely impacts on the environment and their
compliance with the various established guidelines. Some Antarctic
Treaty nations (in particular Australia and New Zealand) have already started to deploy observers aboard the major cruise vessels.
Australian Antarctic Division (1995:36) reports that during the 1994-
1995 season, the first Australian observer was placed aboard the
Kapitan Khlebnikov during its visit to the Australian Antarctic Territory and the Ross Sea region. The task of the observer was to observe
shipboard safety including lifeboat drills, helicopter and Zodiac operations, and environmental management such as environmental education and the behavior of tourists on the ship and ashore. The results
of these observations were summed up as follows: "The observer was
satisfied with overall compliance with relevant Antarctic Treaty
guidelines and Australian legislation, the quality of oral and written
briefings on appropriate behavior while in the Antarctic, and safety
aspects."

Scott (1993:13), an Antarctic scientist and guide aboard the forty-
three passenger *Akademik Vavilov* in the Antarctic Peninsula area,

stresses that her only concern about Antarctic tourism is the same concern she has about all human presence in the South, which is that no human presence should have a negative impact on the wildlife and the environment. Most important, she states that "As a group, the passengers on the tourist ships that I have been associated with have had a far greater appreciation, awareness and understanding of the practical needs for protecting and conserving Antarctic wildlife and environment," than many expeditioners or the crews of the ships supporting both.

Ledingham (1993:12) adds his observations in an article titled, *Reflections of an Antarctic tour guide.* He notes that the behavior of tourists is monitored by lecturers, guides and Zodiac drivers, to ensure they don't get too close to any animals. When people have to be told to move back, it is usually because of over-enthusiasm rather than a deliberate contravention of the rules. Ledingham assesses the environmental effects of tourist vessels around East Antarctica and the Ross Sea as presently negligible. He notes that the impact of passengers ashore is minimal, and that after they have returned to their vessel there is little or no sign of their passage. He concludes that "The environmental impact is miniscule compared with that of long-term expeditioners in national operations."

During cruises observed by the author in the Antarctic Peninsula, on average two to three Zodiac landings per day were carried out. This resulted in the author visiting many of the most popular landing sites. Passengers usually spent between two and three hours ashore at each site. Due to the smaller number of passengers aboard the *Professor Khromov* and the *Akademik Boris Petrov,* slightly longer landings were made than those undertaken during the voyage of the larger *Alla Tarasova.* After going ashore, passengers were again advised of "no-go zones" and were given another reminder of the IAATO and ATCP guidelines for tourist behavior in Antarctica. In compliance with the guidelines, no food was taken ashore and no toilet facilities were provided ashore. Passengers were reminded to stay clear of the wildlife. People were then free to explore around the vicinity of the landing sites—most of them doing so alone or in small groups of three or four. Some opted to accompany one of the lecturers/guides in order to get a deeper understanding of the geology, fauna, and flora of the sites visited. The "explorers" among the groups observed were very few, and there was a direct correlation between age and exploring. Only younger passengers were observed wandering some distance away from the landing sites. There was very little visible impact of visitors on the wildlife and flora, and visitors behaved in a very respectful way, kept their distance from wildlife, and were just happy to be in such a fascinating place. Despite these very positive observations on visitor behavior, there is a small group of visitors who require close observation by guides during their time ashore. These include:

1. Photographers who wander off in search of the "perfect" shot. One photographer was observed climbing a snow-covered ridge, which may have had some hidden crevasses, to get a better angle for a photograph. By his action he endangered himself and potentially also the success of the cruise. Should a serious accident occur, the expedition leader would have had little choice but to turn the ship around and head back to the nearest landing strip on King George Island, or worse, to Ushuaia, three days' sailing across the Drake Passage.

2. Overanxious birdwatchers. During one of the landings in the South Orkney Islands the author participated in an excursion to seek the elusive snow petrel, which was known to nest in the cliffs of the island. A group of five people, under the guidance of an expert birdwatcher, made their way across moss beds toward the cliffs. Despite the best intent, stepping on the mosses could not be avoided on several occasions. Nesting skuas were also disturbed, and several of them left their nests and dive-bombed members of the party.

3. Tourists from non-English-speaking backgrounds. Instructions tend to be given mainly in English, leaving those without a working knowledge of the language largely uninformed. As a result, on one cruise, two Spanish-speaking passengers were observed smoking while ashore at Hannah Point. The expedition leader acted quickly and the cigarettes were extinguished.

4. Members of the crew did not appear to be familiar with Antarctic guidelines. On one occasion, passengers were called to the aft deck to have a look at the night's harvest—several ice fish complete with krill in their mouths were displayed by the crew. While ashore, members of the Russian crew had to be reminded that smoking was prohibited.

Points 1 and 3 were also seen as a concern in the environmental audit that was carried out by Poles Apart for an American based Antarctic tour operator. Poles Apart (1994:31) states that professional photographers and passengers of non-English-speaking background often approached wildlife too closely. Non-English-speaking passengers seemed to suffer from "a dilution of instructions via translation" and came from countries where environmental issues do not have the priority they are given in Antarctica.

CONCLUDING COMMENTS

Judging by the accounts provided by those who have observed Antarctic tourism, there would appear to be little justification in portraying tourism as a particularly threatening Antarctic activity.

Wherever there is human endeavor, there will always be an impact and the risk of accidents. This holds true for any part of the world, and it is acknowledged that the Antarctic is a particularly hostile and dangerous environment for tourism operations. Although tourists may have on rare occasions caused some highly localized impacts on the fauna and flora, on a grander scale, these impacts have been minimal. Tourists, who pay large amounts of money to experience Antarctica, are exceedingly motivated to preserve what they have come to see. Their impacts while ashore can be further mitigated by the continuation of cruises that involve lecture programs and by observance of the IAATO and ATS guidelines for the conduct of tourism in Antarctica. Most Antarctic tourists are environmentally conscious and do not set out to intentionally cause harm to the Antarctic environment. In fact, it can be argued that the most threatened life form in Antarctica is the human being (tourist and scientist alike) rather than the wildlife and flora of the continent. Thus, health and safety rather than environmental issues should dominate future debates of commercial Antarctic tourism.

This chapter discussed the perceived environmental impacts of tourism in Antarctica and concluded that reporting is at times based on exaggeration and generalization and that the scientific facts available at this stage do not support the notion of tourists as the destroyers of Antarctic wildlife and flora. A significant increase in visitor numbers to the same sites may, however, lead to as yet unidentified long-term cumulative impacts, and such sites will need to be monitored closely.

It is argued that given the demonstrated goodwill of Antarctic tourists and the keen financial interest in the maintenance of the near-pristine Antarctic environment by Antarctic tour operators, as well as the watchful eye of the Antarctic Treaty Parties, tourism in Antarctica is at present a sustainable activity.

Chapter 6

Antarctic Tourists:
Motivations, Expectations, and Images
of Antarctica As a Tourist Destination

In an investigation into commercial tourism in a remote location such as Antarctica, it is important that the subjects at the core of much of the debate are understood. As was outlined in the previous chapter, tourists are seen by some as posing a potential threat to the Antarctic environment, and as such, they deserve closer analysis. It is, for example, necessary to establish their demographic backgrounds, their images of Antarctica as a tourist destination, and their expectations of an Antarctic holiday. As Stonehouse and Crosbie (1995:22) point out: "It is clearly important to know what tourists themselves seek from their experience, and whether their demands differ significantly from what tour operators provide for them." This chapter introduces surveys that have been conducted by various researchers and discusses the findings of the surveys conducted by the author.

VISITOR PROFILES IN THE LITERATURE

Only a very limited number of Antarctic visitor surveys have been reported in the literature. Examples include Codling (1982b), who reported her firsthand observations aboard a Society Expedition cruise to the Antarctic Peninsula region but only provided a breakdown of passengers by nationality. From her writings it does not appear that she used a structured questionnaire approach to probe deeper into the backgrounds of passengers. Enzenbacher carried out survey work during the 1992-1993 season, but no results have been published. Professor John Marsh (1991 and personal communication 1995) carried out a passenger survey during a 1991 voyage to the Antarctic

Peninsula aboard a Chilean vessel leaving from Punta Arenas. He reported only the following percentages of his sample of eighty passengers:

- Main countries of residence: Chile, 45 percent; United States, 24 percent
- Gender distribution: 56 percent male and 44 percent female
- Age: 7 percent under 21; 80 percent between 21 and 60; 13 percent over 60
- First Antarctic visit: 96 percent
- Traveling partners: 40 percent alone; 43 percent with relative; 17 percent with friends
- Membership in environmental organization: 28 percent
- Wish to return: 41 percent

Because Chilean ships play virtually no role in today's commercial Antarctic tourism, Marsh's results may not be suitable for generalization. His sample is also heavily skewed toward Chilean nationals, a group of people hardly represented at all on other commercial cruises. His findings nevertheless provide an interesting comparison to those obtained by other authors, including this writer.

As part of its 1994-1995 Observer Program, the Antarctic Unit of the Tourism Board of Tierra del Fuego (INFUETUR) in Ushuaia, Argentina, also provided a brief overview of visitor profiles. Four cruises were observed. Table 6.1 reveals that on large and small cruise vessels alike, the average age of passengers was above fifty years. Regarding the nationalities of passengers, the dominance of citizens of the United States can be noted on the smaller vessels, whereas South Americans made up the largest number of passengers on the one large cruise vessel in Antarctica in 1994-1995.

In contrast to the above vessels, passenger statistics for 1994-1995 made available to the author for the *Hanseatic* and *Bremen* revealed the following nationality mix: German (39 percent), American (26 percent), Swiss (7.7 percent), Japanese (7.4 percent), Austrian (6.3 percent), Argentinian (5.7 percent), and other nationalities (7.9 percent). Putting these figures into context, it is interesting to note that German-owned and operated vessels are also predominantly used by German speakers.

It is of value to contrast the passenger profiles provided by Hanseatic Tours with those provided by NSF, which annually compiles in-

TABLE 6.1. Sample Visitor Profiles by Nationality and Age Leaving from Ushuaia, 1994-1995

	%
Akademik Sergei Vavilov (n = 69)	
Nationality:	
United States citizen	87
Canadian, Australian, Italian, Bolivian, Dutch	13
Average age: 53 years (minimum 29; maximum 82)	
Professor Molchanov (n = 33)	
Nationality:	
United States citizen	97
British	3
Average age: 52 years (minimum 27; maximum 79)	
Livonia (n = 37)	
Nationality:	
United States citizen	65
British	11
Dutch	8
German	5
Other	11
Average age: 53 years (minimum 25; maximum 79)	
Eugenio Costa (n = 918)	
Nationality:	
Argentinian	52
Brazilian	43
Other	6
Average age: 55 years (minimum 2 months; maximum 94)	

Source: INFUETUR, 1995.

formation collected from Antarctic tour operations that are members of IAATO.

As Table 6.2 shows, tourists from the United States were the dominant group of visitors, with German and British passengers ranking second and third. The NSF data provided in the report did not go beyond reporting actual passenger numbers and their nationalities. The most likely reason for this is that because of commercial sensitivities, other demographic or psychographic details of passengers are difficult to obtain.

By the end of the millennium, the domination of Antarctic tourism by visitors from the United States was even more pronounced than shown in Table 6.2. Figures provided by the National Science Foun-

TABLE 6.2. Cruise Tourists by Country, 1995-1996 and 1996-1997

Country	1995-1996		1996-1997	
	Passengers	%	Passengers	%
United States	3,382	36.7	3,503	47.8
Germany	1,061	11.5	777	10.6
United Kingdom	857	9.3	475	6.5
Japan	661	7.2	510	7.0
Australia	410	4.5	680	9.3
Switzerland	192	2.1	280	3.8
Austria	174	1.9	78	1.1
Canada	159	1.7	254	3.5
France	95	1.0	93	1.3
Argentina	94	1.0	—	—
Others	736	8.0	561	7.7
Unknown	1,391	15.1	9	0.1
Total	9,212	100	7,322	100

Source: National Science Foundation 1997a (compiled from information provided by Antarctic tour operators).

dation (2000) show that during the 1999-2000 season 52.43 percent of all ship-based tourists came from the United States. Only six other countries contributed significantly to visitor arrivals in the south: Germany (8.93 percent), United Kingdom (8.78 percent), Australia (7.61 percent), Canada (4.61 percent), Japan (2.93 percent), and Switzerland (2.13 percent). All other countries accounted for 10.02 percent, and the nationality of 2.56 percent of tourists was unknown.

A further survey was carried out by Girard (1996:80), who worked as a member of the Project Antarctic Conservation (PAC) team at Hannah Point during the 1993-1994 season (which lasted from November 1 to March 20). She mentions the emergence of new segments of the market in the form of Japanese, Taiwanese, and Chinese passengers aboard the eleven cruise ships that operated in the region. Girard calculated that during this season, 8,000 passengers spent a combined 40,000 days in Antarctica. She gives the nationalities of passengers as 50 percent North American, 38 percent European (including 25 percent German), 6 percent Australian, 3 percent Asian, 2 percent South American and South African). The median age reported by Girard was fifty-five years. She went further and investigated the motivations of visitors. She also reported her observations of tourists aboard cruise vessels and ashore and included several recommendations with regard to tourist conduct in Antarctica.

The final, and most comprehensive, visitor surveys were carried out by the New Zealand Department of Conservation (DOC) (Cessford and Dingwall 1996:1). The surveys were carried out during the 1992-1993 and 1993-1994 seasons among cruise passengers to New Zealand's sub-Antarctic islands. The New Zealand observers were responsible for the distribution and collection of questionnaires, which no doubt increased the response rate considerably. Strictly speaking, the sub-Antarctic islands are not included in this investigation, but it can be argued that visitors to the sub-Antarctic share many of the characteristics of their counterparts who visit Antarctica itself. Furthermore, Cessford and Dingwall's study surveyed many passengers on vessels that were visiting the sub-Antarctic islands prior to proceeding to the Ross Sea area. Thus, passengers aboard these vessels can fairly be described as Antarctic tourists. The survey obtained 458 fully usable responses (Cessford and Dingwall 1996:10), which represents the most comprehensive sample reported in the literature.

> It [the survey] reveals that visitors were from more affluent and older sectors of society, were often retired or from professional backgrounds, included a high proportion of women compared with participants in other outdoor recreation activities, and had a high degree of conservation group involvement. Visitor satisfaction was high and favored features of their visits were experiences of natural environments and wildlife, and the enhanced opportunities for conservation learning.

More specifically, visitor characteristics reported by Cessford and Dingwall (1996:11) show that 69 percent of visitors were above age fifty; that the gender balance was close to equal; visitors generally were either New Zealanders, Australians, or Americans; 30 percent of the sample were retired; among those still working, professionals were predominant; and 59 percent of the sample were members of a conservation group. Other findings obtained by Cessford and Dingwall will be included in the discussions of the findings of the surveys conducted by the author where a comparison is appropriate.

From the Arctic, Stonehouse and Crosbie (1995:23) report the results of an unpublished preliminary survey carried out by Crosbie among eighty-eight ship passengers in northern Canada:

> . . . two-thirds gave wildlife, history and education as their primary reasons for visiting, while one third were there primarily for recreation and photography. Wildlife and scenic beauty were particular attractions, more so than aspects of Inuit culture. . . . As a group the passengers were conservation conscious: about half were members of conservation societies. . . . These were experienced tourists, one third of whom, surprisingly, had already visited Antarctica.

Taking note of the above surveys, the author's aim is to contribute to the better understanding of Antarctic tourists by providing visitor profiles, characteristics, expectations, and motivations of Antarctic travelers. The results of the various surveys conducted are reported in the next section.

BACKGROUND OF THE VISITOR SURVEYS

The survey method, also known as the questionnaire technique, is one of the most commonly applied techniques in tourism research. Kerlinger (1973:410) states, "Surveys are studies of large and small populations by selecting and studying samples from the population to discover the relative incidence, distribution, and interrelation of variables." Pizam (1987:70) adds, "Sample surveys are conducted when the study of the population is impossible, difficult or costly."

As was outlined in Chapter 4, 9,212 shipborne visitors reached Antarctica during the 1995-1996 summer season. A further 5,092 overflight passengers made the trip to Antarctica aboard Qantas charter flights during the two seasons of 1994-1995 and 1995-1996. The following surveys were carried out: (1) surveys of Antarctic travelers aboard ten cruise vessels prior ($N = 159$) and after ($N = 138$) an Antarctic visit during the 1994-1995 and 1995-1996 seasons; and (2) surveys of passengers aboard Antarctic overflights during the 1994-1995 and 1995-1996 seasons ($N = 484$) as well as the 1996/97 season ($N = 1,312$).

In his research the author discovered that conducting surveys of Antarctic travelers is not an easy task. The design of the questionnaires was a combination of open-ended and closed formats. Open-ended responses were seen as useful where questions probed the attitudes and expectations of travelers. The questionnaire design process was greatly facilitated by the author's stay at the Scott Polar Research Institute at the University of Cambridge in England. There he made the acquaintance of Dr. Bernard Stonehouse, the founder of Project Antarctic Conservation, which aims to establish baseline data for the sustainable management of Antarctic tourism. After discussions with Dr. Stonehouse, the author was invited to become a member of the PAC team, and it was decided that his contribution was to concentrate on the profiles, attitudes, and motivations of Antarctic travelers. Two shipborne passenger survey instruments, one to be completed before arriving in Antarctica and one after the visit, were developed. A separate instrument was designed to capture the profiles of overflight passengers. To get the questionnaires into the hands of the passengers, the cooperation of Antarctic tour operators was essential. This was, however, at times a very difficult task. In December 1994 and January 1995, the author was permitted to travel aboard two Quark cruise ships, where he was able to personally distribute the survey instruments. Dr. Stonehouse traveled aboard several Quark vessels and distributed questionnaires. The airborne survey questionnaires were kindly distributed by Croydon Travel aboard several of their overflights.

The number of fully usable seaborne survey questionnaires returned at the end of the 1994-1995 season was small. It was decided to continue sampling during the 1995-1996 season. A substantial effort was made to get as many Antarctic tour operators to participate in the surveys as possible. To give the reader an idea of the difficulties encountered in conducting visitor surveys in remote locations (and to send a caution message out to those who may be tempted to carry out their own survey work in isolated regions), the process is described in full.

During 1995, the author approached all known Antarctic tour companies, asking them to participate. At that time, agreement to distribute the questionnaires was obtained from Marine Expeditions (Canada), Quark Expeditions (United States), Greg Mortimer Mountain Services/World Expeditions (now Aurora Expeditions), Adventure Associates, Southern Pride (all Australia), and Hanseatic Tours (Germany). Croydon Travel, the organizers of Antarctic overflights, again agreed to distribute questionnaires aboard their flights. An acquaintance of the author, Alan Parker, a lecturer aboard the cruise ship *Vavilov,* and Dr. Stonehouse also agreed to take questionnaires with them for distribution during their voyages. In an attempt to survey passengers on diverse tours, the author also approached Adventure Network International (United Kingdom), Orient Lines (the operator of the *Marco Polo*), Southern Heritage Tours (New Zealand), and John Splettstoesser, the spokesperson for IAATO, for assistance.

Despite follow-ups, no response was received from ANI, Southern Heritage, and Splettstoesser. Orient Lines advised that they did not wish to participate in the survey. By the end of the 1995-1996 season in March 1996, completed survey questionnaires were received from Croydon Travel, Adventure Associates, Hanseatic Tours, and through the efforts of Dr. Stonehouse. As for the other operators, the results were disappointing. Southern Pride, a new company that was to operate cruises to the Ross Sea, went into liquidation before its ship even arrived in Australia. Greg Mortimer Mountain Services did not take the questionnaires along to Antarctica, and Parker was not allowed to distribute the questionnaires aboard the *Vavilov.* Quark Expeditions and Marine Expeditions replied with apologies that it had not been possible to distribute the questionnaires aboard their vessels.

Thus the number of returned questionnaires during the 1995-1996 season was again relatively small. The results presented in this section therefore may be seen only as indicative of the passengers aboard the surveyed ships and planes. Ship-based survey results will be compared with survey results obtained by other researchers (in many cases even more limited), to see whether there is commonality with regard to visitor profiles.

The lesson to be learned from the ship-based Antarctic passenger surveys is that, unless a researcher is personally distributing the questionnaires to passengers, only very limited results can be obtained. It is therefore suggested that future visitor surveys be carried out by requesting tour operators to mail questionnaires to their clients *before* their departures for Antarctica and that the passengers be asked to return completed survey forms to either the operator or directly to the researcher.

Table 6.3 provides the names of the ships involved in the surveys as well as the size of the samples obtained. Although a total of ten vessels was involved in the surveys, an analysis of Table 6.3 reveals that the majority of responses received came from only three vessels:

TABLE 6.3. Ships Involved in the Surveys and Sample Sizes

Ship	Responses		
	Before	**After**	**Total**
1994-1995			
1. *Alla Tarasova*	18	12	30
2. *Alla Tarasova*	52	33	85
3. *Professor Khromov*	25	21	46
1995-1996			
4. *Marine Explorer*	17	15	32
5. *Marine Explorer*	41	32	73
6. *Kapitan Khlebnikov*	–	18	18
7. *Bremen*	2	2	4
8. *Bremen*	4	3	7
9. *Hanseatic*	–	1	1
10. *Hanseatic*	–	1	1
Total	**159**	**138**	**297**

Notes:

1. Dates: November 15 to December 3, 1994; Ushuaia-Antarctic Peninsula-Falkland Islands; because of ice and weather conditions, group did not get to land on the continent.
2. Dates: December 12 to December 30, 1994; Falkland Islands-South Georgia-South Orkneys-Antarctic Peninsula-Ushuaia; author traveled on this cruise; stormy seas reduced response rate for the "after" survey.
3. Dates: December 30, 1994 to January 10, 1995; Ushuaia-Antarctic Peninsula-Cape Horn-Ushuaia; author traveled on this cruise.
4. Dates: November 16 to November 30, 1995; Ushuaia-Falkland Islands-Antarctic Peninsula-Ushuaia; vessel is also known as *Professor Multanovskiy.* Renamed for the 1996-1997 season *Marine Intrepid.* Maximum passenger number is 46.
5. Dates November 30 to December 13, 1995; Ushuaia-Antarctic Peninsula-Ushuaia.
6. Dates: January 1 to February 1, 1996; Adventure Associates distributed questionnaires to 36 of their passengers toward the end of a semicircumnavigation of Antarctica. Ushuaia-Antarctic Peninsula-Ross Sea-Hobart.
7. Dates: December 19, 1995 to January 6, 1996; Antarctic Peninsula region.
8. Dates: January 13 to February 18, 1996; Antarctic Peninsula region.
9. Dates: January 4 to January 15, 1996; Antarctic Peninsula region.
10. Dates: February 15 to March 6, 1996; Antarctic Peninsula region.

Alla Tarasova (38.7 percent), *Marine Explorer* (35.3 percent), and *Professor Khromov* (15.5 percent). By comparison, the contributions of survey results from the *Kapitan Khlebnikov* (6 percent) and the *Bremen* and *Hanseatic* (a combined 4.4 percent) were insignificant.

Thus, the results obtained from the shipborne passenger surveys provide mainly an indication of profiles, characteristics, and attitudes of passengers aboard small to medium-sized Antarctic cruise vessels operating in the Antarctic Peninsula. While this may be seen as a limitation of the study, it should be kept in mind that it is small to medium-sized vessels that make the most trips to Antarctica and that the Antarctic Peninsula is by far the most visited region. Future research opportunities exist in comparing the visitor profiles obtained by the author with visitor profiles of passengers aboard icebreakers and large vessels such as the *Marco Polo.*

ANALYSIS OF SHIPBORNE TOURIST RESPONSES PRIOR TO LANDING IN ANTARCTICA

A total of 159 fully usable responses were received for the first survey, which passengers completed prior to reaching Antarctica. Several of the questions were open-ended, and it was therefore necessary to categorize responses. The following variables were used for the questions relating to motivation, image, and mood/atmosphere:

- Tourist access (ship, air, inaccessibility, not a tourist destination)
- Environment (pollution by tourists, polluted by scientists, pristine, hostile)
- History (historic exploration, historic sites)
- Flora (all plants)
- Science (scientific stations, research)
- Climate (cold, windy)
- Geographic features (mountains, ocean, icebergs, glaciers, snow)
- Mood (peaceful, exciting).

After responses had been categorized, the data was entered into Statistical Package for the Social Sciences and a frequency analysis was first carried out. For clarity, percentage responses have been rounded off to the nearest percentage point, and thus totals may not add up to 100 percent.

Table 6.4 provides an overview of the characteristics of the visitors. It shows that, in line with surveys reported in the literature, the majority of passengers were in the "mature" age groups, with only 25 percent being under the age of forty-five years. Fifty-one percent

TABLE 6.4. Visitor Profile Characteristics (N=159)

Characteristics	%	Characteristics	%
Age group		**Traveling Partner**	
18-25	2	Alone	30
26-35	8	With partner	38
36-45	15	With friend	16
46-55	21	With family	14
56-60	16	With colleague	1
61-65	14	No response	2
66-70	15		
71-80	7	**Employment status**	
over 80	3	Retired	40
		Employed	57
Gender		Home duties	1
Male	54	No response	3
Female	45		
		Occupation	
Place of residence		Professional	70
United States	50	Clerical	9
United Kingdom	13	Trade	3
Australia	9	Blue collar	3
South Africa	8	Other	7
Germany	3	No reply	9
Scandinavia	3		
Canada	3	**Member in environmental**	
Other	9	**organization**	
No reply	1	Yes	50
		No	48
Previous Antarctic visit		No response	2
None	81		
One	11		
Two	5		
More than two	4		

Source: Author based on shipborne surveys, 1994-1995 and 1995-1996.

fell into the forty-six to sixty-five age group, and the largest single age group was forty-six to fifty-five years old (21 percent). Cessford and Dingwall (1996:11) stated that 69 percent of their survey respondents were over fifty years of age, while in the author's surveys 75 percent were over forty-six.

Slightly more males (54 percent) than females (45 percent) responded to the questionnaire, while the sample by Cessford and Dingwall (1996) consisted of nearly equal numbers of males and females.

Slightly over 50 percent resided in the United States. Compared with the NSF data shown in Table 6.2, Americans were slightly overrepresented. People from other countries that tend to feature prominently in Antarctic tourism—the United Kingdom, Australia, and South Africa—were all well represented in the sample. Compared to the NSF data, German tourists were underrepresented in the survey. This is explained by the fact that most responses were obtained from passengers aboard relatively small vessels, whereas Germans tend to prefer to travel on larger, more luxurious ships such as the *MS Bremen* and *MS Hanseatic.*

Most respondents (81 percent) had never been to Antarctica. However, 11 percent had been once before, 3 percent had visited twice, and 4 percent had traveled there more than twice. The most-traveled individual had been there seventeen times. The Antarctic Peninsula (15 percent) and the Ross Sea (8 percent) were the regions most visited by those who had been to Antarctica before.

Nearly 30 percent traveled alone, and nearly 70 percent traveled with a partner. Most respondents traveled as part of a group. These were frequently organized by independent travel agents in the home countries of passengers.

Almost 40 percent were retired, compared to 57 percent who were employed. Seventy percent of survey respondents classified themselves as professionals. Given the high cost of Antarctic tourism, high incomes are needed to afford it. Professionals are generally associated with above-average incomes, and they are thus more likely to have the necessary disposable income to undertake a voyage to Antarctica.

The percentages of those who were members of environmental organizations (50 percent) and nonmembers (48 percent) were nearly equal. By contrast, results obtained by Cessford and Dingwall (1996) showed a slightly higher percentage of membership in an environmental organization (59 percent).

Of particular interest was the question of which other cold-climate regions passengers had visited. As Table 6.5 shows, the most frequently visited cold-climate destinations were sub-Arctic Alaska (21 percent), Northern/Arctic Europe (16 percent), and the Andes (15 percent). The high percentage of respondents who stated that they had visited Alaska may be explained by the fact that 50 percent of the sample were from the United States. Alaska is easily accessible from

TABLE 6.5. Previous Cold Climate Regions Visited*

Region	%
Sub-Arctic Alaska	21
Northern/Arctic Europe	16
Andes	15
Himalayas	12
Arctic Canada	10
Greenland	8
Arctic Russia	7
Arctic Alaska	6
Svalbard	5

Source: Based on shipborne surveys, 1994-1995 and 1995-1996.

Note: *Multiple response (237 responses).

all parts of the United States, and the high percentage of passengers who had visited it did not come as a surprise. The finding may indicate that people who have seen one of the polar regions are also likely to want to experience the other. More research is needed to verify this point, however.

In addition to cold-climate regions, many respondents had also visited other remote locations around the globe, ranging from Pitcairn Island and Easter Island to Inner Mongolia. One respondent summed up the previous travel experiences of Antarctic passengers surveyed when he stated, "You name it, I have been there." The fact that Antarctic travelers are highly experienced has to be taken into account when the Antarctic product is marketed and, in particular, when the product is being delivered. Given their extensive travel experience, total honesty in advertising and excellence in the operation of the tours are vital if customer complaints are to be avoided.

An interest in finding out why people chose to visit the far South when so many other less hostile and difficult-to-reach destinations are available led to the inclusion of a question probing motivations for undertaking the voyage. Table 6.6 provides percentage responses in descending order. It highlights that the most important motivation was to see and experience Antarctic wildlife (18 percent), with an additional 6 percent listing penguins as their motivation for travel. Thus, a total of 24 percent of responses fell into the category of Antarctic fauna.

TABLE 6.6. Motivation for Undertaking a Voyage

Attributes	%
Wildlife	18
Curiosity	12
Scenery	7
Remoteness	7
Adventure	6
Penguins	6
Photography	5
Pristine environment	5
History	4
Status	4
Beauty	3
Icebergs	3
Want to learn about the Antarctic	3
Family reasons	3
Dates were suitable	2
Always wanted to go	2
Glaciers	1
Mountains	1
All else	8

Source: Based on shipborne surveys, 1994-1995 and 1995-1996.

Note: Multiple response (416 responses).

Given the predominance of images of penguins, seals, flying sea-birds, and, to a lesser extent, whales in the brochures of tour companies and in the many coffee-table books on Antarctica, this result did not come as a surprise. Interestingly, respondents also indicated that their curiosity (12 percent) had led them to travel to the region. To a lesser degree the scenery (7 percent) and the remoteness of the region (7 percent) were also important motivations. Perhaps somewhat surprisingly, respondents were not greatly motivated by the history of Antarctic exploration (4 percent) and, even more surprising, did not mention science and scientific stations at all. The lack of interest in historic events may be attributed to the fact that most survey results were obtained on cruises to the Antarctic Peninsula, which is mostly associated with wildlife and scenery, while the Ross Sea region is generally seen as being of greater historic significance. Scott, Shackleton, Amundsen, and Borchgrevink are well-known figures associated with the Ross Sea, and several of their huts are visited on cruises to this region.

When a cross tabulation between motivation for visiting and gender was carried out, several interesting results were obtained. Of the respondents who chose the "wildlife" variable, 55 percent were male and 45 percent were female. Males accounted for 61 percent of the variable "adventure" (39 percent were female), and 60 percent of responses for "photography" came from men (40 percent female).

As far as adventure goes, it has to be pointed out that Antarctic cruises offer relatively little. Adventure implies a certain element of the unexpected, of high risk and uncertain outcomes. The format of Antarctic cruises is fairly predictable; the only variables are the actual sites at which landings are made (due to weather, ice, and wildlife conditions). This in itself is not adventure. The closest passengers get to experiencing adventure is when they get into the Zodiacs and are driven ashore. During these Zodiac rides, particularly in inclement weather (high seas and strong winds), passengers may feel a sense of adventure because there is a real risk of someone falling overboard into the near-freezing water.

The images people hold of Antarctica as a tourist destination were probed in the next question. Table 6.7 shows that the main images held by respondents were the fauna (particularly penguins), ice features, and, to a lesser degree, environmental attributes. Historic features were again only of minor importance, and scientific stations did not rate at all.

The images passengers held thus correlated closely with their motivations to visit. Many passengers held an image of Antarctica as a place where wildlife, in particular penguins, could be viewed, and this motivation was strong enough for them to undertake the voyage. The fact that penguins are indeed big drawing cards in tourism is evidenced by the more than 500,000 people who annually visit the Phillip Island Penguin Parade in Victoria, Australia.

With regard to the kind of atmosphere or mood people expected to experience during their time in the Antarctic, Table 6.8 indicates that the positive attributes of peace, excitement, beauty, and awe far outweighed the one negative attribute listed, a hostile climate. This indicates that passengers were generally in a highly positive mood prior to reaching the Antarctic. It was interesting to compare these findings with those obtained after passengers had visited. The cross tabulation of atmosphere and mood by sex showed that 59 percent of those who chose the variable "exciting" were male.

TABLE 6.7. Images of Antarctica as a Tourist Destination Prior to Arrival

Attributes	%
Penguins	14
Wildlife	10
Whales	4
Seals	5
Birds	4
Total fauna	**37**
Icebergs	12
Ice	6
Snow	4
Glaciers	2
Total ice features	**24**
Scenery	5
Mountains	2
Ocean	2
Total scenic features	**9**
Beauty	3
Total mood attributes	**3**
Inaccessible	5
Cold	4
Unspoiled	4
Hostile	2
Windy	1
Total environmental attributes	**16**
Historic exploration	2
Historic sites	1
Total historic attributes	**3**
Total all else	**8**

Source: Based on shipborne surveys, 1994-1995 and 1995-1996.

Note: Multiple response (480 responses).

The question of passengers' main interest while ashore was seen as crucial. First, from a commercial perspective, if passengers held interests that could not be fulfilled while ashore, disappointment and dissatisfaction would result. Second, if passengers' main interest ashore was, for example, to go for long hikes or to climb mountains, increased environmental pressures would be placed on the sites visited by the greater dispersal of people. As Table 6.9 shows, the main interest of passengers was the wildlife (a combined score of 57 percent of responses). Taking photographs (11 percent) and looking at

TABLE 6.8. Atmosphere/Mood Expected

Attributes	%
Exciting	22
Awe	21
Peace	17
Beauty	9
Hostile	7
Curious	3
All else	20

Source: Based on shipborne survey results, 1994-1995 and 1995-1996.

Note: Multiple response (253 responses).

TABLE 6.9. Main Interest While Ashore

	%
Wildlife	56
Scenery	11
Take photographs	11
Ice features	6
Flora	3
Historic sites	1
Scientific stations	1
Everything	3
Just to be there	3
All else	3
No response	1

Source: Based on shipborne survey results, 1994-1995 and 1995-1996.

Note: Multiple response (308 responses).

the scenery (11 percent) were also of interest. Historic sites and scientific stations were practically of no interest at all.

Table 6.10 tabulates answers to the question, "How many years ago did you make the decision to visit Antarctica?" It was expected that Antarctic travelers had a long-term fascination with the continent and that most of them had decided long before to visit. The results show that this expectation was only partially fulfilled; 36 percent of respondents stated that they had decided to visit six or more years before. What was surprising was the high proportion of respondents who had decided on a visit within the previous year (35 percent). Table 6.11 shows that the high cost of Antarctic travel was seen as the single most important factor that had prevented respondents from visiting sooner. Given the constraints under which tourism takes place—remote location, lengthy sea passages, limited season, and limited availability of suitable vessels—a substantial increase in expedition-type cruises is not likely to occur in the near future. Larger vessels such as the *MS Rotterdam,* previously mentioned, have the ability to provide cheaper packages, but they offer different experiences.

TABLE 6.10. Years Since Travel Decision Was Made (*N* = 159)

Years	%
Within last year	35
Two to three years ago	20
Four to five years ago	8
Six or more years ago	36
No response	1

Source: Based on shipborne survey results, 1994-1995 and 1995-1996.

TABLE 6.11. Barriers to Travel

Reason	%
Cost	42
Lack of time	21
Visit other places first	13
Didn't know how to	12
Family commitments	6
All else	4
No response	4
No barrier	2

Source: Based on shipborne survey results, 1994-1995 and 1995-1996.

Note: Multiple response (220 responses).

ANALYSIS OF SHIPBORNE ANTARCTIC TOURIST RESPONSES AFTER VISITING THE ANTARCTIC

The second survey was conducted to investigate whether respondents' visit had changed their opinions with regard to Antarctica as a tourist destination and to probe their levels of satisfaction as well as to investigate the likelihood of a return visit. Another purpose was to determine possible improvements to product delivery. A total of 138 fully usable responses were received. For comparison, data for the prearrival survey are also provided in Table 6.12.

Table 6.12 shows that the characteristics of passengers who responded to the after-visit survey were very similar to those of respondents who had filled in the questionnaire prior to arriving in Antarctica. Apart from establishing demographic profiles, the after-visit survey probed several other aspects. One of these was whether, after experiencing Antarctica by ship, passengers would recommend it to their friends as a holiday destination. A total of 87 percent of respondents stated that they would, and 10.9 percent said they would not. Another 2.1 percent did not reply. Also, 15.9 percent of those who said that they would recommend Antarctica to their friends as a vacation destination stated that they would do so only to some of their friends, in particular to those who had an interest in wildlife and remote locations. A further 4.3 percent voiced concern over Antarctic tourism, with several respondents disliking the term "vacation destination" and suggesting that one should speak of an "experience" rather than a "destination." Although this comment is appreciated, there is little doubt that Antarctica is a tourist destination, albeit a very remote and special one. Once people start to pay money to see a place, the location has developed into a tourist destination even if there is no local population to reap the benefits of their expenditures. It is important that Antarctica is treated as a tourist destination (a Lonely Planet guide to Antarctica by Rubin was published in 1996) rather than a mythical land beyond the horizon. Once this is acknowledged, tourism planning and development measures, which have proven their worth at other locations around the globe, can be investigated and applied.

When asked whether they thought that tourism in its present form should be allowed to continue, 87.7 percent of respondents said "yes," 10.1 percent said "no," and 2.2 percent did not reply. While there was overwhelming support for the kind of tourism that currently exists, it should be noted that 21.7 percent of respondents who

TABLE 6.12. Visitor Profile Characteristics After and Before Visit

Characteristics	After visit (N = 138) %	Before visit (N = 159) %
Age group		
18-25	3	2
26-35	5	8
36-45	13	15
46-55	25	21
56-60	13	16
61-65	16	14
66-70	14	15
71-80	7	7
over 80	2	3
Gender		
Male	49	54
Female	51	45
Place of residence		
United States	44	50
United Kingdom	15	13
Australia	19	9
South Africa	9	8
Germany	2	3
Scandinavia	2	3
Canada	1	3
Other	7	9
No reply	2	1
Traveling partner		
Alone	33	30
With partner	44	38
With friend	9	16
With family	13	14
With colleague	–	1
No response	1	2
Employment status		
Retired	41	40
Employed	56	57
No reply	3	1
Occupation		
Professional	72	70
Trade	3	3
Clerical	9	9
Home duties	1	3
Other	7	7
No reply	8	9

Source: Based on shipborne survey results, 1994-1995 and 1995-1996.

had stated that tourism should continue as it is did so under the pro-
viso that it should be strictly controlled. Only 1.4 percent stated that
tourists came back from Antarctica as ambassadors for the preservation
of the region. Given that tourists are often referred to as "Antarctic
ambassadors," this finding is interesting. It would appear that tourists
do not see themselves as ambassadors, but that other groups, in particular tour operators, like to attach this label to them.

An important component of the visitor surveys was the question of
the image of Antarctica as a tourist destination. In this after-visit survey, the question of image was included to see whether having visited
Antarctic shores had significantly changed the image passengers held
of the region. Table 6.13 provides an overview of images held.

Not surprisingly, several respondents now also mentioned specific
Antarctic sites. The three most mentioned were Deception Island,
Lemaire Channel, and Hannah Point on Livingston Island in the
South Shetland Islands.

When analyzing the results reported in Table 6.13, the following
observations can be made:

- Scientific bases and historic sites were mentioned by very few
  respondents.
- The Antarctic flora was not mentioned at all.
- Fauna, in particular penguins, was mentioned most often.
- Scenic features such as scenery, mountains, and the ocean rated
  highly.
- Ice in its various forms featured strongly.
- Among the mood attributes, "beauty" was the most common
  term used to describe the image now held of Antarctica.

Several further observations can be made: (1) The images passengers held before arriving were also largely the ones they held after
their visit. This indicates that tour brochures prepare clients well for
what to expect from a voyage south. (2) Some relatively minor
changes in image occurred: "fauna" declined by 8 percent, "ice features" by 4 percent, and "inaccessibility" by 3 percent. The largest
percentage increase in responses was recorded for the attribute "scenery," which rose from 5 to 10 percent. This increase is explained by
the fact that brochures, Antarctic articles and books, and Antarctic
videos and TV programs can only offer a poor substitute for seeing
Antarctica firsthand. Thus it is no surprise that, once exposed to the

TABLE 6.13. Comparison Between Images of Antarctica As a Tourist Destination After and Before Visit

	After %*	Before %**
Penguins	11	14
Wildlife	9	10
Whales	1	4
Seals	4	5
Birds	4	4
Total fauna	**29**	**37**
Ice	5	6
Icebergs	9	12
Glaciers	3	2
Snow	3	4
Total ice features	**20**	**24**
Scenery	10	5
Mountains	4	2
Ocean	2	2
Total scenic features	**16**	**9**
Beauty	9	3
Total mood attributes	**9**	**3**
Pollution by tourists	3	2
Unspoiled	4	4
Antarctic light	2	–
Inaccessible	2	5
Cold	1	4
Windy	1	1
Hostile	1	2
Total environment attributes	**14**	**16**
Scientific bases	1	–
Pollution caused by science	1	–
Total scientific attributes	**2**	**0**
The early explorers	1	2
Historic sites	–	1
Total historic attributes	**1**	**3**
Total all else	**3**	**8**

Source: Based on shipborne survey results, 1994-1995 and 1995-1996

Notes: *Based on 429 responses. **Based on 480 responses.

grandeur of the scenery, passengers think of it when recollecting their experiences. When cross tabulating main images by sex, no great differences existed between the images held by males and females.

The question of what mood or atmosphere passengers had experienced during their visit was also included. Results are displayed in Table 6.14, which shows that the main attributes passengers used to describe the mood they had experienced in Antarctica were awe, excitement, beauty, and satisfaction. The "all else" category included many different attributes that, because of their diversity, could not be grouped together. A comparison with Table 6.8 shows that mood/atmosphere expected correlated well with what was actually experienced.

A cross tabulation between sex and mood/atmosphere revealed a substantially higher female response (59 percent) than male response (41 percent) to the variable "awe." With regard to the mood variable "satisfied" the results were reversed. Men (69 percent) seemed to feel more satisfied than women (31 percent) did.

The following three questions were included to assess which shore activities passengers had enjoyed most and to see whether they had wanted to undertake any additional shore activities. It was expected that answers to these questions would give an indication of potential changes in the type of product tourists may demand in the future.

As Table 6.15 shows, wildlife and scenery as well as simply being in Antarctica dominated the responses. Once again, historic sites and

TABLE 6.14. Mood or Atmosphere Experienced During Visit

	%
Awe	26
Exciting	16
Beauty	16
Satisfied	7
Happy	6
Peaceful	6
Solitude	3
Hostile	2
New	1
All else	17

Source: Based on shipborne survey results, 1994-1995 and 1995-1996.

Note: Multiple response (207 responses).

TABLE 6.15. Shore Activities Most Enjoyed by Passengers

	%
Watching the animals	23
Watching the penguins	20
Watching the birds (excluding penguins)	10
Just being there	10
Scenery	9
Everything	6
Watching the mammals	3
Zodiac rides	5
Taking photographs	1
Scientific bases	1
Flora	1
Ice features	1
Historic sites	1
All else	9

Source: Based on shipborne survey results, 1994-1995 and 1995-1996.

Note: Multiple response (207 responses).

scientific stations were of minimal importance. Given the concerns sometimes voiced by representatives of National Antarctic programs with regard to visits to their research facilities and the efforts in protecting historic sites, it could be argued that Antarctic tourists would be quite happy not to visit either. Future Antarctic products may well exclude scientific bases and historic sites, at least in the Peninsula area, and concentrate on wildlife and scenery, which clearly is what tourists seek. As far as itinerary design is concerned, the main justification for including scientific stations is that they provide a diversion from viewing wildlife and watching the scenery. Meeting people who live and work in Antarctica gives the place a human dimension that it otherwise lacks completely. The science carried out at the various stations, where it is accessible to tourists at all, is of very little importance to them. During one of the author's cruises in December 1999, aboard the *Boris Petrov,* no stations were visited at all, and none of the passengers seemed to be concerned about it. During another cruise the Russian base of Bellingshausen as well as the Chilean station Eduardo Frei were visited. There was no evidence of the type of science that is carried out at these bases—instead passengers were shown the

Chilean gymnasium and the Russian gift shop. One passenger commented that seeing the bases was the lowlight of the Antarctic cruise! Shopping for Antarctic souvenirs such as T-shirts, badges, coffee mugs, and key rings may indeed be a bigger attraction at the bases than the science that is carried out.

Table 6.16 demonstrates that many passengers felt that they would have liked to carry out other shore activities. At first glance, this would indicate a certain dissatisfaction with the existing tourism product. Many of the "yes" responses, however, are easily explained by the answers shown in Table 6.17.

Many of the "land on the continent" and "visit king and emperor penguins" responses came from passengers on cruises that, due to weather and ice conditions, could not visit all the planned sites. Passengers should be advised in the brochures that they cannot expect to see emperor or king penguins during their cruises to the Antarctic Peninsula—kings nest on the sub-Antarctic islands, while emperors can be found much farther south and mainly during the Antarctic winter. This indicates that tour operators have to continue to be care-

TABLE 6.16. Additional Shore Activities ($N = 138$)

	%
Yes	58
No	40
No reply	2
Total	**100**

Source: Based on shipborne survey results, 1994-1995 and 1995-1996.

TABLE 6.17. Additional Shore Activities Requested

	%
Land on the continent	32
Visit king and emperor penguins	22
Land at more sites	14
Longer stay ashore	16
Go for longer hikes	15

Source: Based on shipborne survey results, 1994-1995 and 1995-1996.

Note: Multiple response (80 responses).

ful in the way they word their brochures, as otherwise passenger disenchantment may become a problem. Landing at more sites also rated highly while the actual time spent ashore did not seem a cause for major concern. This finding, however, is somewhat contradicted by the results shown in Table 6.18, which shows that longer shore stays were the most frequently requested improvements.

These findings are similar to those obtained by Cessford and Dingwall (1996) for visits to New Zealand's sub-Antarctic islands. They report, "These results suggest that the main improvements to visits desired by small vessel visitors were increased onshore time and more visit opportunities and freedom. A similar proportion of large vessel visitors also desired greater onshore time" (p. 24). During the author's voyage to the Ross Sea during January and February 1997, many passengers complained about the duration of time ashore, which in some cases was no more than one hour.

When asked whether they would like to visit Antarctica again sometime in the future, 50 percent of respondents said yes, 45 percent said no, and 5 percent did not reply. These figures indicate that considerable potential for repeat business exists. The places people would like to visit on a return trip to Antarctica are shown in Table 6.19.

Most responses were obtained from passengers cruising in the Antarctic Peninsula region, and it is therefore not very surprising that on another visit to Antarctica many respondents wanted to visit other parts of the continent, in particular the Ross Sea.

Table 6.20 reports answers to questions with regard to activities enjoyed most and least while aboard the vessels. Given that on most cruises more than 80 percent of the passengers' time is spent on board the vessel (rather than ashore), it is important to know which activities passengers are most interested in.

TABLE 6.18. Activities Enjoyed Least While Ashore

	%
Shore visits were too short	15
Nothing	13
Pollution caused by science/whaling	8
More control of tourists is needed	6
Return to ship	1
All else	56

Source: Based on shipborne survey results, 1994-1995 and 1995-1996.

Note: Multiple response (142 responses).

TABLE 6.19. Preferred Region of Future Visit

	%
Ross Sea region	22
Sub-Antarctic islands	11
Antarctic Peninsula	11
Interior of the continent	10
Weddell Sea	8
Australian Antarctic Territory	6
All else	12
None	16

Source: Based on shipborne survey results, 1994-1995 and 1995-1996.

Note: Multiple response (241 responses).

TABLE 6.20. Activities Enjoyed Most and Least While Aboard

	%
Most (208 responses)	
Lectures	32
Interaction with other passengers	20
Views from the ship	15
Cruising itself	13
Food	8
Interaction with crew	5
All else	7
Least (141 responses)	
Seasickness and other ailments	21
Length of time in getting to Antarctica	19
Food (too much, etc.)	6
Nothing	4
All else	28
No reply	22

Source: Based on shipborne survey results, 1994-1995 and 1995-1996.

Table 6.20 shows that lectures given as part of the cruise program are seen as a vital and welcome component of voyages to Antarctica. This is indeed a positive finding, since it is during these lectures that passengers are introduced to the various aspects of the Antarctic environment. It can be argued that the more passengers are aware of, for example, the conditions under which Antarctic wildlife exists and under which Antarctic science is carried out, the more environmental

sensitivity they will show while ashore. Operators are advised to take
note of the strong approval rating lectures received and to continue
the involvement of qualified lecturers in their Antarctic programs.

The high proportion of passengers who stated that interaction with
other passengers was one of the activities they enjoyed most aboard
the vessel was somewhat unexpected. It was thought that Antarctic
passengers might be individualistic and that they would not value
contact with other passengers very highly. No surprise was the finding that passengers enjoyed the cruise itself and the associated viewing of scenery. As was previously mentioned, most time on Antarctic
voyages is spent onboard the vessel, and viewing the Antarctic scenery from the ship is an important component of the tour product.

Given the reputation of the Drake Passage as one of the roughest
stretches of ocean in the world, it did not come as a surprise that passengers listed seasickness as among the most unpleasant aspect of
their voyage. For the time being operators can do relatively little to
assist their clients in this matter. While a great variety of seasickness
remedies are on the market, there does not seem to be one that completely prevents seasickness at all times.

The length of time needed to reach Antarctica was also a concern.
Some passengers, however, were of the opinion that the time it took to
get to the Antarctic Peninsula and the associated discomforts were the
price one had to pay to experience the last frontier. This physical distance and the discomforts experienced in getting to Antarctica, in particular to the more distant Ross Sea, will continue to be major constricting
factors in the development of ship-based Antarctic tourism.

Despite the discomforts mentioned, the overall level of enjoyment
of cruises was very high. Table 6.21 shows that many passengers
thought the voyage had been far more enjoyable than they had ex-

TABLE 6.21. Level of Enjoyment of Antarctic Voyage (*N* = 138)

	%
Much more enjoyable than expected	41
Somewhat more enjoyable than expected	26
About as enjoyable as expected	28
Less enjoyable than expected	2
Much less enjoyable than expected	1
No reply	1

Source: Based on shipborne survey results, 1994-1995 and 1995-1996.

pected. Although it could be argued that people who pay substantial amounts of money for a relatively short holiday experience would naturally be inclined to say that they have enjoyed the experience, the high level of satisfaction is nevertheless a very positive finding that should encourage operators to continue with the current small- to medium-scale, lecture-supported pattern of Antarctic cruising.

CHARACTERISTICS OF OVERFLIGHT PASSENGERS AND THEIR IMAGES AND ATTITUDES TOWARD ANTARCTICA AS A TOURIST DESTINATION

Seeing Antarctica from above rather than from sea level is a completely different way of experiencing the region. As was previously outlined, Antarctic overflights were popular in the 1970s and, after a fifteen-year break, resumed during 1994-1995. Little has been written about the profiles of people who flew to the Antarctic during the first series of flights, and to this author's knowledge no comprehensive visitor surveys were carried out aboard these flights.

Through close cooperation with Phil Asker, the managing director of Croydon Travel, the author was permitted to survey passengers on several flights during the 1994-1995 and 1995-1996 seasons. The author hypothesized that people who opted to fly to Antarctica for the day did so because it was the only way that they could afford to see it. Given the much greater affordability of overflights, it was also expected that overflight passengers would be much younger and that the percentage of professional people among them would be substantially lower compared to shipborne tourists. The most important questions addressed through these surveys were the following:

1. Do passengers who fly to Antarctica for the day have different characteristics from those who visit Antarctica by ship?
2. Are the images and characteristics of Antarctica as a tourist destination identified by overflight passengers different from those identified by shipborne passengers?
3. Are the motivations of passengers for undertaking an overflight different from those visiting Antarctica by ship?
4. How likely are overflight passengers to visit Antarctica by ship after they have seen the continent from the air?

The following section analyzes the data obtained from the overflight surveys and contrasts the findings with those obtained from the various shipborne surveys. Questionnaires were included in a folder, which each passenger received on board, and public announcements were made during the flights requesting passengers to complete the questionnaires. It was not possible to control the time during which passengers completed the survey, and as a consequence, some passengers may have answered the questions prior to seeing Antarctica while others may have completed the questionnaire on the return flight. The questionnaire was kept short to minimize inconvenience to passengers. Table 6.22 shows the characteristics of the sample of passengers.

The 1994-1995 surveys were carried out during all six flights, which carried a total of 2,134 passengers. The 1995-1996 surveys were restricted to the first three flights (QF 2601, QF 2602, and QF 2603), which carried a total of 902 passengers. Very few respondents had been to Antarctica before. One respondent stated that he had been to Antarctica aboard a flight in 1977. This observation again raises the question: has someone been to a place, in this case Antarctica, if they have overflown it? The answer is probably no. Otherwise people would "have been" to all the places they overfly, for example, on a long-distance flight between Australia and Europe. If one accepts that people overflying a foreign country do not count as international visitors to that country, then Antarctic overflight passengers also cannot be counted as Antarctic tourists.

As Table 6.23 shows, several differences existed between the profiles of ship and air tourists. While 29 percent of ship passengers were in the age group sixty-one to seventy, only 20 percent of air passengers fell into this category. This was, however, made up by the higher proportion of those over seventy-one on flights (14 percent), so that both samples showed a remarkable 38 percent of passengers over the age of sixty-one. The gender distribution was interesting to note. Shipborne respondents were more likely to be male (54 percent) than female (45 percent), while on the overflights females (58 percent) outnumbered males (40 percent). The employment status of both samples was identical, with 57 percent being employed and 40 percent being retired. There was, however, a significant difference in the kind of work respondents did. Professionals dominated both samples (57 percent for the overflights and 70 percent for the ship-based surveys). The higher proportion of professional people on the ships can

TABLE 6.22. Characteristics of the Sample of Overflight Passengers, 1994-1995 and 1995-1996 (*N* = 484)

	%
Age group	
under 18	0.4
18-25	6
26-35	9
36-45	13
46-55	19
56-60	15
61-70	20
71-80	14
over 80	4
No response	1
Gender	
Male	40
Female	58
No response	2
Place of residence	
Australia	97
Overseas	3
Employment status	
Employed	57
Retired	40
No response	3
Occupation	
Professionals	57
Previous visit to Antarctica	
No	97
Yes	3

Source: Based on overflight surveys, 1994-1995 and 1995-1996.

perhaps be explained by the price of the cruises, which are out of reach of many "ordinary" workers.

Passengers were asked what motivated them to undertake an overflight. A great variety of responses was received. Table 6.24 shows that the uniqueness of the region was the strongest motivation for going on a flight to Antarctica.

TABLE 6.23. Passenger Profiles Aboard Overflights and Aboard Ships

	Overflight (N = 484) %	Ship Prior to Visit (N = 159) %
Age group		
18-25	6	2
26-35	9	8
36-45	13	15
46-55	19	21
56-60	15	16
61-70	20	29
71-80	14	7
over 80	4	3
No response	1	–
Gender balance		
Male	40	54
Female	58	45
No response	2	–
Employment status		
Employed	57	57
Retired	40	40
No response	3	1
Occupation		
Professional	57	70

Sources: Based on overflight surveys, 1994-1995 and 1995-1996, as well as shipborne surveys, 1994-1995 and 1995-1996.

Table 6.25 provides an insight into the images and characteristics overflight passengers expected of Antarctica as a tourist destination. Findings will be contrasted with those obtained from shipborne tourists in a later section of this chapter.

In the successful marketing of any tourism product it is important to establish what expectations consumers have of the experience they purchase. Table 6.26 shows that good views, learning about Antarctica, the scenery, memories, and experiences were high on the list of expectations of overflight passengers. The 2 percent who had hoped for wildlife viewing would obviously have been disappointed since penguins are difficult to see from 2,000 feet above ground!

To assess the likelihood of air travelers becoming seaborne Antarctic tourists, the following question was asked: "After experiencing

TABLE 6.24. Motivations for Undertaking the Flight

	%
A unique trip to a unique region	23
Always wanted to go to the Antarctic	12
Just wanted to see the Antarctic	12
Fascinated by the Antarctic	10
An experience	10
It was a present	8
The plane trip appealed	6
Family reasons	5
Adventure	5
Other	9

Source: Based on overflight survey results, 1994-1995 and 1995-1996.

Note: Multiple response (649 responses).

the Antarctic from above, how likely would you say is it that you would undertake an Antarctic cruise within the next three years?" Results shown in Table 6.27, indicate that 38 percent of the sample stated that they were likely or more than likely to visit the region by ship within the next three years. This appears, however, to be more a case of wishful thinking rather than reality, since very few cruise bookings have been made by overflight passengers (Asker, P., personal communication 1996).

Given the predominance of Australians aboard the flights, it is perhaps not surprising that the majority of respondents stated that if they were to travel by ship, it would be to the AAT or to the Ross Sea (see Table 6.28). These are the parts of the Antarctic that overflight tourists would be most familiar with, since it is here that the reported endeavors of Antarctic figures such as Mawson, Scott, Amundsen, and Shackleton took place. By contrast, the Antarctic Peninsula area is relatively unknown to Australian travelers, a fact that is reflected in the outbound figures from Australia to South America. During 1994, fewer than 10,000 Australians ventured to South America, which is a prerequisite for boarding an Antarctic Peninsula cruise.

During the 1996-1997 season, the survey was repeated. Profiles of passengers and their likelihood of undertaking an Antarctic cruise are shown in Tables 6.29 and 6.30.

TABLE 6.25. Images and Characteristics of Antarctica As a Destination

	%
The early explorers	3
Historic sites	1
Total historical attributes	**4**
Scientific bases	1
Total science attributes	**1**
Wildlife	3
Penguins	4
Sea mammals	1
Total Fauna attributes	**8**
Beauty	6
Pristine	7
Exciting	2
Peace	1
Total positive attributes	**16**
Cold	3
Windy	1
Hostile	2
Remote	7
Total negative attributes	**13**
Ice	8
Mountains	8
Icebergs	6
Glaciers	5
Snow	5
Total ice features	**32**
Danger from too much tourism	2
Environmental concerns	2
Vastness of Antarctica	6
Scenery	8
Ocean	1
Wilderness	2
Other	7

Source: Based on overflight surveys, 1994-1995 and 1995-1996.

Note: Multiple response (1,133 responses).

TABLE 6.26. Expectations of Overflight

	%
Good views	18
Learn more about Antarctica	13
Pleasure	12
Scenery	11
Memories	10
An experience	10
Just as it was	6
See icebergs	3
Photo/video opportunities	3
Wildlife viewing	2
A dream come true	2
Adventure	1
No expectations	1
Other	8

Source: Based on overflight surveys, 1994-1995 and 1995-1996.

Note: Multiple response (657 responses).

TABLE 6.27. Likelihood of Undertaking an Antarctic Cruise Within Three Years ($N = 484$)

	%
Very unlikely	26
Unlikely	33
Likely	25
Very likely	10
Definitely	3
No response	3

Source: Based on overflight surveys, 1994-1995 and 1995-1996.

COMPARATIVE PERCEPTUAL IMAGES OF ANTARCTIC VISITORS

As stated previously, it was of interest not only to establish similarities or differences between the seaborne and overflight passengers but also to investigate how their images of Antarctica as a holiday destination differed. Chi-square significance testing was carried out to determine the significance levels of the relationships between the re-

TABLE 6.28. Most Preferred Region for Cruise (*N* = 484)

	%
No response	39
Australian Antarctic Territory	22
Antarctic Peninsula	14
All of the above	11
Ross Sea	10
Sub-Antarctic Islands	4

Source: Based on overflight surveys, 1994-1995 and 1995-1996.

TABLE 6.29. Profiles of Overflight Passengers, 1996-1997

	%
Age group (*n* = 1,277)	
under 18	1.3
18-25	7.7
26-35	7.8
36-45	13.5
46-55	20.8
56-60	13.5
61-70	18.6
71-80	12.5
over 80	4.2
Gender (*n* = 1,262)	
Male	43.8
Female	51.4
Occupation (*n* = 1,248)	
Manager/administrator	17.3
Professional	26.4
Paraprofessional	3.3
Tradesperson	5.3
Clerk	3.4
Salesperson	2.6
Laborer	1.3
Student	3.6
Domestic Homemaker	10.3
Plant and machine operator	1.9
Other	24.5
Member in conservation group (*n* = 1,220)	
Yes	13.4
No	86.5

Source: Based on overflight surveys, 1996-1997.

TABLE 6.30. Likelihood of Undertaking an Antarctic Cruise Within the Next Three Years ($N = 1,248$)

	%
Very unlikely	30
Unlikely	34
Likely	23
Very likely	9
Definitely	4

Source: Based on overflight surveys, 1996-1997.

sponses received from the various surveys (see Table 6.31). To facilitate analysis, attributes were grouped into the following categories: inaccessible, landscapes, negative imagery, positive imagery, fauna, human intervention, and other. The significance test was carried out to test three separate relationships: (1) images before and after visit by ship; (2) images before visit by ship and on overflights; and (3) images after visit by ship and on overflight.

Comparison of Images Held Before and After Visit by Ship

The most significant changes occurred with regard to the positive images category, which included variables such as beauty, peace, and uniqueness. With a confidence level above 99.99 percent it can be stated that passengers on their return from Antarctica held a far stronger image of these attributes than prior to their visit. This is perhaps not surprising given that values such as the beauty and peace of a place such as Antarctica are difficult to imagine prior to a visit. At the same time that positive mood images increased, negative ones decreased. Passengers now thought of the region as being less cold, windy, and hostile than they had previously stated. This interesting finding is most likely based on the fact that Antarctica is always described, among other things, as the coldest and windiest continent. While this is true for parts of the continent, it does not hold true for the coastal regions of the Antarctic Peninsula and, to a lesser extent, the Ross Sea. The summer minimum air temperatures in the Peninsula region are around zero degrees Celsius and, even if one takes the wind chill factor into account, are far less severe than even mild winters in most of North America or northern Europe. It follows that tour operators would be well advised to stress to their clients that if ade-

TABLE 6.31. Chi-Square Test of Significance of Image of Antarctica

Variable	Chi Obtained		
	Ships Before/After	Ship Before/ Overflight	Ship After/ Overflight
Inaccessible	2.77	8.42*	25.4*
Landscape	2.59	20.17*	14.97*
Fauna	5.33*	155.19*	72.67*
Human intervention	0.11	6.49*	6.49*
Negative images	6.32*	0.02	10.43*
Positive images	36.98*	17.61*	5.27*
Other	2.93	0.28	3.13
Confidence level chi-square			
0.005	7.88		
0.0010	6.66		
0.025	5.02		
0.050	3.84		
0.100	2.71		

Source: Overflight survey results, 1994-1995 and 1995-1996, as well as seaborne surveys, 1994-1995 and 1995-1996.

Note: *Significant at 0.05.

quate protective clothing is worn, cold and wind should be no barriers to visiting the region.

Perhaps surprisingly, the variable "fauna" declined after passengers had seen Antarctica. One explanation could be that people were very familiar with the imagery of Antarctic wildlife, particularly penguins, before they went on their trip. Seeing them only confirmed that they actually looked like the images passengers had been exposed to prior to reaching the area (through books and brochures). Thus, other, more unexpected images, such as the sheer beauty of the place, dominated their impressions.

Comparison of Images Held by Ship and Overflight Passengers Prior to Seeing Antarctica

The only variables that showed no significant difference between the two samples were "other" and "negative imagery." Thus both groups thought of Antarctica as a cold, windy, and hostile place to spend a holiday.

The biggest difference was found with regard to the fauna variable, which was mentioned far less often by overflight passengers. In particular, whales, seals, and flying seabirds were mentioned much less often by these passengers. Since penguins still received a substantial number of mentions, it could be argued that the depth of knowledge of the Antarctic fauna was much shallower among overflight passengers than among their seaborne counterparts. That is, overflight passengers may have only "high profile" wildlife in mind.

With regard to the variables "inaccessible" and "landscape," the two groups of respondents were also significantly different. Overflight passengers were more inclined to think of Antarctica as inaccessible/remote and possessing grandiose landscapes (including mountains and ice features). At the same time, they were more likely to associate more positive mood images such as uniqueness, peace, and beauty with the destination than their shipborne counterparts.

CONCLUDING COMMENTS

The surveys of shipborne Antarctic travelers correlated well with previously published work. Respondents tended to be very experienced travelers, were of mature age and professional, and came from developed countries. The images and expectations they held of Antarctica as a holiday destination were largely confirmed by their visit. The surveys of the overflight passengers broke new ground in the sense that no such surveys had previously been carried out. They make a significant contribution to the understanding of a unique component of the Antarctic tourism product.

Chapter 7

The Future of Antarctic Tourism

As previously outlined, Antarctica is a unique continent without an indigenous population, without an owner, and without an existing tourism infrastructure. Current types of tourism taking place there have been analyzed in the preceding chapters, and visitor numbers have been traced back to the mid-1950s. The primary aim of this study is not to forecast visitor numbers but to investigate what type of tourism may be most popular in the medium to long term. For the forecasting of future patterns of tourism development at most other tourist destinations, the literature describes several quantitative forecasting techniques that could be employed (see for example Archer 1987:77-85, who outlines the most popular techniques including time series models, causal approaches, and systems models). The range and type of new tourism products that may be developed at a destination can likewise be determined relatively easily by looking at cases at other, similar destinations. Were one to investigate the future directions of beach tourism at an as yet undeveloped tropical island, one could easily draw examples of development from places such as Bali, Fiji, and the Caribbean islands. By tracing the development history of other beach destinations, one would arrive at a relatively accurate picture of how tourism at the new destination was most likely going to develop.

In the Antarctic context there are very few, if any, destinations one could study to establish future trends. The quantitative techniques mentioned do not take into consideration the unique conditions under which Antarctic tourism must take place; limited access to the continent because of the question of continued availability of suitable vessels, in particular relatively low-cost Russian ships, and the possible introduction of larger aircraft for tourism purposes, are variables that would be difficult to incorporate into such models. Likewise, the potential for the introduction of site-based accommodation in Antarctica would be a restricting factor for modeling tourism demand.

Taking note of these constraints, the author decided that the Delphi method, which relies on expert opinions rather than on historical data, was the most appropriate technique. The application of the Delphi method to a tourism-based problem is relatively rare.

BACKGROUND OF THE DELPHI METHOD

The Delphi method, named after the Greek oracle, was developed by Helmer and others at the Rand Corporation. The procedure of the method is as follows. A problem area is identified for which a forecast is needed, a panel of experts is selected, and an initial survey questionnaire is mailed out to the panel members. After panelists have completed the questionnaire, it is returned to the organizer of the Delphi study. The organizer compiles the responses and feeds them back to the respondents in a second round of questionnaires to allow panel members to alter their opinions in light of comments made by other panelists. Wilson and Keating (1990:10) list the following six steps in the conduct of a Delphi study:

1. Participating panel members are selected.
2. Questionnaires asking for opinions about the variables to be forecast are distributed to panel members.
3. Results from panel members are collected, tabulated, and summarized.
4. Summary results are distributed to the panel members for their review and consideration.
5. Panel members revise their individual estimates, taking account of the information received from the other, unknown panel members.
6. Steps 3 through 5 are repeated until no significant changes result.

Armstrong (1985:117) lists three features that are important for the success of a Delphi study:

1. The respondents are experts in the subject area.
2. There is more than one round—that is, the experts are asked for their opinions on each question more than one time.
3. Controlled feedback is provided. Respondents are told about the group's responses on the preceding round. On Round 2 and later

rounds, respondents with extreme answers are sometimes asked to provide reasons, which are summarized anonymously for the next round.

Advantages of the method are that "Experts are kept apart so that their judgements will not be influenced by social pressure or by other aspects of group behavior" (Wheelwright and Makridakis, 1985: 325). Because the anonymity of panelists is guaranteed by the Delphi director, communication between panelists with regard to the study is unlikely. Wheelwright and Makridakis (1985:325) also list a number of disadvantages of the method. These include "insufficient reliability, oversensitivity of results to ambiguity of questions, different results when different experts are used, difficulty in assessing the degree of expertise, and the impossibility of predicting the unexpected." They do, however, point out that these complaints are only relative and that the method "should be judged in terms of the available alternatives." For the task at hand no other method was seen to be superior.

The Delphi method does not require a historical data series, other than what is in the knowledge base of the panel members, and therefore does not necessarily reflect patterns that may have existed in the past (Wilson and Keating 1990:360). This observation is particularly important for forecasting future types of tourism development in the Antarctic region, because the aim was to identify whether future developments may be significantly different from those taking place today. In the author's opinion, an extrapolation of past visitor trends would not have provided satisfactory answers. The Delphi method, unlike many forecasting methods, does not have to produce a single answer as its output. Instead of reaching a consensus, the Delphi approach can result in a spread of opinions, since there is no particular attempt to get unanimity. The objective is to narrow down the quartile range as much as possible without pressuring the respondents. Thus, justified "deviant" opinion is permitted by this approach (Wheelwright and Makridakis 1985:325).

THE DELPHI TECHNIQUE APPLIED TO TOURISM

While the Delphi technique has been used successfully in a variety of other fields, its application to tourism-related matters has thus far been sporadic. Yong, Keng, and Leng (1989) investigated future scenarios and marketing implications for the Singaporean tourism industry and found the technique useful. Green, Hunter, and Moore (1990a, 1990b) applied the Delphi technique to assess the environmental impact of a tourist development, an old textile mill (Salt's Mill), in Bradford, England. Their study concentrated on the impacts of the development of a single enterprise, while the author's research sought to establish future trends for a remote continent.

In summing up their findings, Green, Hunter, and Moore (1990b: 120) note that the Delphi approach provided a helpful evaluation of impacts associated with the development of Salt's Mill and that it exposed the major issues related to the development. They caution that "Until it can be tested in a range of different environments, including those of particular ecological sensitivity, it is difficult to be dogmatic about the reliability of the methodology developed in this article."

In a reply to Green, Hunter, and Moore, Wheeller, Hart, and Whysall (1990) are critical of several aspects of the study. One of the major criticisms is the mix of the panel members. The author took note of this criticism and proceeded with great care to assemble a representative Delphi panel of Antarctic experts.

METHOD AND PANEL SELECTION

When panelists were selected, care was taken to choose experts who could represent the broad spectrum of parties concerned with a diversity of Antarctic tourism aspects. The following groups of experts were identified as potential participants on the panel:

1. Environmental organizations
2. Antarctic tour operators
3. Antarctic Treaty Parties and other government bodies
4. Academics who had published in the field
5. Antarctic experts and practitioners

Individuals and organizations were identified through the literature and at Antarctic and tourism conferences the author attended. After potential panel members had been identified, the initial questionnaire was developed. This was mailed to ninety-three potential panel members with a letter and a brief biography of the author. After several follow-ups, thirty-five fully usable responses to the following questions were received:

1. Do you think that tourism is a legitimate use of Antarctic resources? Yes or No. If you answered "yes," please go to question 2. If your answer was "no," please explain why.
2. What would you say is presently the most appropriate type of tourism taking place in the Antarctic region? Why?
3. In your opinion, what are the impacts of current tourism activities on the Antarctic environment?
4. What type of tourism activity would you expect to be *the most common* form of tourism activity taking place in the Antarctic region in twenty-five years' time? Why? Where in the Antarctic region do you think this type of tourism will mainly take place?
5. What do you see as the possible barriers for the development of the type of tourism you have outlined in question 4?
6. What impacts do you think the type of tourism activity you have outlined will have on the natural and created environment of the Antarctic region?
7. What other types of tourism activities could you envisage taking place in the Antarctic region in twenty-five years' time? Where would they take place and what impacts would they have on the natural and created environment?
8. What impacts do you think the established scientific stations in Antarctica are having on the natural and created environment of Antarctica?
9. Do you have any other comments with regard to the future of tourism in Antarctica?

The length of responses ranged from a few lines per question to several pages on individual questions. All responses were transcribed by the author, collated, and mailed back to the panel of experts for additional comments. Panel members were invited to change their opinions on the various points in light of responses received from other panel members (the anonymity of all panel members was guaranteed since no names appeared on the summary report). It was of great interest to the author to note how firmly respondents believed in the answers they had provided in the first instance. Only three responses were received, and all of them stated that the respondent did not want to change his or her opinions and had nothing to add to what he or she had previously stated.

Strengths and Weaknesses of the Panel

Table 7.1 lists the participants in the study. The thirty-five panel members represented a broad cross-section of Antarctic interests. Greenpeace and the World Wide Fund for Nature are the two environmental organizations represented. The Australian Conservation Foundation did not reply to the request to participate but has a policy that states: "In view of the sensitivity of the Antarctic environment, and the environmental impacts of tourism, and the need to protect Antarctica's wilderness character the ACF believes that commercial and private tourism ventures should not be permitted" (ACF 1990). All Antarctic Treaty Parties were approached. Two key players, the United States Antarctic Program (USAP) and the British Antarctic Survey (BAS), declined to participate, which can be seen as weakening the collective views of the panel.

Among the Antarctic tour operators the most notable was Lars-Eric Lindblad, who in 1966 pioneered commercial Antarctic tourism in its present, ship-based form (Lindblad passed away in 1994). His comments carry significant weight because they are based on nearly thirty years of experience of conducting tours to Antarctica and other remote locations around the globe. The combined views of the Antarctic tour operators were expressed by their spokesperson, John Splettstoesser. Operators and charterers of large and small ships were included on the panel. Two companies that were the dominant force in Antarctic tourism in 1996 (Quark Expeditions and Marine Expeditions) unfortunately did not participate on the panel. The views of Quark Expeditions with regard to future tourism developments in Antarctica, however, were expressed by the president of the company, Lars Wikander, during a lecture aboard the *Alla Tarasova* in December 1994. These views were broadly in line with those of the panel of experts. It also must be noted that since the survey was conducted Society Expeditions has changed ownership. This fact, however, does not diminish the views expressed by Peter Cox, then director for planning and operations. Of particular importance is the inclusion of Anne Kershaw, managing director of Adventure Network International, which provides the only land-based tourism product by flying passengers to the interior of the continent. ANI's operations can be seen

TABLE 7.1. Members of the Delphi Panel

Environmental organizations
Cassandra Phillips, Antarctic and Cetacean Officer, World Wide Fund for Nature
    International
Janet Dalziell, Antarctic Campaigner, Greenpeace Australia

Antarctic tour operators
Peter Cox, Director, Planning and Operations, Society Expeditions
Warwick Deacock, Manager, World Venture
Erwin Flathmann, Manager, Passenger Operations, Transocean Tours
John Splettstoesser, Spokesperson for IAATO
Lars-Eric Lindblad
Victoria Underwood, CTC Manager, Antarctic Operations, Explorer Shipping
    Company/Abercrombie & Kent
Anne Kershaw, Adventure Network International
Greg Mortimer, GMMS/World Expeditions

Antarctic Treaty Party representatives and other government representatives
Dr. Chang, Director, Polar Research Centre, Korea Ocean Research Institute
A. Karlguist, Director, Swedish Polar Research Secretariat
Ian Hay, Policy Section, Australian Antarctic Division
Captain Antonio Carlos Monteiro, Manager, Brazilian Antarctic Program
Dr. Heinz Kohnen, Director, Alfred Wegener Institute fuer Polar und
    Meeresforschung
J. Castellvi, Secretaria General del Plan Nacional de I+D, Madrid
R. Schorno and Sander van Bennekom, Antarctic Program coordinators,
    Netherlands
Malcolm MacFarlane, New Zealand Antarctic Program (personal views)
Maria Luisa Carvallo Cruz, Ministerio de Relaciones Exteriores, Instituto
    Antartico Chileno
Jean Page, Department of Foreign Affairs, Canberra
Fiona May, Commonwealth Department of Tourism, Canberra

Academics
Dr. Bruce Davis, University of Tasmania
Prof. Colin Michael Hall, Victoria University, Wellington
Dr. Richard Herr, University of Tasmania
John Manning, Manager, Geodesy, AUSLIG
Prof. John Marsh, Trent University, Canada
Prof. Valene Smith, California State University, Chico
Dr. Bernard Stonehouse, Scott Polar Research Institute, University of Cambridge
Dr. Nigel Wace, Australian National University

Antarctic experts and practitioners
Dr. Phillip Garth Law, Melbourne
Dr. Paul Dingwall, Department of Conservation, Wellington
Robyn Graham, Australian Antarctic Foundation (personal views)
Richard Voelker, Program Manager, Science and Technology Corp., Washing-
    ton
Dr. Geoff Mosley, Melbourne (personal views)

as a potential forerunner of future, perhaps larger scale, Antarctic tourism developments. Greg Mortimer's contribution based on his experiences as geologist, mountaineer, tour leader, and tour operator was especially welcome.

Several of the panel members in the academic category are leading figures in the field of Antarctic tourism. Dr. Bernard Stonehouse has spent the last fifty years conducting research in Antarctica and heads up the Project Antarctic Conservation team at Scott Polar Research Institute. Dr. Valene Smith, Professor John Marsh, Professor Colin Michael Hall, Dr. Bruce Davis, Dr. Richard Herr, and Dr. Nigel Wace have all contributed to the Antarctic tourism debate.

The outstanding contributor among the Antarctic experts is Dr. Phillip Law, who in 1954 established Mawson, Australia's first station on the continent. Dr. Dingwall was approached via his involvement in the IUCN. Dr. Geoff Mosley, although responding as a private citizen, provided an environmental viewpoint, and Richard Voelker approached the issue with a technical background based on his expertise in marine technology. The inclusion of John Wilson, the station leader at the Australian Davis station during 1992-1993, was particularly appreciated since his comments provided an insight into how Antarctic expeditioners feel about Antarctic tourism issues.

In total, the panel represents a diverse group of people that can be seen as representative of parties that have interest in Antarctic tourism affairs. The expertise and standing of panel members leads to the conclusion that results obtained from the study represent a realistic assessment of current and future developments.

The following section presents a summary of responses received and discusses the answers that were obtained. Many respondents went to great length to answer the seven questions, and the panel contributed many thousands of words. The panel members were assured that their responses would be treated as confidential and that their statements would not be attributable to them as individuals. As a result, the answers provided in the next section do not provide the usual citations of authors.

LEGITIMACY AND PREFERRED PRESENT TYPES OF TOURISM IN THE ANTARCTIC

The first question asked was "Do you think that tourism is a legitimate use of Antarctic resources?" All respondents agreed that tourism is a legitimate use of Antarctic resources. One respondent stated that in his opinion, tourism was not a *use* but an *impact.* Several additional answers were provided by the panel. These are broken down into the various categories of respondents.

Tour Operators

- Yes. *Responsible* tourism that respects the ecology of Antarctica is not only legitimate but in my opinion also a use of Antarctic resources that can be a great stabilizer and of vital importance to the survival of the white continent.
- It is the well-informed traveler who will *critically observe* the scientific community and other possible NGO activities. As an *Ambassador to Antarctica* (which is what all "tourists" visiting Antarctica become) they will be *very watchful* of any legislation their congressmen might be pushing for that might be harmful to Antarctica.
- I am sure that tourism is just about the only legitimate use of Antarctic resources at this time. If we are talking about exploiting mineral resources, wildlife resources such as making gloves of penguin skins, we need very careful studies of the impact of such activities. Oil, is of course, another possibility which is very disturbing. I would think that such exploitation is far off simply because of what it would cost. Furthermore, there is plenty of oil in Nigeria, Indonesia, Mexico, etc., which is now unsold.

Antarctic Treaty/Government Representatives

- Yes, when it occurs in an ecologically sustainable way.
- Yes. Regulations under the Antarctic Treaty set out guidelines on the conduct of tourism in Antarctica. The Protocol on Environmental Protection to the Antarctic Treaty Protocol requires environmental impact assessment for all activities, including tourism.

Academics

- Yes. "Legitimate" in that it transgresses no laws. Whether it is appropriate, or desirable or even manageable or sustainable is another matter.

Panel respondents reiterated what Treaty Parties have acknowledged in Recommendation VIII-9 (Heap 1990:2602): ". . . that tourism is a natural development in this Area and that it requires regulation." Thus the responses clearly indicate that commercial tourism in Antarctica is an acceptable use of Antarctic wilderness and wildlife resources. The only organizations that disagree with this view are the Australian Conservation Foundation and the Wilderness Society, both of which have a policy that no tourism should be allowed in Antarctica. Both organizations were invited to participate on the panel, but neither of them responded. As in all other tourist destinations around the world, remote or not, there is no argument that care must be taken to avoid jeopardizing the resource on which tourism is based. As was discussed in Chapter 4, tour operators organized under IAATO have developed and implemented guidelines that to date have ensured sensitive conduct of tourism in Antarctica.

In response to the question "What would you say is presently the most appropriate form of tourism taking place in the Antarctic region?" there was consensus among the panel members that shipborne tourism was most appropriate. Several mentions were also made of air-supported adventure tourism of the kind conducted by ANI, and some respondents also opted to name a type of tourism (mainly ecotourism), rather than the mode of transport used. The impacts of tourism on the Antarctic environment have been discussed previously. The panel assessed the overall impact of current tourism activities as being very small. As to the type of negative impacts tourists might have, despoliation of vegetation, disturbance to wildlife, and disruption of science stood out as the most mentioned types of impacts. These are also the impacts most commonly cited in the literature.

THE FUTURE OF COMMERCIAL TOURISM IN ANTARCTICA AND ITS IMPACTS

Forecasting future developments in tourism is never an easy task, but it is particularly difficult in a part of the world where previous experiences cannot readily be extrapolated into future developments. The kind of tourism activities that have taken place in Antarctica to date—ship-based, small-scale land-based tourism with air support, and overflights—may well be the only forms of tourism that Antarctica will ever experience. Antarctica is at present a cruise destination, but many island destinations, including Australia, Japan, New Zealand, and Tahiti, started out as cruise destinations. When ships were the only mode of transport to reach these islands, visitor numbers were very small. Once aircraft began to replace ships as the main mode of transport to these islands, their relative isolation ended and visitor numbers increased substantially. Several possible tourism development scenarios can be hypothesized in the Antarctic context:

1. Antarctica could remain a cruise destination without any tourism-related land infrastructure (there are few other places where this is the case).
2. Antarctica could remain primarily a cruise destination, but permanent tourist facilities could be established, most likely near existing scientific stations and most likely in the Antarctic Peninsula region.
3. A combination of fly/cruise tourism may develop whereby passengers fly to an Antarctic airfield and from there are transferred to their cruise vessels.
4. Permanent, air-supported large-scale facilities along the lines of the previously proposed Project Oasis near Australia's Davis station may develop.
5. A combination of all the above may provide the tourism product of Antarctica in the twenty-first century.

This chapter investigates the most likely future developments of Antarctic tourism by drawing on the literature and on the responses from the Antarctic panel of experts.

Future Antarctic Tourism in the Literature

Law (1977), quoted by Lovering and Prescott (1979:99), writing about the future of tourism in Antarctica, states: "Strong tourist pressures would develop if air access could be developed in conjunction with a palatial hotel amidst Antarctic surroundings of great natural beauty and within easy reach of glaciers, mountains, penguin rookeries, seal colonies and with a reasonably sunny summer climate." Law mentioned the Ross Sea and the Antarctic Peninsula as two possible sites for such a venture. He saw the huge capital cost of building such a hotel, coupled with an immense recurrent cost associated with its use only during the summer season as a major problem. As a solution to this problem he suggested, ". . . a better solution to the accommodation problem would be to use an ice-strengthened luxury passenger ship moored for about 6 weeks at an appropriate site to act as a floating hotel for 3 or 4 successive tourist loads delivered to a nearby airfield" (Law 1977, quoted in Lovering and Prescott 1979:99). He pointed out that two such airfields already existed, one at McMurdo and the other at the Argentine station of Marambio on Seymour Island. Both of these airfields are capable of handling C-130 transport planes. Nearly twenty-five years later, Law's 1977 proposal has not come to fruition, despite the fact that several new airfields are now available in Antarctica (for example, at the Chilean station of Teniente Rodolfo Marsh on King George Island and at the British base at Rothera in the Antarctic Peninsula). The reasons for the lack of air-supported tourism in Antarctica are political—Antarctic Treaty Parties and scientists still see Antarctica as their territory, and they are in no rush to share it with tourists—and economic—flights that involve landings are very dependent on favorable weather conditions, and flight delays pose a high commercial risk for the operators.

Law's other suggestion, that there would be a great circle air route from Melbourne to Buenos Aires that would overfly parts of Antarctica, has also not come into being. Unlike Law's suggestion that the flight would pass over McMurdo, thus enabling passengers to have a good look at Antarctica from above, current Aerolineas Argentinas flights do not get much closer than 2,000 miles to the geographic South Pole. Passengers may on occasion spot floating icebergs but will not sight the continent itself. (Qantas Airways also flies the route from Australia to Buenos Aires, but these direct flights likewise do not go far enough south for passengers to get a view of Antarctica.)

Interestingly, Antarctica New Zealand (1996:1) appears to be taking a very commercially oriented approach toward Antarctica and, in particular, tourism. Its mission statement is: "Antarctica New Zealand will provide leadership in developing, promoting and realizing opportunities for New Zealand from international involvement in Antarctica and the Southern Ocean." Referring to the organization's strategic goal with regard to the commercial framework, Antarctica New Zealand (1996:11) states: "Antarctica New Zealand will provide a framework to facilitate appropriate commercial and tourism opportunities for New Zealanders in a way that is consistent with New Zealand's values and obligations in the Antarctic and Southern Ocean." Given the strong business orientation of its board of directors (Cowie, Jim, personal communication 1997), this statement could be interpreted to mean that Antarctica New Zealand may consider becoming directly involved in for-profit tourism activities. These could conceivably include flying tourists from Christchurch to McMurdo, allowing them to spend some time at Scott Base, and taking them on snowmobile and helicopter excursions to natural and historic sites in the McMurdo Sound region.

The following section analyzes the responses from the panel with regard to the most likely future of tourism in Antarctica. The panel was asked the following questions with regard to future tourism developments: "What type of tourism activity would you expect to be the *most common* form of tourism activity taking place in the Antarctic region in twenty-five years' time? Why? Where in the Antarctic region do you think this type of tourism will mainly take place?"

As Table 7.2 shows, shipborne tourism was clearly seen as the most likely form of tourism in twenty-five years. This coincides with the panel's assessment that shipborne tourism was currently the most appropriate form of tourism taking place. Interestingly, only four respondents predicted that overflights would be common in twenty-five years. As outlined in Chapter 4, overflights resumed in 1994 and have continued since, but it remains to be seen whether they will still be as popular in twenty-five years as they are today.

In addition, the following all received one mention:

- Ship- or airborne with short-term accommodation ashore
- Mooring tourist ships to provide summer hotels to which tourists travel by air
- Airborne short-term visits to available airstrips in the Antarctic Peninsula
- Airborne visits to the continent proper with associated localized development
- Increased number of hard runways
- Increase in adventure tourism overland by ski or snowmobile
- Hotel-based tourism in the Antarctic Peninsula
- Tour operators could invest in some land-based infrastructure
- Governments could gain foreign exchange by permitting land-based tourism in their sector

TABLE 7.2. Most Common Form of Antarctic Tourism in Twenty-Five Years (*N* = 35)

Type of Tourism	%
Ship-based	53.7
Air-supported	22.2
Land-based	11.1
Overflights	7.4
Eco/wilderness/adventure	5.5

Note: Multiple responses (54 responses).

Table 7.3 shows that the panel members had very little doubt that the Antarctic Peninsula would continue to be the region where tourism would mainly take place in the long term. Panel members who had stated that they thought the Antarctic Peninsula would be the location for most tourism gave the following reasons: (a) easy accessibility; (b) variety of wildlife; and (c) climatic conditions, including sea ice conditions. These three points are also the main reasons why Antarctic tourism is so highly concentrated in the Peninsula region today.

The responses focused on wildlife, scenery, and historic sites, but visits to scientific stations received only one response. Table 7.4 summarizes the reasons given for the panel's opinions. Except where indicated otherwise, all reasons given received only one mention.

Several other comments were received:

- Bigger hotels might be established
- Not likely that overflights will be reactivated
- Number of cruise companies will decline as result of Madrid Protocol
- No big change expected, but number of tourists and modes of transport will progress
- Regulation of visitation frequency of certain places of touristic interest may be necessary
- Specific requirements for ships and staff
- Specific qualifications for ships and staff
- Ecological tourism/small scale ecotourism
- SSTI (Sites of Special Tourist Interest) will be established
- All shores will be visited, including the Australian Antarctic Territory

TABLE 7.3. Most Likely Locations of Future Antarctic Tourism Activities

Location	%
Antarctic Peninsula	65.2
Ross Sea	10.9
Sub-Antarctic Islands	10.9
South Pole	4.3
East Antarctica	2.2
All Antarctic shores	2.2
AAT	2.2
Other	2.1

Note: Multiple response (46 responses).

Barriers to the Development of Future Tourism

The panel was asked what they saw as the possible barriers for the types of tourism they had suggested would dominate in Antarctica in 2020. The possible barriers mentioned most were cost of operating tours and regulation.

Cost of Operating Tours and Cost for Clients

The mention of cost (nine responses) suggests that panel members were very aware of the fact that Antarctic tourism is among the most expensive tourism products to operate and to purchase. The panel suggests that ship-based tourism will continue to dominate the market, and it is therefore unlikely that prices for tours will fall significantly. On the contrary, cruise prices aboard small to medium-sized vessels, most of which are of Russian or Estonian registry, will most probably rise as the former Soviet countries progress farther down the path of capitalism.

The only way in which cruises can become cheaper is if larger vessels are employed. In 1998-1999 the *Marco Polo* was the largest vessel operating in Antarctic waters, and on all its four cruises carried between 447 and 573 passengers (National Science Foundation 1999:1), but the vessel has a capacity of 800 passengers. The cost of catering for additional passengers would probably amount to no more than US$50 per day. Thus additional berths could be sold cheaply, thereby increasing the profits of the operator. There is, however, considerable opposition to the use of large vessels in Antarctic waters, notably also from the Antarctic tour operators organized under IAATO. They de-

TABLE 7.4. Reasons for Most Common Types of Future Tourism

Shipborne
Financially feasible/commercially viable (6 responses)
Less environmentally degrading (2 responses)
No need for infrastructure
Flexible with regard to the market and location
Increasingly sophisticated ships
Likely to be most favored by regulations
Most convenient form of access to coastal areas
Safer

Air supported
Most convenient to remote areas
Airborne, land-based large-scale tourism

Overflights
Most technologically feasible
Easy and cheap

Hotel based
In Antarctic Peninsula because of territorial claims and economic feasibility

cided to cancel the probationary IAATO membership of Orient Lines after its repeated breach of the IAATO guidelines that limit the maximum number of passengers to be carried on a single Antarctic vessel to 400 (Victoria Underwood and Denise Landau, personal communication 1996).

Attracted by the dawn of the new millenium, the 1999-2000 season saw some of the largest vessels ever travel to Antarctica. The largest was the *MS Rotterdam,* a ship with twelve decks, a draft of 8.1 meters, and a length of 238 meters that is capable of carrying 1,600 passengers. It is operated by the U.S.-based Holland America Line Westours, Inc. and carried 936 passengers and 656 crew during its voyage south (National Science Foundation 2000). The two other vessels were the 850-person *Ocean Explorer* (operated by World Cruise Company of Canada) that carried 889 passengers on two cruises, and the 830-passenger *Aegean* (operated by Marine Expeditions Inc., a Canadian company that previously introduced relatively inexpensive Antarctic cruises aboard small Russian vessels) that carried 912 passengers on its two voyages. Initially the *MS Rotterdam* planned to land passengers at the Argentinian station of Esperanza but, following consultation with Antarctic experts, the plan was abandoned. Instead the ship cruised past some of the most scenic spots in the South Shetland Islands and along the western side of the Antarctic Peninsula.

Regulation

The second most nominated barrier was regulation, which received six responses. This suggests that at least some of the panel members were of the opinion that regulations imposed by the Treaty Parties under the Madrid Protocol and by national governments may have serious implications for the conduct of Antarctic tourism. To date, however, these regulations have not been unduly harsh, and they are somewhat less restrictive than those imposed on the sub-Antarctic islands of Australia and New Zealand (see Chapter 2). Tour operators accept regulations under the Madrid Protocol and act accordingly. Under the protocol, operators are obliged to seek the approval of the respective Antarctic authorities of their home countries prior to undertaking tours in Antarctica. In countries such as the United States and Australia, such approval is only given after an Initial Environmental Evaluation (IEE) is carried out. Examples of such IEEs include those carried out by Croydon Travel for the Antarctic overflights and by Peregrine Adventures and Aurora Expeditions for overnight camping ventures in the Antarctic Peninsula. The regulations under the Madrid Protocol therefore should not be seen as a barrier by the industry but rather as a measure that ensures "best practice" in Antarctic tourism. The protocol helps keep tourism environmentally sustainable and contributes to making the activity economically sustainable as well. Visitors to this remote continent expect to find near-pristine conditions and are willing to pay for them. The associated economic returns will ensure that operators will continue to be eager to maintain the beauty of Antarctica.

Other Barriers

Numerous other barriers were mentioned by the panel of experts. The following received two mentions each:

- Opposition by environmental organizations
- Lack of demand for Antarctic tours
- Intra-industry disputes
- Need for authorized guides aboard ships adds cost

The following statements received one response each. For convenience these are listed in alphabetical order:

- Barriers needed to keep tourism within boundaries
- Capacity to deal with oil spills, etc.
- Conflicting itineraries among tour operators
- Cost of infrastructure
- Enforcement
- Failure to meet standards of the Protocol
- Government restrictions
- Hazards and safety limitations
- Ignorance and romantic ideas of the nature of Antarctica
- Insurance
- International law
- Jurisdiction
- Liability
- Limitations of tourism in conservation areas
- Need for regulation/education (control number of tourists)
- Not sufficient infrastructure available for mass air tourism
- Opposition by Antarctic stations for tourists to visit
- Opposition from environmentalists to air-supported, land-based tourism
- Overcrowding (in the Peninsula area)
- Prohibit construction of hotels
- Prohibit entrance to certain areas
- Restrictions might make the Antarctic tourism product unattractive to the consumer
- Safety aspects
- Scientists and environmentalists who want to keep Antarctica closed to nonscientists
- Stricter controls on visiting wildlife areas through placing sites off-limits, restricting numbers, or requiring environmental impact assessments
- Suitable wheel-based landing strips
- Unreasonable requirements for vessel operations

Impacts of Most Common Types of Future Antarctic Tourism

The panel was next asked a question with regard to the impacts of future Antarctic tourism activities on the natural and created Antarctic environment. Responses are summarized below. The following impacts of future Antarctic tourism activities were all mentioned once except where indicated in parenthesis.

General Tourism/Visitor Impacts

- Important to make sure that commercial activities such as tourism are not allowed to cloud the spirit of the Antarctic Treaty (psychological impact).
- Some more infrastructure, especially on King George Island.
- In general, more knowledge is needed on the exact impacts of tourist activities. Further study is required.
- Not an impact but a risk factor which could produce an impact. Risks of all human activities in the Antarctic are greater than anywhere else.

Scale of Impacts on Sites Visited

- We hope it will be almost zero, but it is difficult to say.
- If conducted responsibly I do not believe that tourist activities have any adverse impact—and this entails the impact from the vessels carrying tourists and the impacts of the tourists themselves.
- Little, if any, as long as the Codes of Conduct continue in operation and are adhered to by all operators in Antarctica.
- The most expected impact caused by tourism activity is the large number of tourists.
- Very little if governed.
- Can be one-off or cumulative.
- Limited if a good management regime is in place.
- Local damage but increased global awareness of the importance of environmental protection.
- Small impacts overall—but concentrated at few sites.
- Almost none on the environment as a whole.
- Still minimal, assuming the Protocol is in force.
- Should visitor numbers become too great, the cumulative impact may become greater than the sum of the parts.
- Cumulative and geographical impacts resulting from a concentration of activities in particular locations.
- Impacts as now—possibly worse if not regulated.

- If carried out in a responsible manner such as outlined in IAATO objectives and guidelines, the impact will be minimal and most likely cause no harm to the natural environment.
- As yet unknown—studies need to be undertaken at Chilean Base Marsh to see impacts on the environment.
- No in-depth studies exist to determine the exact magnitude of impacts.
- No more impacts than tourism has at present; possibly a net result could be slightly less impacts if operators are encouraged to cooperate with national programs and combine their operations to use existing facilities.
- Up to now tourism has had only a beneficial impact in that returning tourists have pressured their governments to clean up the environment surrounding their stations.

Regulation of Impacts/Management of Impacts

- As regards certain small regions, which receive concentrated attention, controls and restrictions of various kinds can be implemented to prevent any substantial undesirable results.
- Environmental Impact Assessment conditions and all Protected Areas have management plans which should prevent any land-based tourist installations (hotels) being built.
- Emergency response procedures should be elaborated urgently.
- More protection of historic sites and interpretation.
- All tourism needs to have guidelines to avoid negative impacts.

Exclusions/Limits of Development

- On-shore facilities including wharf structures should be prohibited or at least minimized.
- No land-based installations such as hotels should be allowed.

Impacts of Shipborne Tourism

- Impacts of sightseeing cruises would be minimal.
- The size of ships (number of passengers and crew) may well need limiting.
- Shipwrecks are always a danger.
- Negligible, if properly organized and if limited in number of passengers and in frequency.

- If tourist numbers increase and larger ships will enter the Antarctic, then this will create a need for larger facilities to divert tourists from scientific stations; i.e., this means there will be more infrastructures specifically to support tourism. The current infrastructure for science may/will not be able to support this expansion. The impact may be limited to specific areas, such as the Peninsula.

Impacts of Airborne Tourism

- High impact if infrastructures like airports, hotels, etc. will be built.
- If more flights, more accidents eventually a major search and rescue problem.
- The number of airplanes will always be limited; the Pole will always be only for the very rich.

Impacts of Land-Based Tourism

- Hotel-based tourism in the Antarctic Peninsula: Substantial impact in the immediate surrounds—primarily in pollution and sewage control. Some impact on flora and fauna and the physical environment.

Impacts of Adventure Tourism

- Uncontrolled adventure tourism: high impact.
- More adventure tourism—eventually a major search and rescue problem.

Impacts on the Land

- Litter
- Waste production and disposal
- Noise pollution
- Contamination (even if slight) of the land
- Displacement of flora and fauna
- Pollution through dumping, burning, incineration, sewage, and release of fuel into the environment, both terrestrial and marine

Impact on Wilderness and Scenic Values

- The concentration on readily accessible sites will have increased human impact on wilderness values, physical landscape, and endemic biota
- Crowding
- Reduction of wilderness values

Impacts on the Sea

- Pollution of enclosed anchorages by sewage
- Contamination (even if slight) of the sea

Impacts on the Natural Environment (Flora and Fauna)

- Tourism has impacts on the fauna (four responses) and flora (three responses).
- There have been reports by researchers (Dr. Trivelpiece) that have indicated that penguin populations have actually increased in some places that are visited by tourists. I do not believe that enough baseline data has been collected to date to even be able to understand population dynamics of the various types of wildlife. Until scientists understand why the [Adélie and Chinstrap penguin] populations themselves increase and decrease, how can anyone determine whether or not tourists are affecting these numbers?
- The impact on the natural environment depends on the numbers and behavior of visitors.
- Very little impact on the natural environment, provided that onshore facilities including wharf structures are prohibited or at least minimized.
- Disturbance of wildlife by too many visitors or visits that are too frequent; inappropriate behavior by tourists toward wildlife.

Impacts on Historic Sites

- The natural vegetation is of course extremely vulnerable and not much can be said about the effects on birds and penguins. The behavior of the people is crucial. Ten careless people can do more damage than 1,000 responsible people.

- Significant increases in visitor numbers may diminish the wilderness value of Antarctica, as well as place pressures on the environment, in a cumulative sense.
- Potentially significant if not controlled on wildlife breeding habitat and areas of rich lichen and mosses.

Impacts on Scientific Work and Stations

- Disruption of scientific programs (three responses).
- Understanding of science and people working in the Antarctic.
- The impact to the created environment (mostly scientific stations) will be minimal if visits are properly coordinated between operators and Antarctic program managers. The impact should be lessened by the fact [that] these visits should be both educational and in support of the programs which are funded by the taxpayer.
- Some considerable impact on the "created" environment—particularly on scientific stations and their operation, unless restrictions are imposed and observed.

OTHER TYPES OF FUTURE TOURISM ACTIVITIES IN ANTARCTICA

The panel was asked further questions with regard to future tourism developments in Antarctica: "What *other* types of tourism activities could you envisage taking place in the Antarctic region in twenty-five years' time? Where would they take place and what impacts would they have on the natural and created Antarctic environment?" The following sections summarize the answers received.

Adventure Tourism

The panel foresaw an increase in adventure tourism activities in Antarctica including inland, around the geographic South Pole, in the Antarctic Peninsula and the Transantarctic Mountains accessible from McMurdo. Possible adventure activities mentioned included mountain climbing, downhill and cross-country skiing, ballooning, whale watching, surfing, sailing, and sledging. An increase in private expeditions (some for the purposes of record or publicity seeking) with the associated problems of Safety and Rescue was also expected.

A possible increase in the number of yachts visiting the region and volunteers doing research as a vacation were also mentioned. Potential impacts of adventure activities were generally perceived as being low because all will have to comply with regulations under the Madrid Protocol.

By the year 2000, several of these predictions had already come true. During the 1999-2000 season, more private expeditions than ever operated in Antarctica, the number of commercial yachts in the South increased significantly, and adventure activities such as mountaineering, diving, and sea kayaking were introduced by commercial operators.

Airborne Tourism

Some panel members thought that in the future larger airplanes may land on blue ice runways, small groups may fly to inland destinations, and the use of small aircraft and helicopters to access new areas would increase. It was generally perceived that air-supported tourism would have higher impacts than ship-based tourism, but it was noted that the overall impact would still be small.

Four panel members also foresaw that overflights would resume which, indeed, they have. They thought that although these flights would have minimal impacts, they had the potential to lead to noise pollution, and those flights required altitude regulation. (A minimum altitude of 10,000 feet above sea level and 2,000 feet above ground was established for the Qantas/Croydon Travel overflights.)

Land-Based Tourism

- Hotels: major impacts (locally) not acceptable.
- Land-based resorts—impact on wildlife and wilderness values.
- Probably more pressure to have permanent or semipermanent tourist accommodation or other infrastructure.
- Any natural area such as Antarctica can attract the whole gamut of human activities. Pressure will be strongest on "land" to see wildlife at close quarters.
- Camping holidays. Could be low impact or devastating, according to how managed.
- It is likely that land-based tourism activities would have a higher impact on the Antarctic environment than shipboard-

based activities. The infrastructure required for both land and airborne forms of tourism, including permanent structures and landing strips, would have a significant impact on the Antarctic environment. Noise pollution (which disturbs local fauna) and the cumulative impacts of tourism would also be likely to increase. While this is the case, potential does exist for land-based tourism facilities to be developed which are appropriately planned and managed and which do not have a detrimental effect on the Antarctic environment.

- Possible interest in land-based accommodation (again, subject to Protocol requirements).

Shipborne Tourism

- Short-term ship-based visits—Antarctic Peninsula; Ross Sea; selected sites in East Antarctica.
- Impact would be dependent on numbers and frequency of ships and domestic control applicable to the tour operators.

Yacht-Based Tourism

- More yachts
- Perhaps more small expeditions using yachts
- Small, yacht-based charters—mostly around the Antarctic Peninsula
- Private yachts, especially around peninsula and islands
- Yachting: big impact because of total lack of control, therefore must be regulated

Other Comments

- Depending on international laws and agreements in the next twenty-five years, the following type of tourism might well be possible: Tourists spending their vacation in South America, the Falklands, Australia, and New Zealand might "interrupt" the vacation for a short visit of Antarctica. They might stay in a small hotel in Antarctica for two or three days, do excursions by boat, guided by a group of scientists. After that they return to their holiday resort in South America. Regions: mainly Antarctic Peninsula, Victoria Land, and the South Pole. The impact would depend on the organization in Antarctica. It is very concentrated on one place and other areas are left alone. Passengers would have to fly to Antarctica and this would have, of course, higher impact on the environment. In general it is difficult to say what the impacts might be.

- Great danger remains that people will visit Antarctica outside the regulation system. Policemen on the continent are not feasible so information and education are the only means to keep those people out of the Antarctic region. The impacts of those tourists can be considerable. Besides this, exclusive trips to inaccessible parts of Antarctica will still be organized. However, due to the high costs of such projects, they will be limited.
- The Environmental Protocol will severely limit the types of future activities taking place—by scientists, explorers, and tourists alike. As mentioned earlier, the costs of doing business will be much more expensive than at present.

Restrictions and Management

- Inland camps, fuel dumps, etc., should be very limited.
- Hopefully, there will not be many hotels and airports because they would have an impact. Military activities, which we have been able to avoid up to now, would of course impact the environment.
- Tourism has to be managed under certain guidelines.

Regions/Areas Where Tourism Will Take Place

- Another possible region is that section of the Transantarctic Mountains accessible from McMurdo.
- Mainly Peninsula but increasingly Ross Sea and elsewhere in the Peninsula.

Other Comments

The panel was asked whether they had any other comments with regard to the future of Antarctic tourism. They provided the following comments.

Environmental Organizations

- Antarctic tourism is obviously a matter of concern at the moment because of dramatic increases in the past couple of years. Our organization is worried about the impacts of such an increase. However, the issue should not mask the impacts of governmental activity, which, owing to its more permanent nature, is still having more serious impacts. Probably the aspect least well addressed at present is the cumulative impacts of governmental and nongovernmental activities. Mechanisms are still inadequate to address the problem of predicting, spotting, and acting to prevent or mitigate cumulative impacts. Please note that in answering the questions, I have talked about tourism really as commercial tourism. After substantial thinking about the issue, my organization has concluded that the word "tourism" is not particularly useful when considering environmental impacts, and in fact the impacts of all visitors to the Antarctic should be addressed equally. When it is necessary to split visitors up into categories for further analysis, the word "tourism" is too broad, as, even if it is defined as commercial tourism, it covers too many very different sorts of activities, at very different scales.

Antarctic Tour Operators

- Responsible tourism and Antarctica should be able to coexist to their mutual benefit.
- The future of tourism in Antarctica should continue as long as people are interested in seeing the continent, but tourism must maintain its present high level of responsibility in order to continue without being compromised by overregulation. As long as tour operators maintain a coordinated body that adheres to acceptable codes of environmental conduct, there should be few problems that might surface and which could create new regulations that could impact heavily on the industry, possibly driving some or all companies out of the market.
- I would like to see the cooperation that exists between tour operators, national scientific organizations such as the NSF, from all parts of the world continue.

- It is a critical time in history where data on impacts of tourism is being collected by Antarctic Treaty nations. The key to suitable tourism development in Antarctica lies with setting numbers for visitation at *all* possible sites. I believe that regulated tourism can be undertaken in Antarctica in sympathy with the environment.

Antarctic Treaty Party Representatives and Other Government Representatives

- It is not possible to deter or keep tourism from Antarctica. Nor is it feasible for tourist companies to teach their customers not to make some impact on the Antarctic.
- Likely to be a continuing increase in the number of visitors to Antarctica. Even if there is some inconsistency from one year to the next, the underlying trend should be of growth.
- The Council of Managers of National Antarctic Programs has been studying rules for tourism in Antarctica. In the near future, I believe that we will have an equilibrated tourism activity without disturbing the fragile Antarctic ecosystem.
- Tourism is legitimate, but it should be wisely managed and organized; there should be strong regulations on number and frequency, on the areas of visits as well as on the kind of tourism.
- The emphasis will be on "responsible" tourism activity—conducted in accordance with the Protocol and Treaty.
- There can be positive impacts of tourism on the Antarctic environment, especially of trips with minimal impact, [so] that passengers can become much more aware of Antarctica (all its aspects) and become promoters of good tourist practice in Antarctica and raise public awareness of specific Antarctic issues.

Academics

- Tourism will expand. This can please a lot of people [and] build political support for conservation and science but may threaten the environment. This is OK if managed cooperatively—governments, bases, operators, and public. Antarctic tourism can

serve as [a] model of ecotourism, and there are also applications for the Arctic. Antarctic tourism is in the economic interest of Argentina and Chile especially.
- Cultural heritage sites will become an increasingly important attraction but many will be damaged. Tourism will become increasingly associated with national claims. A future energy crisis will be the greatest limiting factor on tourism development.
- There is a need to recognize that different factors arise in different parts of Antarctica. I am not convinced voluntary codes of conduct will suffice.
- Private base hotels are likely, but most sites with ready access already have scientific stations built on these sites.
- Antarctic tourism will continue and diversify.
- Tourism should continue at present rate and level—the development of IAATO and USNSF monitoring policies are important developments to ensure environmental/sustainable tourism. The public has a right to visit the continent—especially since most tourists are well-educated and concerned visitors, and not the "sand/sea/sex" tourists of Caribbean/Tahiti resorts.

Antarctic Experts and Practitioners

- I would like my mum and my kids to be able to see [it]—after all, why should it be the preserve of [an] elite few?
- Tourism will inevitably grow and diversify, but the rate of growth and the scope of diversification are difficult to predict. It will expand its geographic extent—overcrowding will open new area[s], as will the use of icebreakers.
- Tourist operators have generally been quick to respond to concerns about their activities and have been keen to demonstrate that they can responsibly self-regulate. These responsible operators should be encouraged to continue in their good habits by national operators cooperating with them more closely.
- Tourism should be encouraged—assuming reasonable safeguards exist. An educated population will take steps to preserve the environment. One problem that may occur is that different countries have varying safeguards to minimize pollution.

Summary of the Opinions of the Panel

The following points sum up the collective opinions of the panel of Antarctic experts:

1. Tourism is a legitimate activity in Antarctica, and shipborne tourism is currently the most appropriate form. It is also seen as the most likely major form of Antarctic tourism in twenty-five years.
2. The majority of Antarctic tourism activities will continue to take place in the Antarctic Peninsula region.
3. The greatest barriers to the various scenarios raised by the panel were seen to be the cost of operating tours and, as a result, the costs to clients. Furthermore, issues of increased regulation of tourism under the ATS were raised.
4. More adventure products such as skiing, ballooning, and mountain climbing were seen as other tourist activities that might form part of the Antarctic tourism product.

Despite the great diversity of interests represented by panel members, responses received with regard to impacts and future directions of tourism were very similar. In summing up the panel's responses, it becomes clear that respondents did not foresee any drastic changes in the Antarctic tourism product. Instead, it seems that some fine tuning and diversification of existing shipborne products will take place.

Dennis Collaton, managing director of Adventure Associates (personal communication 1995), is also of the opinion that the Antarctic tourism product will continue to be delivered in its present form. He sees overflights as the only recent innovation and suggests that the more adventurous products will continue to serve only a small percentage of all travelers to Antarctica. Collaton also recognizes that the more ships operate in Antarctic waters, the greater the pressures will be on the wildlife sites visited.

As far as ship-based tours are concerned, the 1996-1997 circumnavigation of Antarctica was a product refinement rather than a new form of tourism. The 12,000-mile circumnavigation took place from November 24, 1996, to January 27, 1997, a total of sixty-six days, and started and finished in Stanley, Falkland Islands. The icebreaker *Kapitan Khlebnikov* carried around 100 passengers at a price of between US$29,990 per person in triple share accommodation and

US$39,900 in twin-share accommodation. Because of high costs to operators and clients, it is not expected that this type of product will be frequently available in the future (Denise Landau, personal communication 1996).

As outlined previously, the panel made the point that among "other" future tourism developments, it expected an increase in more adventurous tourism activities. This process has already started. In January 1996, Greg Mortimer conducted the first ship-based expedition for climbers and photographers. According to Mortimer (personal communication 1996), a group of thirty people spent a "night" camping on a snow ridge on Petermann Island at the southern end of the Lemaire Channel. Furthermore, the tourists climbed several mountains in the vicinity of the Lemaire Channel, including Mount Scott. As previously mentioned, such activities require at least an IEE to demonstrate that activities have no more than a transitory impact on the environment. This was prepared and subsequently approved by the Australian Antarctic Division.

Stonehouse (1995a) describes Petermann Island in the Scott Polar Research Institute (SPRI) publication *Management Recommendations for Visitor Sites in the Antarctic Region:*

> . . . over half of Petermann Island is ice covered . . . and snow cover persists on the ice-free stretches, well into January and February. . . . Visitors need to be warned that snow fields merge with ice caps . . . and the ice may be slippery, especially when thinly covered with fresh snow.

He lists the attractions of the island as penguins, skuas, Dominican gulls, Antarctic terns, blue-eyed shags, sheathbills, petrels, sea mammals, rocks, soils, and vegetation as well as scenic attractions. He makes the following important points with regard to the management of Petermann and the nearby Hovgaard and Pléneau islands:

> These islands provide relatively simple landings and safe local walking. Ease of access to the ice cliffs of Petermann Island is a possible hazard for over-enthusiastic walkers. There is little vegetation in need of protection: only the penguin colonies, the shags of Petermann Island, and the elephant seal wallows of Pleneau Island appear to need special management care. (Stonehouse 1995a:10-11)

Stonehouse's comments and the author's personal observations at the site make it clear that, provided all litter is taken back to the ship and portable toilet facilities are provided (as indeed they were during the Mortimer expedition), there is no reason to deny tourists the simple pleasure of spending a night ashore at suitable sites. According to Greg Mortimer (personal communication 1996), the camping and climbing activities received an overwhelmingly favorable response from clients. In December 1999, the author was engaged by Peregrine Adventures as a naturalist/guide and Zodiac driver and had the opportunity to participate in an overnight camp at Portal Point, the NE part of the Reclus Peninsula. The process went as follows. The expedition leader selected the site based on the criteria that it must be safe for passengers and not occupied by wildlife. Tents and sleeping bags were transported ashore by Zodiacs before passengers were landed. Once ashore, passengers were responsible for setting up their tents within the area specified by the expedition leader. In line with IAATO regulations, no food was taken ashore. A sealable plastic drum lined with a plastic garbage bag and filled with snow acted as a temporary toilet facility. At the completion of the camp the next morning the contents were returned for proper disposal aboard the cruise vessel. A total of forty people spent five hours camping ashore and all they left behind were their footprints in the deep snow and memories of a unique experience—having spent a night sleeping out on the Antarctic continent.

In this context, it is noteworthy that a proposal by the Canadian company Marine Expeditions to establish a permanent summer camp for tourists at Turret Point during the 1995-1996 season met with the resistance of other operators and that plans to establish the camp were subsequently dropped. In light of Stonehouse's assessment of Turret Point, this opposition appears to have had more to do with commercial aspects rather than concern for the local environment:

> A very acceptable alternative [to nearby Penguin Island]. There is ample room for walking in an interesting and varied habitat, without close surveillance. Wildlife, though plentiful and easily seen, is concentrated away from the main landing areas and thus far less vulnerable to disturbance. We should like to encourage more expedition leaders to visit Turret Point and fewer to visit Penguin Island, thus removing some of the pressures from an overburdened site. (Stonehouse 1995b:12)

The study found no strong evidence among panel members that airborne tourism, which would include landings on blue ice or rock runways, will be a major factor in Antarctic tourism in the early part of the twenty-first century. This contradicts Charles Swithinbank (personal communication 1993, 1996), who predicts that airborne tourism will expand using both ice runways and the present four conventional runways—Teniente Roldopho Marsh, Marambio, Dumont d'Urville, and Rothera—to take large numbers of tourists to the interior and eventually dominate Antarctic tourism. If Swithinbank's possible, but high-risk, scenario should become reality, Antarctica as a tourist destination would change significantly. As at other island destinations, Antarctic tourist arrivals would increase substantially should wide-bodied aircraft start to land paying tourists on the continent.

Several environmental groups have expressed concern that substantially increased tourist numbers in Antarctica would spoil the last great wilderness. In this context, it is again necessary to keep the size of Antarctica in mind: 14 million square kilometers—nearly twice the size of Australia. Impacts of airborne tourist arrivals would very much depend on where planes would land. Landing 400 passengers from a Boeing 747-400 near a penguin rookery or seal colony, of course, would be out of the question, and would never get approval under Madrid Protocol regulations.

On the other hand, landing the same number of people at an inland site on the South Polar Plateau, maybe somewhere near the geographic South Pole, and allowing them to stay a few days in the "South Pole Hotel" might not have an unacceptably high negative environmental impact since there is no life of any description that could be threatened by visiting tourists (apart from their own lives, of course). (There may, however, be impacts on the science conducted at the particular location.) In the opinion of this author, the Treaty Parties may find it difficult to reject a proposal to land a large civilian aircraft on an inland blue ice runway on environmental grounds. The argument of search and rescue (SAR) would of course be raised, but a commercial operator could insure against this risk, leaving the Treaty Parties with little reason to reject such a proposal. The most likely barrier to such a development taking place, however, is the associated commercial risk.

With regard to other future tourism developments, overflights of the continent will in all likelihood continue. The continued success of overflights from Australia will increasingly see bookings from overseas travelers, which will necessitate greater marketing efforts abroad. This in turn will lead to an increase in cost for the tour operator and hence may lead to higher airfares.

Trans-Antarctic flights from Australia to South America (the new airport in Ushuaia is capable of handling wide-bodied jets) and/or South Africa may also be considered again in the future. There are very few technical reasons why flights of this nature should not take place, and it appears that lack of demand and perhaps lack of aircraft availability may be stopping transpolar flights from becoming reality. In early December 1999, an Air France Concorde visited Ushuaia as a part of a round-the-world flight. There were rumors that the plane would return in January 2000 to undertake an overflight of the Antarctic Peninsula—a scary thought at the speed of sound.

Malcolm Clyde, then managing director of Barrier Reef Holdings, referring to the world's first floating hotel, is quoted by Sandilands (1988:15) as saying, "this is the way they will do the first resorts in Antarctica." Sandilands adds that plans for Antarctica are already afoot (presumably he was referring to the late 1980s "Project Oasis" near Davis in the AAT). The idea of floating hotels in the Antarctic may not be as far-fetched as it may seem at first glance, if one considers the technical specifications of the Floating Hotel (previously moored on the Barrier Reef and in Ho Chi Min City in Vietnam): "it is built with a re-enforced double hull in excess of naval specifications and divided into seven independently fire and flood proofed compartments capable of isolating an Ecocet attack or a collision with an iceberg" (Corbett, quoted by Sandilands 1988:15).

Setting up a scientific base that is entirely or partially funded by tourist visits and which could have scientists from around the world working on projects could successfully merge scientific and tourism interests. Scientific tourism, whereby visitors spend a few days or weeks at the station, could be looked at as an alternative form of tourism, albeit only for a very small number of people. There are numerous underutilized station buildings, such as the Chilean base Gonzales Videla at Waterboat Point in Paradise Bay, that could be used for this purpose. The establishment of such a facility and the subsequent encouragement for tour operators to visit the site could draw attention away from other scientific bases that for one reason or another do not wish to welcome tourists. If tourists directly contribute to the funding of the research, and in exchange are allowed to participate in some of the studies, both parties should be satisfied with the experience.

Another alternative could include developing a tourist facility near the ruins of the abandoned whaling stations at Grytviken or Stromness on South Georgia and to designate the area as a special tourist zone. Such a development may draw visitors away from the Antarctic continent itself. Tours from there to the nearby penguin, albatross, and seal sites could be easily organized and could be well controlled under the guidance of qualified naturalists.

FUTURE DEVELOPMENTS IN ANTARCTIC TOURISM

Potential Increase of Tourists from Asia

Compared to many other tourist destinations, Asian travelers are very underrepresented in Antarctica. During the 1999-2000 season, Asian tourists accounted for only 4 percent of all Antarctic travelers, and Japanese tourists made up 73 percent of all Asian arrivals (National Science Foundation 2000). Given that Asian travelers (in particular from Japan, South Korea, Taiwan, Malaysia, and Singapore) account for many of the arrivals in more mainstream destinations such as Australia and Hawaii, this small number of travelers to Antarctica is somewhat surprising. It does, however, also provide a great opportunity for operators who understand what their Asian clients are looking for. It is likely that Antarctic tourism product will have to be modified significantly if larger numbers of Asians are to be attracted. Given the limited time of vacation leave available to many Asian workers and the distance they have to travel just to get to the gateway ports, travel time is a crucial factor. If, for example, experiences with tour itineraries of Japanese visitors in Australia are an indication, it is highly likely that many of them would not be willing to put up with the length of time and inconveniences caused by crossing the Drake Passage. On many cruises aboard smaller vessels, four or five days are spent crossing and recrossing Drake Passage—a disproportionately long time, considering that the total length of many cruises to the Antarctic Peninsula is only eight to ten days. Weather conditions are also not always favorable and may cause planned landings to be cancelled. The high price of the Antarctic product can lead to considerable visitor dissatisfaction. To meet the needs of Asian travelers, luxurious ships may be used more frequently, perhaps on a cruise-only basis without landings (although vessels such as the *Marco Polo* have not made any great inroads into the Asian market).

To what extent Asian, in particular Japanese, tourists will embrace Antarctica as a tourist destination in the future, and the barriers that must be overcome to meet their needs, deserves further research in the source countries.

Air-Supported Seaborne Tourism

One possible product modification was outlined by Lars Wikander, president of Quark Expeditions, one of the largest Antarctic tour operators, during an address aboard the cruise vessel *Alla Tarasova* in December 1994. This was the possible upgrading of the existing landing strip at the Chilean base of Teniente Rodolfo Marsh on King George Island to allow passengers to fly across Drake Passage before being transferred to waiting cruise ships. Transfers could take place either by Zodiac or by constructing a pier, which could also serve the needs of the numerous scientific bases located on the island. Such a development would have a significant impact on Antarctic tourism. First, it would reduce the travel time to and from the destination: Drake Passage can be crossed by aircraft in two to three hours. Second, and more important, such a development would allow people to actually spend ten days in the Peninsula area instead of the present five.

Air-supported tourism would mean that tourists would have ten days of twenty-four-hour daylight to explore the Antarctic Peninsula. During this time they could potentially visit twice as many sites as are currently visited, which would almost certainly lead to increased demand for "new" and previously unvisited sites and an associated increase in length of stay ashore. From an environmental perspective, both factors have to be viewed with concern. Alternatively, instead of increasing the number of days visitors spend in the region, the same number of vessels currently operating in the region could make twice as many trips if they were based at, say, King George Island. From a commercial perspective such a scenario would appear to be highly desirable. Icebreakers such as the *Kapitan Khlebnikov* could regularly push further south past Marguerite Bay along the west coast of the Antarctic Peninsula.

The potential developments would increase visitor numbers, potentially doubling the current number of 10,000 to 15,000 passengers. In the long run, this could lead to overvisitation of certain sites. At present, the rough voyage across Drake Passage deters many potential travelers from visiting Antarctica. It acts as a buffer between South America and the South Shetland Islands/Antarctic Peninsula. If access was facilitated by flights to a place such as King George Island, this buffer would be taken away, and a new, perhaps less adventurous, less environmentally aware, and more pleasure-oriented type of tourist might begin to emerge in Antarctica.

If aircraft are introduced in any significant numbers to support shipborne tourism operations, Antarctic tourism may change from elite tourism to a form of mass tourism. Flights to King George Island are technically possible all year round using relatively small aircraft such as those used by Aerovias DAP Ltd. (DAP). Sooner or later, despite the adverse weather conditions in the landing area, a tourism entrepreneur will take up the challenge of flying large passenger loads to the South Shetland Islands in order to maximize profits from shipborne tourism operations.

One forerunner to such a development is the reported announcement (Australian Antarctic Division 2000) that the French company Crosieres Australes will coordinate fly-sail operations involving four yachts *(Sarah W. Vorwerk, Fernande, Kotick I,* and *Golden Fleece)* and connecting flights to and from the Argentine Station Marambio on Seymour Island. These trips could involve between seventy and eighty passengers. The Argentine company All Patagonia is understood to be in the process of developing fly-cruise tourism products for the 2001-2002 season that would center on Marambio station on Seymour Island. At the time of writing, there were few details available, but it appears that the company is planning to fly around seventy passengers at a time from Ushuaia aboard a C-130 "Hercules" aircraft to Marambio where they would board an as yet unnamed ice-strengthened vessel (Australian Antarctic Division 2000). Should this lead to significantly increased air-passenger numbers, stringent site management plans for all existing and future sites will have to be developed. The work currently carried out in the Peninsula by the Scott Polar Research Institute Project Antarctic Conservation team under Dr. Stonehouse, and the models used in places such as the Galapagos Islands and the sub-Antarctic islands of Australia and New Zealand, will be invaluable in the development of these management plans. Stonehouse (1995a, 1995b) has already produced *Management Recommendations for Visitor Sites in the Antarctic Region,* which covers recommendations for some of the most visited sites including Cuverville Island, Hannah Point, Petermann Island, Port Lockroy, Penguin Island, and Yankee Harbor.

Use of Underutilized Scientific Stations for Tourism Purposes

Unused scientific stations in the Peninsula area could perhaps be used by tourists. Stations such as the Chilean base of Gonzales Videla at Waterboat Point would lend itself as a site for an Antarctic visitor center and also for some "backpacker-type" accommodation. The area has one great advantage over most other sites: at low tide, visitors can actually walk across to the continent. Setting foot on the continent itself rather than the islands lying offshore is something that seems to be of great significance to tourists. Environmental organizations are opposed to any form of land-based tourism, but, where facilities already exist and where it can be shown that no negative environmental impacts will occur as a result of tourism, there would appear to be little reason not to use them. Provided that site-based tourism at abandoned (and possibly operating) stations is monitored, and that its operation abides by the guidelines set out under the Madrid Protocol and the Antarctic Treaty System, this form of tourism may well find a ready market. Small ships with a capacity of up to fifty passengers could drop visitors off, and they could spend a week exploring the environs of the station on foot and by Zodiac.

CONCLUDING COMMENTS

This chapter addressed the future of commercial Antarctic tourism by drawing on the collective expertise of a panel of experts. It is of interest to compare what has been said previously with what the industry itself thinks will happen. During the symposium "Polar Tourism: Environmental Implications and Management" (which the author attended), held at the Scott Polar Research Institute August 18-21, 1996, John Splettstoesser, speaking on behalf of IAATO, outlined what the organization saw as the most likely future scenarios for Antarctic tourism. The points made in his comments, provided as a one-page handout to the audience, are summarized here.

Shipborne

- Ten to fifteen ships/year, 6,000 to 10,000 visitors/year
- Russian-registered ships will continue, perhaps as majority
- Occasional large ships will skew figures, but many not ice-strengthened, and no landings are made

Airborne

- Adventure Network International has an eleven-year history
- Safety, environmental, operating record
- Temporary summer facilities only
- No threats to wildlife in the interior
- ANI can provide search and rescue for ATPs and tourism activities
- ANI acts as coordinator for emergencies—medical, ship grounding, rescue, etc.
- Overflights (Qantas, potentially Air New Zealand, Chilean, Argentinian)
- Other commercially scheduled airlines (Aerolineas Argentinas)

Yachts

- Probably become more popular, but more organized and coordinated
- Some yacht owners operating commercially
- Need better awareness of Protocol, protected areas, ATP contact offices, "Guidance for Visitors"

Adventure Tourism

- ANI involvement
- Excursions to South Pole, emperor penguin colonies, mountaineering
- Other: hang gliding, paragliding, parachuting, skiing, marathon runs, bicycling, crossings, glider or other aircraft, ballooning, golfing, winter tourism, shore camping, scuba diving, etc.
- No infrastructure; possible use of existing huts (e.g., Danco Island)

In summary, it is likely that cruises and overflights will continue to dominate Antarctic tourism for the foreseeable future. An increase in more adventurous activities has been noted over the past few years, and this trend is likely to strengthen, especially as younger and more energetic people gain the financial means to travel to Antarctica. Unless wide-bodied tourist aircraft will be allowed to land on runways located next to major accommodation facilities, it is unlikely that the number of tourists who set foot on Antarctica will reach more than 15,000 to 20,000 per season by 2010. It is hoped that future travelers who venture to the far south of the world will do so with respect for the places they visit, and that Antarctica will remain what it is today—the world's last great wilderness.

Chapter 8

Observations on the Operation of Tourism in Antarctica

SEABORNE TOURISM IN THE ANTARCTIC PENINSULA

The author made his first observations on how ship-based Antarctic tour operations are conducted and how visitors behave while ashore during two cruises to the Antarctic Peninsula, the Falkland Islands (Islas Maluinas), and to the island of South Georgia. Subsequent observations were made on a voyage to the Ross Sea in January-February 1997, and during December 1999, on two cruises to the Antarctic Peninsula, during which he was employed as naturalist, guide, lecturer, and Zodiac driver. During November and December 2000, he again headed south to participate in three cruises aboard the Peregrine Adventures vessel *Akademik Ioffe*. Observations aboard overflights were carried out during the 1995-1996 season.

The author first visited the Antarctic Peninsula region in December-January 1994-1995. Courtesy of Quark Expeditions, he was able to observe tourism operations and visitors aboard the Russian-registered cruise ships *Alla Tarasova* and *Professor Khromov*. The first voyage, aboard the *Alla Tarasova* (December 13 to December 30, 1994), began in the Falkland Islands (Islas Malvinas) (reached via a Linea Aereas Nacional [LAN] Chile charter flight from Santiago de Chile) and ended eighteen days later in Ushuaia, Argentina. On this voyage the *Alla Tarasova* (now the *Clipper Adventure*) carried sixty-three passengers and a mainly Russian crew of eighty-five. The second voyage, aboard the *Professor Khromov,* started and finished in Ushuaia and lasted from December 30, 1994 to January 8, 1995. The ship carried thirty-six paying passengers and had an all-Russian crew and an American expedition leader. Table 8.1 shows the sites and locations visited during the two cruises.

Site Management

During landings, visitors followed the guidelines issued by IAATO (during the voyage south lectures were given on how to behave while ashore) and kept their distance from the wildlife. There was only one incident, on Coronation Island in the South Orkney Islands, that may have led to some negative impacts on the site visited. A group of four people followed a guide in search of nesting sites of the elusive snow petrel. While they tried to avoid stepping on the mosses that covered most of the ground, some members of the group at times could not avoid leaving a footprint in the plants. While concentrating on selecting the next rock to jump on (to avoid damaging the mosses) members of the group inadvertently came too close to some nesting brown skuas. As a result, the birds left their nests and started to dive bomb. This disruption to the site was caused by a very small number of peo-

TABLE 8.1. Sites Observed in the Antarctic Peninsula Region

Falkland Islands	Stanley (visits to Carcass Island and Westpoint Island had to be canceled due to inclement weather conditions)
South Georgia	Zodiac cruises: Welcome Islets, Rosita Harbor, Hercules Bay, Larsen Harbor, Drygalski Fjord. Abandoned whaling stations: Grytviken, Stromness. Penguin colonies: Salisbury Plain, St. Andrews Bay, Cooper Bay. Wandering albatrosses: Albatross Island.
South Orkneys	Shingle Cove, Coronation Island
South Shetlands	Penguin Island, Arctowski (Polish Antarctic station on King George Island), Melchior Islands, Hydrurga Rocks, Half Moon Island, Hannah Point on Livingston Island
Sites off the Antarctic Peninsula	Cuverville Island, Palmer Station on Anvers Island, Torgersen Island, Petermann Island, Deception Island (Whalers Bay and Bailey Head)
Antarctic Peninsula	Waterboat Point, Almirante Brown (Esperanza Station was scheduled to be visited but could not be reached because of strong winds)
Other sites (only aboard ship)	Paradise Harbor, Neumayer Channel, Lemaire Channel, Cape Horn

ple, and the majority of visitors stayed with the expedition leader in another designated area. This observation highlights the fact that it is not the total number of visitors ashore that may be cause for concern, but small groups of well-meaning but overenthusiastic bird watchers and photographers who need to be monitored closely.

Unlike other maritime destinations, no landing fees are payable in the Antarctic. However, on South Georgia, the Falkland Islands, and Macquarie Island, landing fees are imposed on visiting ships. These range from US$50.00 on South Georgia to AUD$150.00 on Macquarie Island. Such a fee system could be adopted if visitor numbers to the Peninsula were to increase dramatically. Such funds could be used for site monitoring, interpretation, and management, including hardening of sites. Hardening is, of course, not a universally accepted concept, and it could well be argued that making a site more resistant to tourist visits could be an incentive for more visits. The previously mentioned visitor management experiment at Arctowski (Stonehouse, personal communication 1997) will set the standards in this respect. While hardening may be an option for some sites, others may have to be declared off-limits for a season or two to allow the site to recover. The Galapagos model of allocating visitor quotas to specific sites could also be investigated for highly popular sites. This could lead to a product differentiation, which in turn would lead to differential pricing. Dollar figures could be placed on the value of visiting different sites, and passengers would be charged accordingly. Locations such as Whalers Bay, where there is little risk of negative environmental impact from visitors, would be classified as "standard" sites, while locations such as Hannah Point that have high conservation values would be in the "premier" site category. The possibility of designating Sites of Special Tourist Interest, which has been raised by the Antarctic Treaty Parties, could be revisited in this context.

In the future, an effort should be made to improve the ratio of guides to clients. With the current ratio of one guide to every twenty passengers, it can be difficult for the guides to keep an eye on all the passengers in their care, especially if there is a relatively large ice-free area where they can walk. At times passengers are not asked to stay together in a group, and many take the chance to explore the close vicinity of the landing sites on their own. This is understandable from the visitor perspective—many people see Antarctica as the last frontier and while on an "expedition," as cruises are called in Antarctic waters, wish to feel as though they are explorers themselves. Unsupervised visitors may cause some unintended disturbance to the wildlife and flora of the sites they visit, and they may also endanger themselves by, for example, walking on unstable snow slopes. The provision of extra guides would assist in the process but may be resisted by the operators for economic reasons.

SEABORNE TOURISM IN THE ROSS SEA

In January and February 1997, the author visited the Ross Sea region aboard the *MS Bremen.* The voyage also included visits to the Auckland Islands, Campbell Island, and Macquarie Island. The twenty-day voyage started and ended in Hobart. Antarctic sites visited included Cape Adare, Cape Hallett, the Italian station Terra Nova, Cape Evans, Cape Bird, and the Ross Ice Shelf.

Compared to the Antarctic Peninsula, the Ross Sea region attracts only a small number of visitors. Cessford and Dingwall (1996) estimated 800, but the actual number might indeed be less. The region has several constraining factors that limit tourism:

1. The time spent in getting there is far greater than in the Peninsula area. It takes approximately three days to reach the Auckland Islands from Hobart. Campbell Island is another half day of sailing away, and, after a short stay ashore, passengers face another four days of sailing before they reach Antarctica at Cape Adare. This makes for a very long, at times rough and somewhat monotonous trip, which has to be repeated on the way back.
2. Most cruises include visits to the sub-Antarctic islands of New Zealand and Australia. Given that visitor numbers on these islands are restricted to between 500 and 600 passengers per season, the total number of visitors to the Ross Sea is also limited.
3. Climatic conditions, in particular pack ice, fast ice, currents, and wind make detailed plans for landings very difficult. During this author's cruise, planned landings at Possession Island and at Cape Royds were made impossible by climatic conditions. Several other landings, including Cape Adare and Cape Hallett, had to be kept brief because of concerns about changes in the weather.
4. Visits to McMurdo Station and Scott Base are restricted by the ice situation in the ice canal, which is cut through the fast ice by

a U.S. Coast Guard icebreaker at the beginning of the season and kept navigable until the last supply ship leaves in February. During this author's voyage an interesting situation arose. The *MS Bremen,* an ice-strengthened vessel capable of operating in 9/10-ice concentration (this means that most of the sea is covered with ice but there are still enough ice-free areas through which the vessel can travel), approached the northern end of the ice canal. The *Bremen* contacted the captain of the U.S. Coast Guard icebreaker *Polar Sea,* which was in the process of making its way out of the ice canal from McMurdo. The captain of the *Polar Sea* reported 10/10-ice concentration for a length of approximately four miles. Since he was unable (or unwilling) to remain in the area until the *Bremen* had completed her visit to McMurdo, the proposed and prearranged visit to the station had to be canceled. This incident poses at least two problems: (1) Does the NSF have a certain obligation to honor a previously granted permission to visit an American station and, if so, should they not have some influence over the Coast Guard icebreaker? (2) Given that the ice-canal is artificially created, one could argue that it is a man-made waterway and should therefore be treated as such. If a ship's itinerary promises a passage through the Suez or Panama Canal, the tour operator would be expected to have this passage prearranged. If a tugboat is required, the operator would have to arrange for it. Not to do so would most likely be seen as a breach of contract by passengers. It could be argued that the McMurdo ice canal is no different and that it is therefore the responsibility of the cruise operator to arrange for an icebreaker to be on standby whenever a visit to McMurdo is planned and advertised. Of course, this is not a cheap undertaking (and may indeed be very difficult to arrange), but if a visit is advertised in the brochure, and it is cancelled not because of the natural occurrence of ice but rather because of its presence in an artificially created canal, the operator may be liable.

5. The Ross Sea area is steeped in Antarctic history, and landings at the huts of Borchgrevink, Shackleton, and Scott are major attractions. Given that the wildlife in the region consists largely of Adélie penguins (and the odd emperor, gentoo, or chinstrap), however, one has to question whether the historic connection is strong enough to continue to attract passengers.

The management of tourism in the Ross Sea region is made easier by the fact that New Zealand exercises its rights over the Ross Dependency by insisting that a New Zealand observer be aboard the cruise vessels. The role of the observer is to ensure that historic huts are visited in the appropriate way (observers carry the keys to the historic huts), to determine whether landings should or should not be made if there is a particularly sensitive site nearby, and to protect the integrity of the wildlife and of SSSIs by posting lecturers at certain locations.

OPERATIONAL ISSUES

Supply of Vessels

Today Russian ships dominate Antarctic tourism. With the demise of the former Soviet Union, many vessels have become available for charter by companies based outside the Russian Federation. Many of the ships (for example, the *Akademik Boris Petrov, Professor Khromov, Professor Molchanov,* and the *Akademik Ioffe*) are former scientific vessels converted for tourism purposes. This sometimes involves converting the science laboratories into libraries and bars. An expedition leader pointed out that the Russian owners of the vessel do not make any money by operating Antarctic cruise ships. They are lucky if they break even. This raises the question of how long Antarctic tourism will continue in its present form. In the opinion of this author, ship-based Antarctic tourism will decline once Russian companies start charging full market rates for the use of their equipment and/or start organizing these cruises themselves.

Seasonality

Some cruises are undertaken very early in the season (November), when there is a strong possibility that sites on the Peninsula cannot be reached because of heavy pack ice concentrations. One of the reasons these cruises take place is that because of its remoteness, the Antarctic is only one region on a ship's international cruising schedule. Unlike year-round cruise destinations such as the islands of the Caribbean, no ships are permanently located in Antarctic waters. Vessels with their home ports in the Northern Hemisphere typically start their season by cruising the waters around Europe and the Arctic before moving across to North America, the Caribbean, and the coasts of South America. Thus they reach the Antarctic region by early to mid-November. The economics of shipping, like those of any capital-intensive mode of transport, dictate that the vessels must be constantly used in order to be profitable. Thus, even cruises early in the season that may have only very low occupancy rates will still contribute to covering part of the fixed costs of the ship's operations.

Staffing and Communications Issues

Ships sailing under the Russian flag are crewed by Russian nationals, which gives rise to several observations:

1. Crews may be experienced in the Arctic, but may not have Antarctic experience. Although pack ice may look the same in the North as it does in the South, local conditions nevertheless do vary. It would be prudent to require that at least one of the officers commanding the ship has previous Antarctic experience.
2. Communications between expedition leader and captain can be difficult if the leader does not speak Russian and the captain has only a very basic command of English. More stringent language requirements must be put in place to avoid misunderstandings. English language courses for crew members could be conducted on board to assist in the process.
3. Communication between ship's doctors and passengers is difficult if the doctor speaks only Russian and the passengers speak no Russian at all. Any medical officer hired to sail on Antarctic cruise ships must be able to communicate in English if serious mishaps are to be avoided. To address the problem, many companies now provide an English-speaking doctor in addition to the Russian physician.
4. Communication between hospitality staff and passengers can be a problem if no common language exists. Hospitality staff observed often could not communicate with passengers, thus making it awkward for passengers to place orders. A bar woman on board one of the ships (a music teacher from Murmansk) spoke German with all passengers, even though there were only two German-speaking passengers on board.
5. The long and continuous working hours for crew and staff during the three-to-four-month season are cause for concern. Staff

and crew do not get a chance to take a day off (the most they often get is a few hours' shore leave in Ushuaia between cruises). This does not allow them to recharge their batteries to be ready for the next group of passengers. Given that for many people Antarctica truly is the trip of a lifetime, a jaded crew that has already been across the Drake Passage numerous times during the season is not a very desirable prospect.

Zodiac Operations

Zodiacs are the mobile crafts most used in Antarctic tourism operations to land passengers on otherwise inaccessible shores. These boats have proven their worth on many occasions and, provided that they are operated with safety in mind, they pose very little threat to the Antarctic environment or to the tourists who ride in them. There are, however, several serious issues that must be addressed in order to ensure safe operations:

1. Zodiacs should not be in the water if the wind speed is higher than twenty to thirty knots, as there is a danger that they will flip over or be swamped by waves.
2. At least two Zodiacs must be in the water at any one time. On several occasion it was observed that this was not the case. During a landing at Baily Head, only one Zodiac was used to ferry passengers between ship and shore. Due to the absence of effective means of communication (no radio), it would have been impossible to launch the second Zodiac (which at the time was securely fastened on the aft deck of the ship) in time to rescue passengers should the first Zodiac have overturned. Furthermore, in what the author considered to be rough seas, the Zodiac went around Baily Head so passengers could observe penguins and leopard seals. This was an exciting excursion, but it took place out of sight of the ship and without radio communication. In light of the often-cited survival time of a human body in the near-freezing waters of the Antarctic (approximately four minutes), this is a highly dangerous practice. Similarly, during a Zodiac excursion in the Melchior Islands, the two Zodiacs operating became separated. The author traveled on a Zodiac driven by a non-English-speaking Russian sailor who had no radio with him and who had not ensured that the Zodiac was equipped

with a spare fuel tank. Several of the passengers urged the driver to reach a distant shore to observe blue-eyed shags and to get a closer look at some enormous icebergs. The excursion was certainly an exhilarating experience, but it highlighted the deficiencies in Zodiac operations during some cruises. Passengers were standing up in the boat to obtain a better viewing position, thereby threatening the safety of all aboard. Minimum safety standards must be enforced to ensure the safety of passengers on Zodiac excursions.

As a Zodiac driver aboard the *Akademik Boris Petrov* (operated by Peregrine Expeditions), the author experienced the way Zodiac operations should be run. All drivers received a comprehensive introduction to Zodiac operations and were given a detailed operations manual specifically designed for Antarctic conditions. Each Zodiac was equipped with two fuel tanks and carried emergency gear. Drivers were issued Mustang survival suits and waterproof two-way radios.

Accounting for Passengers

Various systems are in place to ensure that no passengers are accidentally left ashore. On board one of the vessels, passengers were requested to turn a tag that carried the cabin number to "red" when passengers departed the ship and to "white" after they had returned. Passengers were warned not to turn tags for each other, as this could lead to confusion and in the extreme to the abandonment of a passenger ashore. This system seemed to work well.

Another vessel used a different method. All passengers are required to wear life preservers before boarding the Zodiacs, which were normally placed on the beach while people explored the sites. The "accounting system" was that if a life preserver was still ashore, someone must also still be ashore. This author confused the system by inadvertently boarding a return Zodiac without wearing the life preserver.

Aboard the *Akademik Boris Petrov,* the names of passengers were counted off when they boarded the Zodiacs and were counted again when passengers came back on board. This system worked well since it uses face-to-face identification, which ensures the person has returned to the ship.

OBSERVATION OF ANTARCTIC OVERFLIGHTS

The flight observed was the first in a series of ten flights scheduled for the 1995-1996 season. After overflying the South Magnetic Pole at approximately 65 degrees south (the spinning compass was shown on the video screen), the Antarctic continent was reached at Dumont d'Urville but, due to heavy cloud cover, no Antarctic features could be seen. Likewise, Mawson's hut at Commonwealth Bay could not be seen because of the clouds. Soon after, near Cape Hudson, the clouds disappeared and the Antarctic continent showed itself in its entire splendor. From an altitude of 5,000 meters the viewing range was between 300 and 400 kilometers, and scenery viewed included glaciers, mountains, snowfields, and the massive Antarctic ice cap. Some of the geographical features observed during the three and a half hours above the continent included: Cape Hudson at the tip of the Mawson Peninsula, Mount Melbourne (a volcano), and Mount Minto, first climbed by a team of Australian climbers in 1988. Mounts Erebus and Terror could be seen in the distance. At Cape Adare the huts erected by Borchgrevink could clearly be seen. In addition, sea ice in various shapes and forms as well as icebergs trapped in the still solidly frozen sea ice could be detected. Overall, the viewing over Antarctica can only be described with clichés such as: fantastic, unbelievable, beautiful, spectacular. The written word is inadequate to describe the Antarctic scenery observed from an aircraft, and the many photographs taken during the flight will only do marginally better to provide people who have not traveled on the flight with an impression of the sheer magnificence of this, the last great wilderness area of the planet.

Technical Details

For the first time the aircraft used was a Qantas Boeing 747-400, equipped with the latest in technology and under the command of one of Qantas's most experienced captains. The aircraft took off with the fuel tanks filled to capacity, carrying a total of 170 tons of aviation jet fuel for the round trip to Antarctica. The captain stated that the aircraft burned 120 tons of fuel during the 11.5-hour flight and that it had a reserve of some 50 tons upon landing in Melbourne. This extra safety margin was seen as important should the aircraft have to change course and therefore have to stay in the air longer than anticipated.

Sixteen different flight paths were available to the captain. They all combined aspects of maximum safety and aerial viewing for the passengers. On this particular flight the course taken was as follows: Melbourne—Hobart—South Magnetic Pole—Dumont d'Urville—Commonwealth Bay—Mertz Glacier—Ninnis Glacier— Cape Hudson—Cape Washington—Mount Melbourne—Cape Hallett—Cape Adare—Hobart—Melbourne, a total distance of 9,000 kilometers.

Safety Issues

Passengers were introduced to the normal aerial safety procedures, including the use of life vests, and were shown the locations of the emergency exits. Interestingly, although the plane carried 408 survival suits (flotation body suits that enable a person to survive for some time in Antarctic waters, where the temperature is around −1.0 degree Celsius), passengers were not made aware of their existence and no instructions were given for how to put them on.

Prior to the resumption of these flights, the issue of flight safety had on occasion been raised. Antarctic overflights are, however, no more dangerous than the scheduled commercial flights between Australia/New Zealand and Argentina. During these so called "polar flights," aircraft overfly a region of the South Pacific Ocean that is within 2,000 miles of the geographic South Pole. In case of an emergency landing in the South Pacific there would be very little chance of rescuing the passengers alive—the nearest airport is thousands of miles away. Yet these flights take place regularly several times a week without any mishaps. It follows that Antarctic overflights carried out on one of the world's most reliable airlines do not pose an unacceptably high risk to those who want to see Antarctica from above.

CONCLUSION

Antarctica has always been and will always be a place for adventurous, curious, and exceptional people. Be they scientists, support staff, or tourists, their strongest motivation for wanting to set eyes on—and where possible set foot on—Antarctica is the lure of the unknown, relatively unexplored southern continent, which, like a giant ice cube, occupies the "bottom" of the world.

This book has investigated current and future developments in commercial Antarctic tourism. The research found that tourism in Antarctica is a legitimate use of Antarctic resources and that it compares favorably to other forms of resource use, including scientific research. Tourism activities are sustainable at present levels and do not have unacceptably high levels of negative impacts. The number of tourists, the modes of transport used, and the sites visited should nevertheless be monitored to ensure that the beauty of Antarctica is not spoiled.

As outlined in this book, commercial tourism has developed despite the harsh climate, but its conduct is only possible with the assistance of all interested parties. The future success of tourism will be measured by the satisfaction of paying visitors with their experience and by the degree of protection that the environment receives. To maximize visitor satisfaction and environmental protection, it is imperative that the cooperation between international tour operators, Antarctic Treaty Parties, and tourists is further developed and strengthened. All parties involved in Antarctic tourism have to date displayed a commitment to preserve the beauty of the continent for future generations, and continued close cooperation will ensure that Antarctic tourism remains what it is today, an outstanding model for international cooperation in the most remote corner of the world.

Antarctica is the final tourism frontier on earth, but it is by no means the final frontier of tourism. Much that has been learned from operating tours in the remote and hostile Antarctic climate—the need for meticulous preparations, self-reliance, safety consciousness, the best available equipment, and consciousness of the operating environment—will one day be of great value in the conduct of tourism in what will be the final human frontier—space.

OPPORTUNITIES FOR FUTURE RESEARCH

This book has investigated tourist profiles and attitudes aboard relatively small vessels. Future research activities could concentrate on passengers aboard large vessels such as the *Marco Polo* or the *Rotterdam* (which did not land passengers). It would be interesting to see whether passenger profiles and expectations on such large vessels differ from those aboard smaller ships. In particular, an investigation into their motivations for undertaking a cruise would be useful. It could be hypothesized that "cruise-by" passengers would be less eager to experience Antarctica and that they would perhaps share many of the characteristics of mainstream cruise passengers in other destinations such as the Caribbean.

Scope also exists to repeat the Delphi study to assess future tourism developments. This could be done in five-year intervals and with a different mix of panel members. Other research opportunities exist in the evaluation of the economic value of Antarctic tourism for gateway cities. Ushuaia, for example, now depends heavily on the annual arrival of thousands of Antarctic passengers.

Comparative research into the nexus between Antarctic and Arctic tourism would also be useful. Questions could address the issues of whether Arctic travelers differ significantly from Antarctic travelers, to what extent Arctic visitors rely on ships as their main mode of transport, and what image they hold of the Antarctic as a visitor destination.

The supply of rather inexpensive Russian vessels has made Antarctic tourism relatively affordable. It is unlikely that this supply of vessels will continue in the long run with the present cost structure. An investigation into the structures and policies of the suppliers of these vessels could be an interesting exercise.

Finally, biologists will no doubt continue to monitor human-wildlife interactions closely in order to establish beyond doubt whether tourists do have an impact on penguins, flying sea birds, and seals.

Bibliography

Acero, J.M. and Aguirre, C.A. 1994. "A monitoring research plan for tourism in Antarctica." *Annals of Tourism Research*, Vol. 21, No. 2, pp. 295-302.

ACF. 1990. Minutes of the 63rd Australian Conservation Foundation Council Meeting, June 9-11, Melbourne.

Adams, R. (Ed.) 1990. *Antarctica—Voices from the Silent Continent.* Hodder and Stoughton, London.

Adventure Associates 1995. "Complete Antarctic circumnavigation." *Adventure News* (Sydney), October, p. 1.

Adventure Associates 1996. *Adventure News* (Sydney), April, p. 2.

Adventure Network International 1992. Antarctic tour brochures. Darien, Connecticut.

Age, The, 1995. P & O Princess Alaska advertisement. January 21.

Allen, 1996. "Eco-resort set for approval." *The Weekend Australian: Property,* May 18-19, p. 2.

Anderson, M.J. 1991. "Problems with tourism development in Canada's eastern Arctic." *Tourism Management,* Vol. 12, No. 3, pp. 209-220.

"The Antarctic: Its potential for tourism" 1984. *Aurora ANARE Club Journal,* No. 14, pp. 44-45.

Antarctic News 1989. "Antarctic ship operators release joint environmental guidelines." Joint press release by Mountain Travel, Society Expeditions, and Travel Dynamics, November 6.

Antarctic Heritage Trust (Undated). "Visitors Guide to the Historic Huts of Antarctica." Christchurch, New Zealand.

Antarctic Treaty Parties 1991. *Governmental and Non-Governmental Activities Concerning the Protection of the Antarctic Environment* (Draft Annex to the Protocol). Madrid, April 22-30.

Antarctic Treaty Parties 1992. *Tourism and Non-Governmental Activities in the Antarctic Treaty Area—Agenda Item 13.* Venice, November 11-20.

Antarctica New Zealand 1996. *New Zealand's Future in Antarctica.* Author, Christchurch.

Antarctica project, 1997. "Recent evidence of climate change in the Antarctic." Newsletter, Vol. 6, No. 1, Washington, DC, p. 3.

Archer, B.H. 1987. "Demand forecasting and estimation." In Ritchie, J.R. Brent, and Goeldner, C.R. (Eds.), *Travel, Tourism and Hospitality Research.* Wiley, New York, pp. 77-85.

Arikaynen, A.I. 1991. "Sustainable development of the Soviet Arctic: Some possibilities and constraints." *Polar Record,* Vol. 27, No. 160, pp. 17-22.

Armstrong, J.S. 1985. *Long-Range Forecasting—From Crystal Ball to Computer.* Second Edition. Wiley, New York.

ASAC 1991. *Antarctic Research Priorities for the 1990s: A Review.* Australian Government Publishing Service, Canberra.

Ashford, D. and Collins, P. 1990. *Your Spaceflight Manual: How You Could Be a Tourist in Space Within Twenty Years.* Headline Book Publishing PLC, London.

ASOC 1997. "Letter to ASOC members." Antarctic and Southern Ocean Coalition, Auckland and Washington, July, p. 2.

Auburn, F.N. 1982. *Antarctic Law and Politics.* Croom Helm Australia, Canberra.

Australian Antarctic Division 1991. *ANARE News* (Tasmania). No. 67, September.

Australian Antarctic Division 1992. *ANARE Antarctic Field Manual,* Fourth edition. Kingston, Tasmania. Australian Antarctic Divison.

Australian Antarctic Division 1993. "The New Antarcticans: Tourism in the Ice." *ANARE News* (Tasmania). No. 73, Autumn pp. 3-12.

Australian Antarctic Division 1994. *Understanding Antarctica.* Series of information brochures, Kingston, Tasmania. Australian Antarctic Division.

Australian Antarctic Division 1995a. *ANARE NEWS,* Autumn, p. 36. Australian Antarctic Division, Tasmania.

Australian Antarctic Division 1995b. *Looking South: The Australian Antarctic Program in a Changing World.* Kingston, Tasmania. Australian Antarctic Division.

Australian Antarctic Division 2000. *Antarctic Non-Government Activity News* <http://www.antdiv.gov.au>.

Bailey, J. 1980. *Antarctica: A Traveller's Tale.* Angus and Robertson, Australia.

Ballantine, J.L. and Eagles, P.F.J. 1994. "Defining Canadian ecotourists." *Journal of Sustainable Tourism,* Vol. 2, No. 4, pp. 210-214.

Barnes, J.N. 1982. *Let's Save Antarctica.* Greenhouse Publications, Richmond, Victoria.

Barr, W. 1991. "Soviet cruise liner in collision with an ice floe near Svalbard." *Polar Record,* Vol. 27, No. 160, pp. 238-239.

Barrowclough, N. 1996. "Our forgotten polar hero." *The Age,* June 29, pp. 26-32.

Bates, G.M. 1983. *Environmental Law in Australia.* Butterworth, Sydney.

Bauer, E.A. 1974a. "Tourism comes to Antarctica." *Oceanus,* Vol. 7, No. 1, pp. 12-19.

Bauer, E.A. 1974b. "The race is on for Antarctica." *International Wildlife,* Vol. 4, No. 6, pp. 42-46.

Bauer, T.G. 1991. "Tourism in Antarctica—past, present and future." In Arthur, T. (Ed.), *Proceedings of the Royal Australian Institute of Parks and Recreation Conference,* Melbourne, Vol. 2, pp. 15/1-15/9. Royal Australian Institute of Parks and Recreation. Dickson ACT, Australia.

Bauer, T.G. 1994a. "The future of commercial tourism in Antarctica." *Annals of Tourism Research,* Vol. 21, No. 2, pp. 410-413. Arizona Hospitality Research and Resource Center. Northern Arizona University.

Bauer, T.G. 1994b. "Tourism development in remote areas—the case of Antarctica." *Proceedings of the Third International Seminar in Tourism Development,* Phoenix, Arizona, pp. 23-28.

Bauer, T.G. and Diggins, T. 1994. "Antarctic tourism: Yes or no." *Habitat,* Vol. 22, No. 3, pp. 32-36.

Bauer, T.G., Jago, L., and Wise, B. 1993. "The changing demand for hotel facilities in the Asia Pacific region." *International Journal of Hospitality Management,* Vol. 12, No. 4, pp. 313-322.

Bauer, T.G. and Shaw, N. 1995. *Voyage to Antarctica.* Video production, CALC Multimedia, Victoria University of Technology, Melbourne, Australia.

Bauer, T.G. and Shaw, N. 1998. *Voyage to Antarctica.* CD-ROM, CALC Multimedia, Victoria University of Technology, Melbourne, Australia.

Baumann, E.J. 1996. "Kreuzfahrten." In Mundt, J. (Ed.), *Reiseveranstaltung.* Oldenbourg Verlag, Munich and Vienna, pp. 295-322.

Bechervaise, J. 1963. *Blizzard and Fire.* Angus and Robertson, Sydney.

Bechervaise, J. 1978. *Men on the Ice in Antarctica.* Lothian Publishing Company, Melbourne.

Beck, P.J. 1986. *The International Politics of Antarctica.* Croom Helm, London.

Beck, P.J. 1988. "A continent surrounded by advice: Recent reports on Antarctica." *Polar Record,* Vol. 24, No. 151, pp. 285-289.

Beck, P.J. 1989. "UN goes green on Antarctica: The 1989 session." *Polar Record,* Vol. 26, No. 159, pp. 323-325.

Beck, P.J. 1990a. "Antarctica enters the 1990s: An overview." *Applied Geography,* Vol. 10, No. 4, pp. 247-263.

Beck, P.J. 1990b. "Regulating one of the last tourism frontiers: Antarctica." *Applied Geography,* Vol. 10, No. 4, pp. 343-356.

Beck, P.J. 1992. "The 1991 UN session: The environmental protocol fails to satisfy the Antarctic Treaty System's critics." *Polar Record,* Vol. 28, No. 167, pp. 307-314.

Beck, P.J. 1994. "Managing Antarctic tourism—A front burner issue." *Annals of Tourism Research,* Vol. 21, No. 2, pp. 375-386.

Bell, C. 1986. "Macquarie Island: Magnificent haven of the furious fifties." *Australian Geographic,* Vol. 1, No. 4, pp. 60-81.

Bickel, L. 1977. *This Accursed Land.* Macmillan, Sydney.

Black, J. and Champion, D.J. 1976. *Methods and Issues in Social Research.* Wiley and Sons, New York.

Blamey, R.K. 1995. *The Nature of Ecotourism.* Occasional Paper No. 21, Bureau of Tourism Research, Canberra.

Bly, L. 1989. "Antarctic tourism worries authorities." *Milwaukee Journal,* September 10 (unpaginated).

Boczek, B.A. 1988. "The legal status of visitors, including tourists and non-governmental expeditions in Antarctica." In Wolfrum, R. (Ed.), *Antarctic Challenge,* Vol. 3. Duncker and Humblot, Berlin, pp. 450-490.

Bogart, P.S. 1988. "Environmental threats in Antarctica." *Oceanus*, Vol. 31, No. 2, pp. 104-107.

Bond, C. and Sigfried, R. 1979. *Antarctica: No Single Country, No Single Sea*. Hamlyn Publishing Group, London.

Bonner, W.N. 1993. *Grytviken Whaling Station: An Introduction for Visitors*. South Georgia Whaling Museum, Grytviken, South Georgia. British Antarctic Survey, Cambridge.

Boo, E. 1990. *Ecotourism: The Potentials and Pitfalls*. World Wildlife Fund USA, Washington, DC.

Boo, E. 1992. *The Ecotourism Boom—Planning for Development and Management*. WHN Technical Paper Series, Paper #2, World Wildlife Fund, Washington, DC.

Boswall, J. 1968. "Every man's Antarctica." *The Listener*, July 11, pp. 40-41.

Boswall, J. 1986. "Airborne tourism 1982-84: A recent Antarctic development." *Polar Record*, Vol. 23, No. 143, pp. 187-191.

Bottrill, C.G. and Pearce, D.G. 1995. "Ecotourism: Towards a key elements approach to operationalising the concept." *Journal of Sustainable Tourism*, Vol. 3, No. 1, pp. 45-50.

Bowden, T. 1989. "Breaking the ice." *The Australian Magazine*, October 21-22, pp. 80-84.

Bowden, T. 1991. *Antarctica and Back in Sixty Days*. Australian Broadcasting Corporation, Crows Nest, Australia.

Bowden, T. 1997. *The Silence Calling*. Allen and Unwin, St. Leonards, Australia.

Bowermaster, J. 1994. "Antarctica: Tourism's last frontier." *Audubon*, Vol. 96, No. 4, pp. 90-98.

Brewster, B. 1982. *Antarctica: Wilderness at Risk*. Friends of the Earth, Sun Books, Melbourne.

British Antarctic Survey (Undated). *Food and Clothing*. BAS, Cambridge, U.K.

Bruchhausen, P. 1996. "The grounding and sinking of the 'ARA Bahia Paraiso.'" In Girard, L. (Ed.), *Ecotourism in the Polar Regions*, Proceedings of the Third Symposium on Polar Ecotourism, St. Petersburg, Russia, October 23-26, 1995, A Pas de Loup, Paris.

Budowski, G. 1976. "Tourism and environmental conservation: Conflict, coexistence or symbiosis?" *Environmental Conservation*, Vol. 3, No. 1, pp. 27-31.

Burke, D. 1994. *Moments of Terror: The Story of Antarctic Aviation*. New South Wales University Press, Sydney.

Burns, J. 1996. "Thrills and chills of Antarctica." *Sunday Herald-Sun*, Melbourne, March 10, p. 75.

Burrows, B., Mayne, A., and Newbury, P. 1991. *Into the 21st Century: A Handbook for a Sustainable Future*. Adamantine Press Ltd., Twickenham, U.K.

Bursey, J. 1957. *Antarctic Night*. Longmans, Green and Co., London.

Butler, R. 1988. *Breaking the Ice: Life and Work in the Frozen Wilderness of Antarctica*. Albatross Books, Sutherland, Victoria, Australia.

Butler, R. and Pearce, D. (Eds.) 1994. *Change in Tourism: People, Places, Processes.* Routledge, London and New York.

Byrd, R. 1930. "The conquest of Antarctica by air." *National Geographic,* August, pp. 127-227.

Calantone, R., Di Benedetto, C.A., and Bojanic, D. 1987. "A comprehensive review of the tourism forecasting literature." *Journal of Travel Research,* Fall, pp. 28-39.

Campbell, D.G. 1992. *The Crystal Desert: Summers in Antarctica.* Secker and Warburg, London.

Canadian Environmental Advisory Council 1991. *A Protected Areas Vision for Canada.* Supply and Services, Canada.

Cardozo, Y. and Hirsch, B. 1989. "Antarctic Tourism '89." *Sea Frontiers* (Miami), Vol. 35, No. 5, pp. 283-291.

Carr, T. and Carr, P. 1998. *Antarctic Oasis—Under the Spell of South Georgia.* Norton, New York.

Carter, M. 1994. "Eco-tourism opens way to Antarctica." *Campus Review,* July 21-27, p. 9.

Castellas, P. 1996. "Tip of the iceberg." *Conservation Gazette,* October, p. 1.

Ceballos-Lascurain, H. 1996. *Tourism, Ecotourism, and Protected Areas. The State of Nature-Based Tourism around the World and Guidelines for its Development.* IUCN, Gland, Switzerland, and Cambridge, United Kingdom.

Cessford, G.R. and Dingwall, P.R. 1994. "Tourism on New Zealand's sub-Antarctic Islands." *Annals of Tourism Research,* Vol. 21, No. 2, pp. 318-332.

Cessford, G.R. and Dingwall, P.R. 1996. *Tourist Visitors and Their Experiences at New Zealand Subantarctic Islands.* Science and Research Series No. 96, Department of Conservation, Wellington.

Chester, J. 1986. *Going to Extremes: Project Blizzard and Australia's Antarctic Heritage.* Doubleday, Sydney and Auckland.

Chester, S.R. 1993. *Antarctic Birds and Seals.* Wandering Albatross, San Mateo, California.

Chester, S. and Oetzel, J. 1995. *South to Antarctica: A Handbook for Antarctic Travelers.* Wandering Albatross, San Mateo, California.

Chidsey, D.B. 1967. *Shackleton's Voyage.* Universal Publishing and Distribution Corporation, New York.

Chipman, E. 1978. *Australians in the Frozen South: Living and Working in Antarctica.* Thomas Nelson, Melbourne.

Chipman, E. 1986. *Women on the Ice.* Melbourne University Press, Carlton South, Australia.

Christensen, T. 1990. *Tourism in Polar Environments—With Special Reference to Greenland and Antarctica.* Unpublished MPhil thesis, Scott Polar Research Institute, University of Cambridge.

Clark, N. 1995. "Being consoled? Virtual nature and ecological consciousness." *Futures,* Vol. 27, No. 7, pp. 735-747.

Cleveland, H. 1993. "The global commons." *The Futurist,* Vol. 27, No. 3, pp. 9-14.

Codling, R.J. 1982a. "The Antarctic experience." *Landscape Design*, November, pp. 14-16.

Codling, R.J. 1982b. "Sea-borne tourism in the Antarctic: An evaluation." *Polar Record*, Vol. 21, No. 130, pp. 3-9.

Codling, R.J. 1995. "The precursors of tourism in the Antarctic." In Hall, C.M. and Johnston, M.E. (Eds.), *Polar Tourism: Tourism in the Arctic and Antarctic Regions*. Wiley, Chichester, pp. 167-178.

Cold Regions Bibliography Project 1991-1997. *Current Antarctic Literature*. Vol. 18-24, Science and Technology Division, Library of Congress, Washington, DC, and Scott Polar Research Institute, University of Cambridge, Cambridge, U.K.

Collins, C. 1994. "Pioneer argues for tourism in Antarctica." *The Weekend Australian,* November 12-12, p. 8.

Collister, R. 1972. "Mountaineering in Grahamland." *Mountain,* No. 24, November, pp. 22-28.

Commonwealth Department of Tourism 1992. *Tourism—Australia's Passport to Growth: A National Tourism Strategy*. Australian Government Publishing Service, Canberra.

Commonwealth Department of Tourism 1994. *National Ecotourism Strategy*. Australian Government Publishing Service, Canberra.

Commonwealth Environment Department 1996. "Sub-Antarctic to be submitted for World Heritage listing." *World Heritage—Australian World Heritage News,* Vol. 1, No. 3, p. 1.

Conklin, D.W., Hodgson, R.C., and Watson, E.D. 1991. *Sustainable Development: A Manager's Handbook*. National Round Table on the Environment and the Economy, Ottawa.

Constant, P. 1999. *The Galapagos Islands*. Odyssey Publications, Hong Kong.

Cook, G. (Ed.) 1990. *The Future of Antarctica: Exploitation vs. Preservation*. Manchester University Press, Manchester.

Cooper, C.P. (Ed.) 1990. *Progress in Tourism, Recreation and Hospitality Management*, Vols. 1-3. Belhaven Press, London.

Corkill, J. (Ed.) 1987. *Tourism and the Conservation Movement*. Proceedings of the North Coast Environment Council's Conference, July 4-5, Grassy Head, New South Wales.

Cousteau, J.Y. 1976. "Reasonable Utopias." *Sierra Club Bulletin*, Vol. 16, No. 16, pp. 25-27.

Crossley, L. 1995. *Explore Antarctica*. Australian Antarctic Foundation and AUSLIG, Cambridge University Press. Cambridge, New York, Melbourne.

Croydon Travel 1995. *Antarctica: Fly to the Land of the Midnight Sun*. Travel brochure, Croydon, Australia.

Croydon Travel 1996. *Antarctica: Fly to the World's Last Great Wilderness*. Tour brochure, Croydon, Australia.

Croydon Travel 1997. *Antarctica*. Tour brochure, Croydon, Australia.

Cumpston, J.S. 1968. *Macquarie Island*. Australian Antarctic Division, Melbourne.

Curry, M., Curry, B., and Curry L. 1992. "Environmental issues in tourism management: Computer modelling for judgemental decisions." *International Journal of
Services Industry Management,* Vol. 3, No. 1, pp. 57-69.

Dammann, E. 1979. *The Future in Our Hands.* Pergamon Press, Oxford.

Davidson, K. 1989. "Journey to the end of the earth—Antarctica holds key role in
future of fragile planet." *San Francisco Examiner,* August 1.

Davis, B. 1987. "Heritage conservation in Antarctic and sub-Antarctic jurisdictions:
The case of Macquarie Island." *Maritime Studies,* Vol. 36, September/October,
pp. 22-27.

Davis, P. 1992. *Planning for a Changing Environment: Administration and Management of South Georgia.* Unpublished MPhil thesis, Scott Polar Research Institute, University of Cambridge.

de Groot, R.S. 1983. "Tourism and conservation in the Galapagos Islands." *Biological Conservation,* Vol. 26, pp. 291-300.

de Kadt, E. 1976. *Tourism, Passport to Development?* Oxford University Press,
New York.

Department of the Arts, Sport, the Environment and Territories 1992. *Antarctic Science—The Way Forward.* Australian Government Publishing Service, Canberra.

Department of the Arts, Sport, the Environment, Tourism and Territories 1991. *Antarctic Research Priorities for the 1990s: A Review.* Australian Government Publishing Service, Canberra.

Department of Lands and Survey, 1987. *Management Plan for the Auckland Islands
Nature Reserve.* Management Plan Series No. NR19, Department of Lands and
Survey, Wellington.

Dingwall, P. 1990. "Antarctic tourism." *IUCN Bulletin,* Cambridge, U.K., June,
pp. 9-10.

Dingwall, P. (Ed.) 1995. *Progress in Conservation of the Subantarctic Islands.* Proceedings of the SCAR/IUCN Workshop on Protection, Research and Management of Subantarctic Islands, Paimont, France, April 27-29, 1992, IUCN,
Cambridge, U.K.

Dingwall, P. and Walton, D.W.H. (Eds.) 1996. *Opportunities for Antarctic Environmental Education and Training.* IUCN, Cambridge, U.K.

Donachie, S.P. 1994. "Henryk Arctowski station—mixing science and tourism."
Annals of Tourism Research, Vol. 21, No. 2, pp. 333-343.

Droescher, V.B. 1996. "Sanfter Tourismus auf die unsanfte Art." *Welt am Sonntag,*
No. 12, March 24, p. 95.

Dukert, J.M. 1965. *This Is Antarctica.* Coward McCann, New York.

Dutton, I.M. 1987. "Environmental management of the proposed floating hotel at
John Brewer reef." *Maritime Studies,* Vol. 32, January/February, pp. 16-21.

Eadington, W.R. and Smith, V.L. 1992. "The emergence of Alternative Forms of
Tourism." In Smith, V.L. and Eadington, W.R. (Eds.), *Tourism Alternatives:
Potentials and Problems in the Development of Tourism* (pp. 1-13). The Univer-
sity of Pennsylvania Press, Philadelphia, Pennsylvania.

Echtner, C. and Ritchie, J.R.B. 1991. "The meaning and measurement of destination image." *The Journal of Tourism Studies,* Vol. 2, No. 2, pp. 2-12.

Ecotourism Association of Australia, 1992. Newsletter, Vol. 1, No. 1.

Edwards, K. and Graham, R. (Eds.) 1993. *Gender on Ice.* Proceedings of a conference on women in Antarctica, AGPS, Canberra.

Elliott, G.R. 1988. "Strategic marketing implications of the changing environment of Australian banking." *International Journal of Bank Marketing* (UK), Vol. 6, No. 5, pp. 5-13.

Encyclopaedia Britannica 1939. "Antarctic regions." Vol. 2, pp. 14-20.

Enzenbacher, D.J. 1991. *A Policy for Antarctic Tourism: Conflict or Cooperation?* Unpublished MPhil in Polar Studies thesis, Scott Polar Research Institute, Cambridge University.

Enzenbacher, D.J. 1992. "Tourists in Antarctica: Numbers and trends." *Polar Record,* Vol. 28, No. 164, pp. 17-22.

Enzenbacher, D.J. 1993. "Antarctic tourism: 1991/92 season activity." *Polar Record* 29 (170): 240-242, Scott Polar Research Institute, University of Cambridge, England.

Enzenbacher, D.J. 1994a. "Antarctic tourism: An overview of the 1992/93 season activity, recent developments, and emerging issues." *Polar Record,* Vol. 30, No. 173, pp. 105-116.

Enzenbacher, D.J. 1994b. "Tourism at Faraday station: An Antarctic case study." *Annals of Tourism Research,* Vol. 21, No. 2, pp. 303-317.

Enzenbacher, D.J. 1994c. "NSF and Antarctic tour operators meeting." *Annals of Tourism Research,* Vol. 21, No. 2, pp. 424-427.

Enzenbacher, D.J. 1995. "The regulation of Antarctic tourism." In Hall, C.M. and Johnston, M.E. (Eds.), *Polar Tourism: Tourism in the Arctic and Antarctic Regions.* Wiley, Chichester, pp. 179-216.

Erize, F.J. 1987. "The impact of tourism on the Antarctic environment." *Environment International,* Vol. 13, No. 1, pp. 133-136.

Evans, C. 1989. "A chilling idea: Tide of tourists at the South Pole—Cigarette butts and luggage tags." *The New York Times,* February 19, pp. 62-63.

Falvey, C. 1996. "QANTAS joins the jumbo mambo." *The Australian,* April 19, p. 27.

Far Horizons 1991. *Journey to Antarctica.* Tour brochure, Author, Tananda, South Australia.

Fiennes, R. 1993. *Mind Over Matter.* Sinclair-Stevenson, London.

Figgis, P. 1993. "Eco-tourism: Special interest or major direction?" *Habitat Australia,* Vol. 21, No. 1, February, pp. 8-11.

Finkel, G. 1976. *Antarctica: The Heroic Age.* William Collins Publishers, Sydney.

Flegg, J., Hosking, E., and Hosking, D. 1990. *Poles Apart: The Natural Worlds of the Arctic and Antarctic.* Pelham Books Ltd., London.

Fogg, G. 1992. *A History of Antarctic Science.* Cambridge University Press, Cambridge and New York.

Fogg, G.E. 1998. *The Biology of Polar Habitats.* Oxford University Press, Oxford.

Fothergill, A. 1993. *Life in the Freezer.* BBC Books, London.

Fox, R. 1985. *Antarctica and the South Atlantic: Discovery, Development and Dispute.* British Broadcasting Corporation, London.

Fraser, W. (Undated). Unpublished report for consideration by the Committee on Merchant Marine and Fisheries, Washington, DC.

Friday, L. and Laskey, R. 1991. *The Fragile Environment.* Cambridge University Press, Cambridge, U.K.

Frome, M. 1974. *Battle for the Wilderness.* Praeger Publishers, New York.

Frome, M. (Ed.) 1985. *Issues in Wilderness Management.* Westview Press, Boulder/London.

Fuchs, V. 1959. *Antarctic Adventure: The Commonwealth Trans-Antarctic Expedition 1955-58.* Cassell, London.

Fuchs, V. and Hillary, E. 1960. *Crossing of Antarctica.* Penguin Books, Mitcham, Victoria.

Galapagos National Park Service (Undated). *Rules for Visiting the Galapagos National Park.* Author, Puerto Ayora, Galapagos.

Galimberti, D. 1991. *Antarctica: An Introductory Guide.* Zagier and Urruty Publications, Miami Beach.

Galimberti, D. and Erdorf, R. 1993. *Antarktis Marco Polo Reisen mit Insider Tips.* Mairs Geographischer Verlag, Hamburg.

Galimberti, D. and Ucha, S. 1995. *Report on Antarctic Tourism Numbers Through the Port of Ushuaia 1994-95.* Instituto Fuegino de Turismo, Oficina Antartida, Ushuaia, Argentina.

Gartner, W.C. 1989. "Tourism image: Attribute measurement of state tourism products using multidimensional scaling techniques." *Journal of Travel Research,* 28, Fall, pp. 16-20.

Gauthier, D.A. 1992. "Sustainable development, tourism and wildlife." In Nelson, J.G., Butler, R., and Wall, G. (Eds.), *Tourism and Sustainable Development: Monitoring, Planning, Managing,* pp. 83-95. Heritage Resources Centre Joint Publication No. 1, University of Waterloo, Ontario, Canada.

Gell, R. 1989. *Antarctica—Future of a Frozen Wilderness.* Houghton Mifflin, Knoxfield, Victoria.

Gibson, L.J. and Miller, M.M. 1990. "A Delphi model for planning 'pre-emptive' regional economic diversification." *Economic Development Review,* Vol. 8, No. 2, pp. 34-41.

Girard, L. (Ed.) 1996. *L'Ecotourisme en milieu polaire (Ecotourism in the Polar region).* Proceedings of the Third Symposium on Polar Ecotourism, St. Petersburg, Russia, October 23-26, A Pas de Loup, Paris.

Glover, S. 1994. "Skating on thin ice: Can Antarctica survive the tourism traffic?" *Australian Geographic,* Vol. 16, No. 5, pp. 24-39.

Gonzales, A. Jr. 1970. "Tourists are getting a foothold on the Antarctic wasteland." *The New York Times,* May 24, p. 29.

Goodman, R.D. 1990. *Antarctica.* Letter to the Editor, *The New York Times,* June 17.

Goodrich, R. 1989. "Dentist tells of trek to South Pole." *St. Louis Post Dispatch,* January 25.

Gorman, J. 1990. *The Total Penguin.* Prentice Hall, New York.

Gray, G.J. 1990. *Tourism in the Antarctic: Current Developments and Future Potential.* Unpublished dissertation for postgraduate diploma in tourism, University of Otago, Dunedin, New Zealand.

Greely, A.W. 1896. "The scope and value of Arctic exploration." *National Geographic,* Vol. 7, No. 1.

Green, H., Hunter, C., and Moore, B. 1990a. "Application of the Delphi technique in tourism." *Annals of Tourism Research,* Vol. 17, pp. 270-279.

Green, H., Hunter, C., and Moore, B. 1990b. "Assessing the environmental impact of tourism development: Use of the Delphi technique." *Tourism Management,* Vol. 11, No. 2, pp. 111-120.

Greenpeace, (Undated). *Deutscher Tourismus in der Antarktis.* Hamburg, Germany.

Greenpeace, (Undated). *The Impact of Tourism in Antarctica.* Greenpeace information sheet.

Grenier, A. 1998. *Ship-Based Polar Tourism in the Northeast Passage: A Case Study.* University of Lapland Publications in the Social Sciences, Rovaniemi, Finland.

Grosvenor, G.H. 1899. "Plans for reaching the South Pole." *National Geographic,* Vol. 10, No. 8, pp. 316-319.

Grotta, D., Grotta, S., and Fisher, A. 1992. "Antarctica: Whose continent is it anyway?" *Popular Science,* Vol. 240, No. 1, pp. 62-70.

Gunn, C. 1988. *Tourism Planning.* Taylor and Francis, New York.

Gunn, C. 1994. *Tourism Planning,* Third Edition, Taylor and Francis, Washington, DC.

Gupta, U.G. and Clarke, R. 1996. "Theory and applications of the Delphi technique: a bibliography (1975-1994)." *Technological Forecasting and Social Change,* 53(3), pp. 185-211, Elsevier Science, New York.

Gurney, A. 1997. *Below the Convergence.* Norton, New York.

Hall, C.M. 1992a. *Wasteland to World Heritage: Preserving Australia's Wilderness.* Melbourne University Press, Carlton South, Australia.

Hall, C.M. 1992b. "Tourism in Antarctica: Activities, impacts, and management." *Journal of Travel Research,* Vol. 30, No. 9, pp. 2-9.

Hall, C.M and Johnston, M.E. (Eds.) 1995a. *Polar Tourism: Tourism in the Arctic and Antarctic Regions.* Wiley, Chichester.

Hall, C.M. and Johnston, M.E. 1995b. "Introduction: Pole to pole: Tourism issues, impacts and the search for a management regime in polar regions." In Hall, C.M. and Johnston, M. (Eds.), *Polar Tourism: Tourism in the Arctic and Antarctic Regions,* Wiley, Chichester, pp. 1-26.

Hall, C.M. and McArthur, S. (Eds.) 1996. *Heritage Management in Australia and New Zealand—The Human Dimension.* Oxford University Press, Melbourne.

Hall, C.M. and Wouters, M. 1994. "Managing nature tourism in the sub-Antarctic." *Annals of Tourism Research,* Vol. 21, No. 2, pp. 355-374.

Hall, C.M. and Wouters, M. 1995. "Issues in Antarctic tourism." In Hall, C.M. and Johnston, M.E. (Eds.), *Polar Tourism: Tourism in the Arctic and Antarctic Regions,* Wiley, Chichester, pp. 147-166.

Hall, L. 1988. "Manhaul to Mt. Minto." *Australian Geographic,* No. 12, Oct-Dec. pp. 28-49.

Hall, L. and Chester, J. 1989. *The Loneliest Mountain: The Dramatic Story of the First Expedition to Climb Mt. Minto, Antarctica.* Simon and Schuster, Brookvale, New South Wales.

Hamilton, R.A. (Ed.) 1958. *Venture to the Arctic.* Penguin Books Ltd., Harmondsworth, U.K.

Handmer, J. (Ed.) 1989. *Antarctica: Policies and Policy Development.* Centre for Resource and Environmental Studies, Australian National University, Canberra.

Handmer, J. and Wilder, M. (Eds.) 1993. *Towards a Conservation Strategy for the Australian Antarctic Territory.* The 1993 Fenner Conference on the Environment, Centre for Resource and Environmental Studies, Australian National University, Canberra.

Hanseatic Tours 1995. "Passenger numbers during the 1994/95 season." Internal document, Hanseatic Tours, Hamburg.

Hansom, J. and Gordon, J. 1998. *Antarctic Environments and Resources—A Geographical Perspective.* Longman, New York.

Harris, S. (Ed.) 1984. *Australia's Antarctic Policy Options.* CRES Monograph 11, Centre for Resource and Environmental Studies, Australian National University, Canberra.

Harrowfield, D.L. 1988. "Historic sites in the Ross Dependency—Antarctica." *Polar Record,* Vol. 24, No. 151, pp. 277-284.

Harrowfield, D.L. 1990. "Conservation and management of historic sites in the Ross Dependency." In Hay, J.E., Hemmings, A.D., and Thom, N.G. (Eds.), *Antarctica 150: Scientific Perspectives—Policy Futures* (pp. 55-66). Proceedings of a conference organized by Environmental Science at the University of Auckland, September 8, 1990, Environmental Science Occasional Publication No. 5, Environmental Science, University of Auckland, New Zealand.

Hart, P.D. 1988. "Bound for 60 south—Taxes, tips, and transfers included: The growth of Antarctic tourism." *Oceanus,* Vol. 31, No. 2, pp. 93-100.

Hay, J.E. (Ed.) 1992. *Ecotourism Business in the Pacific: Promoting a Sustainable Experience.* Conference proceedings, Environmental Science, University of Auckland and East West Centre, Honolulu, Hawaii.

Hay, J.E., Hemmings, A.D., and Thom, N.G. (Eds.) 1990. *Antarctica 150: Scientific Perspectives—Policy Futures.* Proceedings of a conference organized by Environmental Science at the University of Auckland, September 8, 1990, Environmental Science Occasional Publication No. 5, Environmental Science, University of Auckland, New Zealand.

Heacox, K. 1998. *National Geographic Destinations: Antarctica, the Last Continent.* The Book Division, National Geographic Society, Washington, DC.

Headland, R. 1989. *Chronological List of Antarctic Expeditions and Related Events.* Cambridge University Press, Cambridge, U.K.

Headland, R.K. 1992a. *The Island of South Georgia.* Cambridge University Press, Cambridge, U.K.

Headland, R.K. 1992b. "Delimitation and administration of British dependent territories in Antarctic regions." *Polar Record,* Vol. 28, No. 167, pp. 315-318.

Headland, R.K. 1993. "Polar treaties and committees." *Polar Record,* Vol. 29, No. 168, pp. 1-12.

Headland, R.K. 1994. "Historical development of Antarctic tourism." *Annals of Tourism Research,* Vol. 21, No. 2, pp. 269-280.

Headland, R.K. and Keage, P.L. 1985. "Activities on the King George Island group, South Shetland Islands, Antarctica." *Polar Record,* Vol. 22, No. 140, pp. 475-484.

Healy, R.G. 1988. *Economic Consideration in Nature-Oriented Tourism: The Case of Tropical Forest Tourism.* FPEI Working Paper No. 39. Research Triangle Park, North Carolina: Forest Private Enterprise Initiative.

Heap, J. (Ed.) 1990. *Handbook of the Antarctic Treaty System,* Seventh Edition. Polar Publications, Scott Polar Research Institute, University of Cambridge.

Heap, J.A. 1991. "Has CCAMLR worked? Management policies and ecological needs." In Joensen-Dahl, A. and Ostreng, W. (Eds.), *The Antarctic Treaty System in World Politics.* Macmillan in association with the Fridtjof Nansen Institute, London.

Hedgpeth, J. 1970. "Discussion on tourism." In Holdgate, M.W. (Ed.), *Antarctic Ecology.* Academic Press, London, p. 952.

Herber, B.P. 1992. "The economic case for an Antarctic world park in light of recent policy developments." *Polar Record,* Vol. 28, No. 167, pp. 293-300.

Herr, R.A. 1993. "Antarctic tourism: Australia, regulation and the industry." In Handmer, J. and Wilder M. (Eds.), *Towards a Conservation Strategy for the Australian Antarctic Territory* (pp. 91-107), Centre for Resource and Environmental Studies, Australian National University, Canberra.

Herr, R.A. and Davis, B.W. (Eds.) 1994. *Asia in Antarctica.* Centre for Resource and Environmental Studies, Australian National University with Antarctic Cooperative Research Centre, Canberra.

Herr, R.A., Hall, H.R., and Haward, M.G. (Eds.) 1990. *Antarctica's Future: Continuity or Change?* Tasmanian Government Printing Office for Australian Institute of International Affairs, Hobart.

Higham, T. (Ed.) 1991. *New Zealand's Sub-Antarctic islands—A guidebook.* Department of Conservation, Invercargill, New Zealand.

Holdgate, M.W. 1987. "Changing habitats of the world." *Oryx,* Vol. 21, No. 3, pp. 149-159.

Holdgate, M.W. 1990. "Antarctica: Ice under pressure." *Environment*, Vol. 32, No. 8, pp. 5-9, 30-33.

Holdgate, M. 1996. *From Care to Action: Making a Sustainable World.* IUCN, Earthscan Publications, London.

Holzhauer, J.D. 1991. "Nature's wonderland frozen in time." *The Times*, August 24.

Honey, M. 1999. *Ecotourism and Sustainable Development: Who Owns Paradise?* Island Press, Washington, DC.

Honnywill, E. 1984. *The challenge of Antarctica.* Anthony Nelson, Shropshire, U.K.

Hooper, M.A. 1991. *Facts and Stories from the Frozen South.* Piccolo Books, London.

House of Representatives Standing Committee on Environment, Recreation and the Arts 1989. *Tourism in Antarctica: Report of the House of Representatives Standing Committee on Environment, Recreation and the Arts.* Australian Government Publishing Service, Canberra.

House of Representatives Standing Committee on Legal and Constitutional Affairs 1992. *Australian Law in Antarctica.* Australian Government Publishing Service, Canberra.

Hughes, J. 1994. "Antarctic historic sites: The tourism implications." *Annals of Tourism Research,* Vol. 21, No. 2, pp. 281-294.

Hughes, J. and Davis, B. 1995. "The management of tourism at historic sites and monuments." In Hall, C.M. and Johnston, M.E. (Eds.), *Polar Tourism: Tourism in the Arctic and Antarctic Regions.* Wiley, Chichester, pp. 235-256.

Hummel, M. (Ed.) 1989. *Endangered Spaces: The Future for Canada's Wilderness.* Key Porter Books, Toronto.

Hunter, C. and Green, H. 1995. *Tourism and the Environment: A Sustainable Relationship?* Routledge, London and New York.

Huntford, R. 1979. *Scott and Amundsen: The Race to the South Pole.* Hodder and Stoughton, London.

Huntford, R. 1985. *Shackleton.* Hodder and Stoughton, London.

Hurley, F. 1956. *Shackleton's Argonauts.* Angus and Robertson, Sydney.

Hutchinson, C. 1992. "Environmental issues: The challenge for the chief executive." *Long Range Planning,* Vol. 25, No. 3, pp. 50-59.

Hutchinson Encyclopedia 1995. Tenth edition, Helicon Publishing, Oxford, England.

IAATO 1992a. *Guidelines of Conduct for Antarctica Visitors.* International Association of Antarctica Tour Operators, Office of the Secretariat, New York.

IAATO 1992b. *Guidelines of Conduct for Antarctica Tour Operators.* International Association of Antarctica Tour Operators, Office of the Secretariat, New York.

IAATO 1995. *IAATO News.* International Association of Antarctica Tour Operators, November, Office of the Secretariat, New York.

IAATO 1996. *IAATO News.* International Association of Antarctica Tour Operators, July, Office of the Secretariat, New York.

IAATO 2000. Home page <http://www.iaato.org>.

ICAIR 1995. *Newsletter.* International Centre for Antarctic Information and Research, Christchurch, July.

Info-Svalbard, 1999. *Spitsbergen.* Information brochure, Info-Svalbard, Longyearbyen.

INFUETUR 1994. *Informe sobre el Transito de Turismo Antarcticoa Traves de Ushuaia.* Instituto Fueguino de Turismo, Oficina Antartida, Ushuaia.

INFUETUR 1995. *Informe sobre el Transito de Turismo Antarticoa Traves de Ushuaia.* Instituto Fueguino de Turismo, Oficina Antartida, Ushuaia.

Inskeep, E. 1991. *Tourism Planning: An Integrated and Sustainable Development Approach.* Van Nostrand Reinhold, New York.

IUCN 1991. *A Strategy for Antarctic Conservation.* International Union for the Conservation of Nature, Cambridge, U.K.

Janiskee, R. 1991. "Ecotourism in Antarctica: Too much of a good thing?" Presented at the annual meeting of the Association of American Geographers, Miami.

Joensen-Dahl, A. and Ostreng, W. (Eds.) 1991. *The Antarctic Treaty System in World Politics.* Macmillan in association with the Fridtjof Nansen Institute, London.

Johnson, P. and Thomas, B. 1992. *Choice and Demand in Tourism.* Mansell Publishing, London.

Johnson, S. 1985. *Antarctica—The Last Great Wilderness.* George Weidenfeld and Nicholson Ltd., London.

Johnston, M.E. 1995. "Patterns and issues in Arctic and sub-Arctic tourism." In Hall, C.M. and Johnston, M.E. (Eds.), *Polar Tourism: Tourism in the Arctic and Antarctic Regions.* Wiley, Chichester, pp. 27-42.

Johnston, M.E. and Hall, C.M. 1995. "Visitor management and the future of tourism in polar regions." In Hall, C.M. and Johnston, M.E. (Eds.), *Polar Tourism: Tourism in the Arctic and Antarctic Regions.* Wiley, Chichester, pp. 297-313.

"Jumbo jet to Antarctica" 1977. *Aurora ANARE Club Journal,* Midwinter, pp. 95-100.

Kaltenborn, B. 1993. "Tourism in the high North: management challenges and recreation opportunity spectrum planning in Svalbard, Norway." *Environmental Management,* Vol. 17, No. 1, pp. 41-50.

Kaltenborn, B. and Hindrum, R. 1996. *Opportunities and Problems Associated with the Development of Arctic Tourism—A Case Study from Svalbard.* Directorate for Nature Management, Trondheim, Norway.

Keage, P.L. and Quilty, P.G. 1988. "Future directions for Antarctic environmental studies." *Maritime Studies,* No. 38, January/February, pp. 1-12.

Keltie, J.S. 1897. "The unmapped areas on the earth's surface." *National Geographic,* September, pp. 264-265.

Kerlinger, F.N. 1973. *Foundations of Behavioral Research,* Second Edition. Holt, Rinehart and Winston, New York.

King, H. (Ed.) 1982. *South Pole Odyssey: Selections from the Antarctic Diaries of Edward Wilson.* Rigby Publishers, Adelaide and Sydney.

Kirwan, L.P. 1961. *A History of Polar Exploration.* Penguin Books, Harmondsworth, U.K.

Knight, R.L. and Cole, D.N. 1995. "Wildlife responses to recreationists." In Knight, R.L. and Gutzwiller, K.J. (Eds.), *Wildlife and Recreationists: Coexistence Through Management and Research.* Island Press, Washington, DC, pp. 51-69.

Knight, R.L. and Gutzwiller, K.J. (Eds.) 1995. *Wildlife and Recreationists: Coexistence Through Management and Research.* Island Press, Washington, DC.

Knight, S. 1988. *Icebound: The Greenpeace Expedition to Antarctica.* Century Hutchinson, Auckland.

Kostyal, K.M. 1990. "Antarctica: Voyage to the bottom of the earth." *National Geographic Traveler,* May/June, pp. 45-61.

Kriwoken, L.K. 1991. "Antarctic environmental planning and management: Conclusions from Casey, Australian Antarctic Territory." *Polar Record*, Vol. 27, No. 160, pp. 1-8.

Laseron, C. 1957. *South with Mawson,* Second Edition. Angus and Robertson, Sydney.

Law, P.G. 1977. "Possibilities for exploitation of Antarctic resources." In Vicuna, F.O. and Araya, A.S. (Eds.), *Desarrollo de la Antartida.* Editorial Universitaria, Santiago de Chile, pp. 24-37.

Law, P.G. 1983. *Antarctic Odyssey.* Heinemann, Richmond, Australia.

Law, P.G. 1989. "Developers would but scratch Antarctica." *The Age,* April 26, p. 7.

Laws, R. 1989. *Antarctica: The Last Frontier.* Boxtree Limited, London.

Leat, P. undated. *The Geology of Antarctica.* The British Antarctic Survey, Cambridge, U.K.

Ledingham, R. 1993. "Reflections of an Antarctic tour guide." *ANARE News*, No. 73, pp. 6-7.

Lemonick, M.D. 1990. "Antarctica: Is any place safe from mankind?" *Time*, No. 3, January 15, pp. 36-40.

Levich, S.V. and Fal'kovich, N.S. 1987. "Recreation and tourism in the Southern Ocean and Antarctica." *Polar Geography and Geology,* (pp. 94-102) Vol. 11, April/June.

Lewis, D. 1979. *Voyage to the Ice: The Antarctic Expedition of SOLO.* Australian Broadcasting Commission, Sydney.

Lewis, D. and George, M. 1987. *Icebound in Antarctica.* William Heinemann Australia, Richmond, Victoria.

Ley, W. 1974. *The Poles.* LIFE Nature Library, TIME-LIFE books, TIME-LIFE International, Amsterdam.

Lindberg, K. 1991. *Policies for Maximizing Nature Tourism's Ecological and Economic Benefits.* International Conservation Financing Project working paper, World Resources Institute, Washington, DC.

Lindberg, K., Enriquez, J., and Sproule, K. 1996. "Ecotourism questioned: Case studies from Belize." *Annals of Tourism Research,* Vol. 23, No. 3, pp. 543-562.

Linstone, H.A. and Turoff, M. (Eds.) 1975. *The Delphi Method: Techniques and Applications.* Addison-Wesley, Reading, Massachusetts.

Lipps, J.H. 1978. "Man's impact along the Antarctic Peninsula." In Parker, B. (Ed.), *Environmental Impact in Antarctica.* pp. 333-383. Virginia Polytechnic Institute and State University, Blacksburg, Virginia.

Liversidge, D. 1958. *The Last Continent.* Jarrolds Publishers, London.

Logan, H.F.M. 1990. "Tourism and other activities." In Hay, J.E., Hemmings, A.D., and Thom, N.G. (Eds.), *Antarctica 150: Scientific Perspectives—Policy Futures.* Proceedings of a conference organized by Environmental Science at the University of Auckland, September 8, Environmental Science Occasional Publication No. 5, Environmental Science, University of Auckland, New Zealand, pp. 53-54.

Lovering, J.F. and Prescott, J.R.V. 1979. *Last of Lands: Antarctica.* Melbourne University Press, Carlton South, Australia.

Lyons, D. 1993. "Environmental impact assessment in Antarctica under the Protocol on Environmental Protection." *Polar Record,* Vol. 29, No. 169, pp. 111-120.

MacCannell, D. 1989. *The Tourist—A New Theory of the Leisure Class.* Schocken Books, New York.

MacDonald, E.A. 1969. "Antarctic tourists are not crazy." *Explorers Journal,* Vol. 47, No. 3, pp. 198-202.

MacFarland, C. 1991. "The enchanted and endangered Galapagos Islands: The opportunity to create a model for ecotourism." *Ecotourism, Society Press Briefing,* National Press Club, Washington, DC. May 30.

Mahon, P. 1984. *Verdict on Erebus.* Collins, Auckland, New Zealand.

Manzoni, M. and Pagnini, P. 1996. "The symbolic territory of Antarctica." *Political Geography,* Vol. 15, No. 5, pp. 359-364.

Marine Expeditions 1995. "Tour brochure for the Polar Regions." Marine Expedition, Toronto.

Marsh, J. 1991. "The characteristics of a sample of tourists visiting Antarctica." Paper presented at the annual meeting of the Ontario division of the Canadian Association of Geographers, University of Ottawa, October 26.

Marsh, J. 2000. "Tourism and National Parks in Polar Regions." In Butler, R.W. and Boyd, S.W. (Eds.) (pp. 125-136), *Tourism and National Parks: Issues and Implications.* John Wiley & Sons, Ltd. Chichester, New York, Weinheim, Brisbane, Toronto, Singapore.

Marsh, J. and Staple, S. 1995. "Cruise tourism in the Canadian Arctic and its implications." In Hall, C.M. and Johnston, M.E. (Eds.), *Polar Tourism: Tourism in the Arctic and Antarctic Regions,* Wiley, Chichester, pp. 63-72.

Martin, S. 1996. *A History of Antarctica.* State Library of New South Wales Press, Sydney.

Maslen, G. 1989. "Seven weeks in kingdom of ice." *The Age,* September 19, p. 11.

Mason, P. 1994. "A visitor code for the Arctic." *Tourism Management,* Vol. 15, No. 2, pp. 93-97.

Mathieson, A. and Wall, G. 1982. *Tourism: Economic, Physical and Social Impacts.* Longman, London and New York.

Mawson, D. 1996. *The Home of the Blizzard: The Story of the Australasian Antarctic Expedition 1911-1914.* Wakefield Press, Kent Town, South Australia.

May, J. 1988. *The Greenpeace Book of Antarctica.* Dorling Kindersley Ltd., London.

May, V. 1991. "Tourism, environment and development: Values, sustainability and stewardship." *Tourism Management,* Vol. 12, No. 2, June, pp. 112-118.

McAuliffe, S. 1995. "Strange wonders in a strange land." *Omni,* Vol. 17, No. 4, pp. 56-64.

McGonigal, D. 1995. "Castles of ice and everlasting day." *Australian Accountant,* May, pp. 65-72.

McGowan, A. 1987. "Historical archaeology at Cape Denison, Commonwealth Bay, Antarctica." *Polar Record,* Vol. 24, No. 149, pp. 101-110.

McIntosh, R.W., Goeldner, C.R., and Ritchie, J.R.B. 1995. *Tourism—Principles, Practices, Philosophies,* Seventh Edition. Wiley, New York.

McIntyre, D. and McIntyre, M. 1996. *Two Below Zero.* Australian Geographic, Terry Hills, New South Wales.

Mear, R. and Swan, R. 1989. *In the Footsteps of Scott.* Grafton Books, London.

Mentha, J.L. and Watson, G.F. 1992. *Education, Antarctica, Marine Science and Australia's Future.* Proceedings of the Phillip Law 80th Birthday symposium, April 29, 1992. Royal Society of Victoria, Melbourne.

Mercer, D. 1995. *"A Question of Balance": Natural Resources Conflict Issues in Australia,* Second Edition. Federation Press, Annandale, New South Wales.

Messner, R. 1990. *Antarktis, Himmel und Hoelle zugleich.* Piper, Munich, Germany.

Mickleburgh, E. 1990. *Beyond the Frozen Sea: Visions of Antarctica.* Paladin Grafton Books, London.

Migot, A. (Undated). *The Lonely South.* The Travel Book Club, London.

Milbrath, L.W. 1989. *Envisioning a Sustainable Society: Learning Our Way Out.* State University of New York Press, Albany, New York.

Mill, R.C. 1990. *Tourism: The International Business.* Prentice Hall International Editions, Englewood Cliffs, New Jersey.

Miller, M.J. 1981. *Roald Amundsen—First to the South Pole.* Hodder and Stoughton, Kent.

Ministry of Environment 1992. *Experience Svalbard on Nature's Own Terms.* Norwegian Ministry of Environment. Oslo.

Ministry of Environment and Ministry of Supply and Services 1991. *Ellsmere Island Newsletter.* Ottawa.

Moeller, G.H. and Shafer, E. 1987. "The Delphi technique: A tool for long-range tourism and travel planning." In Ritchie, J.R. and Goeldner, C.R. (Eds.), *Travel, Tourism and Hospitality Research.* Wiley, New York, pp. 417-431.

Monteath, C. 1988. "Tourism grows where no latitude for error exists." *The Press,* Christchurch, New Zealand. June 15, unpaginated.

Monteath, C. 1996. *Antarctica: Beyond the Southern Ocean.* Harper Collins Publishers, Sydney.

Montgomery, B. 1994. "Politics reflect environmental assets." *The Australian*, November 5-6, p. 29.

Montgomery, B. 1996. "Tourist plan to build runway in Antarctica." *The Australian*, September18, p. 4.

Moore, G. 1968. "To Antarctica by sea." *Pacific Discovery*, Vol. 21, No. 4, pp. 10-15.

Moore, M. 1988. "Antarctica—Miners cast their eye on glittering prize." *Habitat*, Vol. 16, No. 4.

Mosley, G. 1986. *Antarctica: Our Last Great Wilderness*. Australian Conservation Foundation, Hawthorn, Victoria, Australia.

Mosley, G. 1989. "A vision within our reach—World Park for Antarctic." *Habitat*, Vol. 17, No. 5, pp. 4-7.

Motive Market Research 1990. *Assessing the Reaction of Christchurch Residents to the Concept of an Antarctic Exhibition Centre*. Motive Market Research, St. Kilda, Victoria, Australia.

Mueller-Schwarze, D. 1984. "Possible human impacts on penguin populations in the Antarctic Peninsula area." *Antarctic Journal of the United States*, special issue, Vol. 19, No. 5, pp. 158-159.

Mueller-Schwarze, D. and Belanger, P. 1978. "Man's impact on Antarctic birds." In Parker, B. and Holliman, M.C. (Eds.), *Environmental Impact in Antarctica*. Virginia Polytechnic and State University, Blacksburg, Virginia, pp. 373-383.

Murray-Smith, S. 1988. *Sitting on Penguins: People and Politics in Australian Antarctica*. Hutchinson Australia, Surrey Hills, New South Wales.

Mussack, I.E.L. 1988. *An Approach to the Management of Tourism in the Antarctic*. Unpublished MSc. thesis, University of Canterbury and Lincoln College, New Zealand.

Nagle, R. 1990. *Penguins*. Mallard Press, Moorebank, New South Wales.

Nash, R.F. 1989. *The Rights of Nature: A History of Environmental Ethics*. University of Wisconsin Press, Madison, Wisconsin.

National Research Council 1993. *Science and Stewardship in the Antarctic*. National Academy Press, Washington, DC.

National Science Foundation 1991a. *Antarctic News Clips*. NSF, Washington, DC.

National Science Foundation 1991b. "Protecting Antarctica: Progress in Chile." *Antarctic Journal of the USA*, Vol. 26, No. 1, pp. 4-11.

National Science Foundation 1991c. "Preserving Antarctica: Treaty nations agree on new environmental protocol." *Antarctic Journal of the USA*, Vol. 26, No. 4, pp. 1-19.

National Science Foundation 1992. *Antarctic News Clips*. NSF, Washington, DC.

National Science Foundation 1993. *Antarctic News Clips*. NSF, Washington, DC.

National Science Foundation 1995a. *Antarctic News Clips*. NSF, Arlington, Virginia.

National Science Foundation 1995b. *Antarctic Conservation Act of 1978*. NSF, Arlington, Virginia.

National Science Foundation 1996. *8th Antarctic Tour Operators Meeting Agenda/ Handouts*. NSF, Arlington, Virginia, July 11.

National Science Foundation 1997a. *9th Antarctic Tour Operators Meeting Agenda/Handouts,* NSF, Arlington, Virginia.

National Science Foundation 1997b. *The United States in Antarctica: Report of the US Antarctic Program External Panel*. NSF, Arlington, Virginia.

National Science Foundation 1998. *10th Antarctic Tour Operators Meeting Agenda/ Handouts*. NSF, Arlington, Virginia.

National Science Foundation 1999. *11th Antarctic Tour Operators Meeting Agenda/ Handouts*. Hamburg, Germany.

National Science Foundation 2000. *12th Antarctic Operators Meeting Agenda/ Handouts*. Hobart, Tasmania, Australia.

Naveen, R. 1991. "The promise of Antarctic tourism." *The Antarctic Century,* No. 7, p. 1.

Naveen, R. 1992. "Recommendations for managing visitors and tourists under the Antarctic Treaty System." Paper presented at the conference Le Tourisme dans les Regions Polaires, Colmar, Alsace, France, April 21-23.

Nelson, J.G., Butler, R., and Wall, G. (Eds.) 1993. *Tourism and Sustainable Development: Monitoring, Planning, Managing*. Department of Geography Publication Series No. 37, University of Waterloo, Quebec, Canada.

New Zealand Antarctic Program 1992. *Antarctic Operations Manual*. Christchurch.

New Zealand Antarctic Research Programme 1993. *Tourist Procedures During Visits to the Ross Dependency*. Christchurch. New Zealand Antarctic Programme.

New Zealand Antarctic Society 1966. "Flight to Chilean base." *Antarctic,* June, p. 293.

New Zealand Antarctic Society 1970a. "Tourists to Antarctica pose ecological threat." *Antarctic,* Vol. 5, No. 12, December, p. 499.

New Zealand Antarctic Society 1970b. "No Antarctic air service before 1972-73 summer." *Antarctic,* Vol. 5, No. 12, December, pp. 500-501.

New Zealand Antarctic Society 1971a. "Tourists find new frontier." *Antarctic,* Vol. 6, No. 1, p. 36.

New Zealand Antarctic Society 1971b. "No concessions to Antarctic tourists." *Antarctic,* Vol. 6, No. 2, p. 51.

New Zealand Antarctic Society 1972a. "Tourist ship aground in South Shetlands." *Antarctic,* Vol. 6, No. 5, March p. 175.

New Zealand Antarctic Society 1972b. "Grounded tourist ship not seriously damaged." *Antarctic,* Vol. 6, No. 6, June p. 219.

New Zealand Antarctic Society 1977a. "First day—Trips to Antarctica." *Antarctic,* Vol. 8, No. 1, March pp. 35-38.

New Zealand Antarctic Society 1977b. "60 hut visitors." *Antarctic,* Vol. 8, No. 1, March p. 23.

New Zealand Antarctic Society 1977c. "Antarctic Centre links eras of exploration." *Antarctic,* Vol. 8, No. 1, March pp. 39-40.

New Zealand Antarctic Society 1977d. "Tourism: Antarctic day-trips by airlines." *Antarctic,* Vol. 8, No. 3, September p. 100.

New Zealand Antarctic Society 1978. "More Antarctic cruises planned next season." *Antarctic,* June pp. 206-207.

New Zealand Antarctic Society 1979. "Plane crash on Mt. Erebus kills 257." *Antarctic,* December pp. 410-412.

New Zealand Antarctic Society 1991a. "Obituaries: Kershaw—legend in a lifetime." *Antarctic,* Vol. 12, No. 1, pp. 28-31.

New Zealand Antarctic Society 1991b. "Antarctic Treaty: Comprehensive protection of Antarctic environment overtakes Minerals Convention." *Antarctic,* Vol. 12, No. 4, pp. 102-104.

New Zealand Antarctic Society 1991c. "Treaty Nations reviewing second draft of Protocol covering environment protection." *Antarctic,* Vol. 12, No. 5, pp. 159-163.

New Zealand Antarctic Society 1991d. "July update: Decision on environmental protection protocol temporarily deferred." *Antarctic,* Vol. 12, No. 6, pp. 199-200.

New Zealand Antarctic Society 1991e. "Visit Antarctica with Quark Expeditions." *Antarctic,* Vol. 12, No. 6, p. 205.

Nicholson, I.E. 1986. "Antarctic tourism—The need for a legal regime?" In Wolfrum, R. (Ed.), *Antarctic Challenge,* Vol. 2. Duncker and Humblot, Berlin, pp. 191-203.

Nimon, A., Schroter, R., and Stonehouse, B. 1995. "Heart rate of disturbed penguins." *Nature,* Vol. 374, No. 30, p. 415.

Nimon, A.J. and Stonehouse, B. 1996. "Penguin responses to humans in Antarctica: Some issues and problems in determining disturbance caused by visitors." In Dann, P., Norman, I., and Reilly, P. (Eds.), *The Penguin: Biology and Conservation.* Surrey Beatty and Sons, Chicago, pp. 420-439.

Norris, B. 1974. "Organized parties no threat in Antarctic." *Antarctic,* Vol. 7, No. 2, pp. 63-64.

Norwegian Ministry of Justice 1993. *Regulations Relating to Tourism and Other Travel in Svalbard.* Oslo.

Nunavut Vacation Planner 1998. <http://www.arctic-travel.com/chapters/flypage.html>. Nunavut Tourism, Iqualuit, Canada.

Nuttall, M. 1998. *Protecting the Arctic: Indigenous Peoples and Cultural Survival.* Harwood Academic Publishers, Amsterdam.

O'Baugh, S. 1995. "The greatest adventure." *Weekend Melbourne Herald-Sun,* October 4, pp. 4-5.

OECD 1980. *The Impact of Tourism on the Environment.* Organization for Economic Corporation and Development, Paris.

Oesterreichischer Alpenverein 1989. *Sanfter Tourismus Theorie und Praxis.* Innsbruck, Austria.

Ommanney, D. 1940. *South Latitude Readers.* Union Limited, London.

Ono, R. and Wedemeyer, D.J. 1994. "Assessing the validity of the Delphi technique." *Futures,* Vol. 26, No. 3, pp. 289-304.

Orams, M.B. 1995. "Towards a more desirable form of ecotourism." *Tourism Management,* Vol. 16, No. 1, pp. 3-8.

Orchard, M. 1970. "Caretaker at Cape Royds." *Antarctic,* Vol. 5, No. 10, pp. 415-417.

Orient Lines 1995. *Antarctica 1995-96.* Tour brochure, Sydney.

Orient Lines 1997. *Antarctica 97/98.* Tour brochure, Sydney.

Parfit, M. 1988. *South Light: A Journey to Antarctica.* Bloomsbury Publishing, London.

Parks and Wildlife Service Tasmania 1993. *One of the Wonder Spots of the World: Macquarie Island Reserve.* Department of Environment and Land Management, Hobart, Tasmania.

Parson, A. 1989. *Antarctica—The Next Decade.* David Davies Memorial Institute of International Studies, Cambridge University Press, Cambridge, U.K.

Patri, J. 1983. *Les Activités Touristiques en Milieu Polaire: Le Case du Continent Antarctique.* Unpublished MA thesis, University of Chile, Santiago.

Peregrine Adventure 1996. *Expedition Cruises Antarctica, the Arctic and Beyond.* Tour brochure, Melbourne, Australia.

Peregrine Adventures 2000. *Antarctica and Islands of the South Atlantic.* Tour brochure. Melbourne, Australia.

Perry, R. 1973. *The Polar Worlds.* A.H and A.W. Reed, Wellington, New Zealand.

Peterson, M.J. 1988. *Managing the Frozen South: The Creation and Evolution of the ATS.* University of California Press, Berkley and Los Angeles.

Pinochet de la Barra, O. 1988. *Antartida: Suenos de Ayer y del Manana.* Ediciones Pedagogicas Chilenas S.A., Santiago, Chile.

Pizam, A. 1987. "Planning a tourism research investigation." In Ritchie, J.R. and Goeldner, C. (Eds.), *Travel, Tourism, and Hospitality Research.* John Wiley and Sons, New York, pp. 63-76.

Pizam, A. and Sussmann, S. 1995. "Does nationality affect tourist behaviour?" *Annals of Tourism Research,* Vol. 22, No. 4, pp. 901-917.

Plage, D. and Plage, M. 1988. "Galapagos wildlife under pressure." *National Geographic,* Vol. 173, No. 1, pp. 123-145.

Plimmer, N. 1993. *Antarctic Tourism: Issues and Outlook.* PATA Occasional Papers Series No. 10, Pacific Asia Travel Association, San Francisco.

Plog, S.C. 1974. "Why destination areas rise and fall in popularity." *Cornell Hotel and Restaurant Administration Quarterly,* Vol. 15, November, pp. 13-16.

Polar Journeys and World Expeditions 1996. *Journeys to the Polar Regions.* Tour brochure, Sydney.

Poles Apart 1993. *IEE Adventure Network International: Antarctic Air Operations.* Adventure Network International, Darien, Connecticut.

Poles Apart 1994. *Environmental Audit: Antarctica and Southern Ocean Cruises of Quark Expeditions.* Quark Expeditions Inc., Darien, Connecticut.

Poncet, S. and Poncet, J.D. 1991. *Southern Ocean Cruising.* Beaver Island, Falkland Islands.

Ponting, H.G. 1927. *The Great White South.* Duckworth, London.

Poon, A. 1994. "The new tourism revolution." *Tourism Management,* Vol. 15, No. 2, pp. 91-92.

Pound, R. 1966. *Scott of the Antarctic.* World Books, London.

Price, M.F. (Ed.) 1996. *People and Tourism in Fragile Environments.* John Wiley and Sons, Chichester.

Priddle, J. undated. *Antarctic Seas.* The British Antarctic Survey, Cambridge, U.K.

Priddle, J. undated. *Antarctic Whales and Seals.* The British Antarctic Survey, Cambridge, U.K.

Pyne, S.J. 1986. *A Journey to Antarctica.* University of Iowa Press, Iowa City, Iowa.

Qantas 1995. *Tourist Overflights of the Antarctic Continent by QANTAS Airways— Post Activity Report.* Sydney.

Qantas 1996. *Tourist Overflights of the Antarctic Continent by Qantas Airways— Post Activity Report,* Qantas Airways, Sydney.

Quark Expeditions 1994. *Antarctica: The Ross Sea and Subantarctic Islands.* Tour brochure, Quark Expeditions, Darien, Connecticut.

Quigg, P.W. 1983. *A Pole Apart: The Emerging Issue of Antarctica.* McGraw-Hill, New York.

Quilty, P. 1990. "The modern environment of Antarctica." *National Parks Journal,* September, pp. 22-26.

Radisson Seven Seas Cruises 1996. *Adventure Series MS Hanseatic.* Tour brochure, Radisson, Fort Lauderdale.

Ralling, C. 1983. *Shackleton.* British Broadcasting Corporation, London.

Ralston, K. 1993. *A Man for Antarctica: The Early Life of Phillip Law.* Hyland House, South Melbourne.

Reader's Digest 1985. *Antarctica—Great Stories from the Frozen Continent.* Reader's Digest, Surry Hills, New South Wales.

Reader's Digest 1990. *Antarctica: The Extraordinary History of Man's Conquest of the Frozen Continent.* Reader's Digest, Surry Hills, New South Wales.

Reader's Digest 1992. *Book of Australian Facts.* Reader's Digest, Surry Hills, New South Wales.

Reedy, J.R. 1964. "Flight across the bottom of the world." *National Geographic,* March, pp. 459-464.

Reich, R.J. 1979. *Tourism in the Antarctic: Its Present Impact and Future Development.* Unpublished thesis for the Diploma in Polar Studies, Scott Polar Research Institute, Cambridge University.

Reich, R.J. 1980. "The development of Antarctic tourism." *Polar Record,* Vol. 20, No. 126, pp. 203-214.

Reinke-Kunze, C. 1996. *Entdeckungsfahrten in die Polarregionen: Antarktis.* Koehler Verlagsgesellschaft, Hamburg.

Reuning, W. 1994. *Antarctic Journal of the United States—Review 1994.* Vol. 29, No. 5, National Science Foundation, Arlington, Virginia.

Richardson, J. 1993. *Ecotourism and Nature-Based Holidays.* Choice Books, Simon and Schuster, Marrickville, New South Wales, Australia.

Ritchie, J.R.B. and Goeldner, C.R. 1987. *Travel, Tourism and Hospitality Research: A Handbook for Managers and Researchers.* John Wiley and Sons, New York.

Roberts, B. 1978. "International co-operation for Antarctic development: The test for the Antarctic Treaty." *Polar Record,* Vol. 28, No. 119, pp. 107-120.

Robeson, J.F. 1988. "The future of business logistics: A Delphi study predicting future trends in business logistics." *Journal of Business Logistics,* Vol. 9, No. 2, pp. 1-14.

Robinson, J.B. 1990. "Futures under glass: A recipe for people who hate to predict." *Futures,* October, pp. 820-842.

Rogers, B.R. 1990. *Galapagos.* Mallard Press, Moorebank, New South Wales.

Rogers, S. 1995. "Expedition South." *Weekend Financial Review,* January 20, p. 5.

Rohde, H. 1989. *Submission to the House of Representatives Standing Committee on Environment, Recreation and the Arts Inquiry in the Antarctic.* Rohde and Partners, Rozelle, New South Wales, Australia.

Rollins, R. 1998. "Using social science research in the management of coastal wilderness settings." In Miller, M.C. and Auyong, J. (Eds.), *Proceedings of the 1996 World Congress on Coastal and Marine Tourism* (June 19-22, 1996, Honolulu, Hawaii) (pp. 165-172). Seattle, WA: Washington Sea Grant Program and the School of Marine Affairs, University of Washington and Oregon Sea Grant College Program, Oregon State University.

Rothblum, E.D., Weinstock, J.S., and Morris, J.F. 1998. *Women in the Antarctic.* The Haworth Press, Binghamton, New York.

Rubin, G. 1996. *Antarctica.* Lonely Planet, Melbourne.

Ryan, C. 1991. *Recreational Tourism—A Social Science Perspective.* Routledge, London.

Ryan, C. 1995. *Researching Tourist Satisfaction.* Routledge, London.

Sandilands, B. 1988. "Tourism has its eyes on Antarctica." *The Bulletin,* February 9, p. 34.

Sanson, L. 1992. "New Zealand's subantarctic islands: A case study in the development of ecotourism policy." In Hay, J. (Ed.), *Ecotourism Business in the Pacific: Promoting a Sustainable Experience* (pp. 141-150). Conference Proceedings Environmental Science, University of Auckland and East West Centre, Honolulu, Hawaii.

Sanson, L. 1994. "An ecotourism case study in sub-Antarctic islands." *Annals of Tourism Research,* Vol. 21, No. 2, pp. 344-354.

Santelmann, N. 1992. "The big ice cube." *Forbes,* September 28, pp. 146-152.

SCAR 1980. *A Visitor Guide to Antarctica.* Scientific Committee on Antarctic Research, Cambridge, U.K.

SCAR 1996. "Decisions, measures, and resolutions adopted at the XIXth Antarctic Treaty Consultative Meeting Seoul, Korea, 8-19 May 1995." *Polar Record,* Vol. 32, No. 181, pp. 184-195.

Schatz, G.S. 1981. "Protecting the Antarctic environment." *Oceanus,* Vol. 31, No. 2, pp. 101-103.

Schillat, M. 1994. *Feuerland: Eine Grenzregion im Spannungsfeld internationaler Interessen 1520-1915.* LIT Verlag, Hamburg.

Scholes, A. 1951. *Fourteen Men: The Story of the Australian Antarctic Expedition to Heard Island.* Allen and Unwin Ltd., London.

"Scientists, tour operators limit cruises to Antarctica." *San Diego Examiner,* January 15.

"A Scotia Arc cruise with Lindblad Explorer" 1983. *Aurora ANARE Club Journal,* No. 8, pp. 9-11.

Scott, J.M. 1947. *The Pole of Inaccessibility.* Hodder and Stoughton, London.

Scott, J. 1993. "Antarctic Peninsula tourism: A guide's impressions." *ANARE News,* No. 73, pp. 12-14.

Scott, J.J. and Kirkpatrick, J.B. 1994. "Effects of human trampling on the sub-Antarctic vegetation of Macquarie Island." *Polar Record,* Vol. 30, No. 174, pp. 207-220.

Scott, K. 1993. *The Australian Geographic Book of Antarctica.* Australian Geographic, Sydney.

Scott Polar Research Institute 1995. *SPRI Review—95. 69th Annual Report of the Scott Polar Research Institute.* SPRI, University of Cambridge, Cambridge, U.K.

Scott, R.F. 1987. *Scott's Last Expedition: The Journals.* Methuen, London.

Shackleton, E. 1932. *The Heart of the Antarctic.* William Heinemann, London.

Shackley, M. 1995. "The future of gorilla tourism in Rwanda." *Journal of Sustainable Tourism,* Vol. 3, No. 2, pp. 61-71.

Shapley, D. 1985. *The Seventh Continent: Antarctica in a Resource Age.* Resources for the Future, Inc., Washington, DC.

Shaw, G. and Williams, A.M. 1994. *Critical Issues in Tourism—A Geographical Perspective.* Blackwell Publishers, Oxford.

Shaw, S.D. 1991. "Call for action on Antarctica." Pacific Asia Travel Association, *PATA—Bali Daily Update,* No. 4, p. 2.

Sitwell, N. 1992. "Worth saving: Getting to the bottom of the world." *Travel and Leisure Magazine,* December, pp. 56-64.

Slater, S. and Basch, H. 1989. "Guidelines for cruising in Antarctica." *The Boston Herald,* December 31 (unpaginated).

Slaughter, R.A. 1988. *Recovering the Future.* Graduate School of Environmental Science, Monash University, Melbourne.

Slaughter, R.A. (Ed.) 1989. *Studying the Future—An Introductory Reader.* Commission for the Future and The Australian Bicentennial Authority, Canberra.

Smith, P. 1992. "Cruising in Mawson's Antarctica." *Australian Geographic,* No. 25, January-March, pp. 97-113.

Smith, R.I.L., Walton, D.W.H., and Dingwall, P.R. 1994. *Developing the Antarctic Protected Area System.* Proceedings of the SCAR/IUCN Workshop on Antarctic

Protected Areas, Cambridge, U.K., June 29-July 2, 1992. IUCN, Cambridge, U.K.

Smith, S.L.J. 1989. *Tourism Analysis.* Longman Scientific and Technical, Burnt Mill, Harlow, U.K.

Smith, V.L. (Ed.) 1989. *Hosts and Guests: The Anthropology of Tourism.* The University of Pennsylvania Press, Philadelphia.

Smith, V.L. 1993. "What have we learned from Antarctica: A tourism case study." Paper presented to the Arctic Tourism and Ecotourism Symposium, 5th World Wilderness Conference/1st Northern Forum, Tromso, Norway, September 24-October 1.

Smith, V.L. 1994. "A sustainable Antarctic—Science and tourism." *Annals of Tourism Research,* Vol. 21, No. 2, pp. 221-230.

Smith, V.L. and Eadington, W.R. (Eds.) 1992. *Tourism Alternatives—Potentials and Problems in the Development of Tourism,* University of Pennsylvania Press, Philadelphia.

Society Expeditions 1990. *Antarctica Visitor Guidelines and Antarctica Tour Operator Guidelines.* Society Expedition, Seattle, Washington.

South China Morning Post 2000. "Cruise line cleans up act." October 2, p. 5. Hong Kong.

Southern Heritage Expeditions 1995. *Antarctica—The Other Side.* Tour brochure, Christchurch. Southern Heritage Expeditions.

Southern Heritage Expeditions 1996. *Mawson's Antarctica.* Tour brochure, Christchurch. Southern Heritage Expeditions.

Sparks, J. and Soper, T. 1987. *Penguins,* Second Edition. Macmillan, Melbourne.

Spence, S.A. 1966. *Antarctica: Its Books and Papers from the Earliest to the Present Time.* Mitcham, Surrey, England.

Splettstoesser, J. and Folks, M.C. 1994. "Environmental guidelines for tourism in Antarctica." *Annals of Tourism Research,* Vol. 21, No. 2, pp. 231-244.

Splettstoesser, J. and Smith, V. 1994. "Antarctic tourism: A successful union for tourism and the environment." Paper presented at the symposium Sustainable Tourism Development at the IIPT Montreal conference Building a Sustainable World Through Tourism, September 12-16. Montreal, Canada.

Splettstoesser, J.F., Headland, R.K., and Todd, F. 1997. "First Circumnavigation of Antarctica by Tourist Ship." *Polar Record* 33(186): 244-245. Scott Polar Research Institute, University of Cambridge, U.K.

Steele, P. 1995. "Ecotourism: An economic analysis." *Journal of Sustainable Tourism,* Vol. 3, No. 1, pp. 29-44.

Steger, W. 1990a. "Into the teeth of the ice—Six across Antarctica." *National Geographic,* Vol. 178, No. 5, pp. 67-93.

Steger, W. 1990b. "Trans-Antarctic crossing planned for 1990." *Antarctic,* Vol. 11, No. 7/12, pp. 300-303.

Stephenson, L. 1993. "Managing visitors to Macquarie Island—A model for Antarctica?" *ANARE News,* No. 73, pp. 8-9.

Stewardson, C. 1997. *Mammals of the Ice.* Sedona Publishing, Braddon, Australia.

Stonehouse, B. 1965. "Counting Antarctic animals." *New Scientist,* Vol. 25, (454) pp. 273-276.

Stonehouse, B. 1990a. "A traveller's code for Antarctic visitors." *Polar Record,* Vol. 26, No. 156, pp. 56-58.

Stonehouse, B. 1990b. *North Pole—South Pole: A Guide to the Ecology and Resources of the Arctic and Antarctic.* Prion, London.

Stonehouse, B. 1992a. "Monitoring ship-borne visitors in Antarctica: A preliminary field study." *Polar Record,* Vol. 28, No. 166, pp. 213-218.

Stonehouse, B. 1992b. "IAATO: An association of Antarctic tour operators." *Polar Record,* Vol. 28, No. 167, October.

Stonehouse, B. 1993. "Shipborne tourism in Antarctica: Scott Polar Research Institute studies 1992-1993." *Polar Record,* Vol. 28, No. 167, pp. 330-332.

Stonehouse, B. 1994. "Ecotourism in Antarctica." In Cater, E. and Lowman, G. (Eds.), *Ecotourism: A Sustainable Option?* John Wiley and Sons, London, pp. 195-212.

Stonehouse, B. (Ed.) 1995a. *Management Recommendations for Visitor Sites in the Antarctic Region: Petermann, Hovgaard, and Pleneau Islands.* Project Atlantic Conservation, Scott Polar Research Institute, University of Cambridge, Cambridge.

Stonehouse, B. (Ed.) 1995b. *Management Recommendations for Visitor Sites in the Antarctic Region: Turret Point and Penguin Island.* Project Antarctic Conservation, Scott Polar Research Institute, University of Cambridge.

Stonehouse, B. 2000. *The Last Continent—Discovering Antarctica.* SCP Books Ltd. (Published in the USA by Odyssey Publishing Ltd. in association with SCP Books Ltd.), Westdene House, Burgh Castle, Norfolk, England.

Stonehouse, B. and Crosbie, K. 1995. "Tourist impacts and management in the Antarctic Peninsula." In Hall, C.M. and Johnston, M.E. (Eds.), *Polar Tourism: Tourism in the Arctic and Antarctic Regions.* Wiley, Chichester, pp. 217-233.

Stonehouse, B., Crosbie, K., and Girard, L. 1996. "Sustainable tourism in the Arctic and Antarctic." In Girard, L. (Ed.), *Ecotourism in the Polar regions,* Proceedings of the Third Symposium on Polar Ecotourism, St. Petersburg, Russia, October 23-26, 1995, A Pas de Loup, Paris.

Sugden, D. 1982. *Arctic and Antarctic: A Modern Geographical Synthesis.* Basil Blackwell, Oxford, U.K.

Sullivan, W. 1963. *Quest for a Continent: The Story of the Antarctic.* McGraw Hill, New York.

Suter, K. 1991. *Antarctica—Private Property or Public Heritage?* Pluto Press, Leichhardt, New South Wales.

Swan, R. 1990. *Icewalk.* Jonathan Cape, London.

Swithinbank, C. 1988. "Antarctic Airways: Antarctica's first commercial airline." *Polar Record,* Vol. 24, No. 151, pp. 313-316.

Swithinbank, C. 1990. "Non-government aircraft in the Antarctic 1989/90." *Polar Record,* Vol. 26, No. 159, p. 316.

Swithinbank, C. 1994. "Non-government aircraft in the Antarctic 1993/94." *Polar Record,* Vol. 30, No. 174, p. 221.

Talmadge, J. 1991. "Antarctic tourism." Paper delivered at the PATA 40th Annual Conference, Bali, April 12.

Tangley, L. 1988. "Who's polluting Antarctica?" *Bio Science,* Vol. 38, No. 9, pp. 590-594.

Tasmanian Department of Parks, Wildlife and Heritage 1991. *Macquarie Island Nature Reserve Management Plan.* Hobart.

Taubenfeld, H.J. 1988. "The Antarctic and outer space: An analogy in retrospect." In Joyner, C.C. and Chopra, S.K. (Eds.), *The Antarctic Legal Regime.* Martinus Nijhoff Publishers, Dordrecht, Netherlands, pp. 269-281.

Terraquest 2000. World Wide Web site <http://www.terraquest.com>.

Thomas, L. 1963. *Sir Hubert Wilkins: His World of Adventure.* Readers Book Club, London.

Thomas, T. 1994. "Ecotourism in Antarctica: The role of the naturalist-guide in presenting places of natural interest." *Journal of Sustainable Tourism,* Vol. 2, No. 4, pp. 204-209.

Thomson, R.B. 1977. "Effects of human disturbance on an Adélie penguin rookery and measures of control." In Llano, G.A. (Ed.), *Adaptations Within Antarctic Ecosystems.* Proceedings of the third SCAR symposium on Antarctic biology, August 26-30, 1974, Smithsonian Institute, Washington, DC, pp. 1177-1180.

Thomson, R.B. 1978. "Transport and tourism in Antarctic development." In Vicuna, F.O. and Araya, A.S. (Eds.), *El desarollo de la Antartida.* Editorial Universitaria, Santiago de Chile, pp. 290-294.

Thwaites, R. 1990. "Across the ice." *Habitat Australia,* Vol. 18, No. 4, pp. 20-23.

Tindle, R.W. 1983. "Galapagos conservation and tourism—11 years on." *Oryx,* Vol. 17, No. 3, pp. 127-129.

Tisdell, C. 1984. *Tourism, the Environment, International Trade and Public Economics.* ASEAN-Australia Joint Research Project, Kuala Lumpur and Canberra.

Tobias, M. 1989. "The next wasteland—Can the spoiling of Antarctica be stopped?" *The Sciences,* New York Academy of Sciences, March/April, pp. 19-24.

Triggs, G. 1986. *International Law and Australian Sovereignty in Antarctica.* Legal Books, Sydney.

Turismo y Hoteles Cabo de Hornos SA 1990. *Adventure Tourism in Antarctica.* Promotional brochure, Santiago de Chile.

Turner, G.A. 1979. "A strategy for the preservation and management of historic sites in the Ross Dependency Antarctica." Department of Lands and Survey, Wellington, New Zealand.

United States Government 1997. "Environmental impact assessment of non-governmental activities in Antarctica." *Federal Register,* Vol. 62, No. 83, April 30, p. 23,538.

Urry, J. 1990. *The Tourist Gaze: Leisure and Travel in Contemporary Societies.* Sage Publications, London.

Valentine, P. 1991. "Nature-based tourism." In Hall, M. and Weiler, B. (Eds.), *Special Interest Tourism* (pp. 105-107), Belhaven Press, London.

Venables, S. 1991. *Island at the Edge of the World.* Hodder and Stoughton, London.

Vicuña, F.O. 1988. "Air traffic in Antarctica—the need for a legal regime." In Wolfrum R. (Ed.), *Antarctic Challenge,* Vol. 3. Duncker and Humblot, Berlin, pp. 397-431.

Vicuña, F.O. 1988. *Antarctic Mineral Exploitation: The Emerging Local Framework.* Cambridge University Press, Cambridge, U.K.

Vidas, D. 1992. "Antarctic tourism: A challenge to the legitimacy of the Antarctic Treaty System?" *IARP Publication Series,* No. 6, pp. 1-35, Fridtjof Nansen Institute, Lysaker, Norway.

Viken, A. 1995. "Tourism experiences in the Arctic—The Svalbard case." In Hall, C.M. and Johnston, M.E. (Eds.), *Polar Tourism: Tourism in the Arctic and Antarctic Regions.* Wiley, Chichester, pp. 73-84.

Wace, B. 1977. "Day trip to Antarctica." *Geographical Magazine,* Vol. 50, No. 2, pp. 137-138.

Wace, N. 1990. "Antarctica: A new tourist destination." *Applied Geography,* Vol. 10, pp. 327-341.

Wall, G. 1994. "Ecotourism: Old wine in new bottles?" *Trends,* Vol. 31, No. 2, pp. 4-9.

West, J.V. 1994. "Antarctic odyssey." *Astronomy,* Vol. 22, No. 10, pp. 14-16.

Wheeller, B. 1991. "Tourism's troubled times—Responsible tourism is not the answer." *Tourism Management,* Vol. 12, No. 9, pp. 91-96.

Wheeller, B. 1993. "Sustaining the ego." *Journal of Sustainable Tourism,* Vol. 1, No. 2, pp. 121-129.

Wheeller, B., Hart, T., and Whysall, P. 1990. "Application of the Delphi technique. A reply to Green, Hunter and Moore." *Tourism Management,* Vol. 11, June, pp. 121-122.

Wheelwright, S. and Makridakis, S. 1985. *Forecasting Methods for Management.* John Wiley and Sons, New York.

Whelan, H. 1996. "Antarctica's new explorers." *Australian Geographic,* Vol. 11, No. 42, April-June, pp. 80-97.

Whelan, T. (Ed.) 1991. *Nature Tourism Managing for the Environment.* Island Press, Washington, DC.

White, A. and Epler, B. 1972. *Galapagos Islands Guidebook.* National Parks Service, Puerto Ayora, Ecuador.

White, K.J. 1994. "Tourism and the Antarctic economy." *Annals of Tourism Research,* Vol. 21, No. 2, pp. 245-268.

Wight, P. 1993. "Ecotourism: Ethics or eco-sell?" *Journal of Travel Research,* Vol. 31, No. 3, pp. 3-9.

Wilder, M. 1992. *Antarctica: An Economic History of the Last Continent.* Department of Economic History, University of Sydney, Sydney.

Wilkness, P.E. 1989. "Polar regions: Research in a changing world." *American Meteorological Society Bulletin,* Vol. 70, No. 2, pp. 160-164.

Williams, W. 1988. *Antarctic Tourism.* Unpublished Graduate Diploma thesis, Kuring-Gai College of Advanced Education, Sydney.

Wilson, J.H. and Keating, B. 1990. *Business Forecasting.* Irwin, Homewood, Illinois.

Woodley, S. 1993. "Tourism and sustainable development in parks and protected areas." In Nelson, J.G., Butler, R., and Wall, G. (Eds.), *Tourism and Sustainable Development: Monitoring, Planning, Managing* (pp. 83-95). Heritage Resources Centre Joint Publication No. 1, University of Waterloo, Waterloo, Ontario, Canada.

World Commission on Environment and Development 1987. *Our Common Future.* Oxford University Press, Oxford, U.K.

Wouters, M. and Hall, C.M. 1995a. "Managing tourism in the sub-Antarctic islands." In Hall, C.M. and Johnston, M.E. (Eds.), *Polar Tourism: Tourism in the Arctic and Antarctic Regions.* Wiley, Chichester, pp. 257-276.

Wouters, M. and Hall, C.M. 1995b. "Tourism and New Zealand's sub-Antarctic islands." In Hall, C.M. and Johnston, M.E. (Eds.), *Polar Tourism: Tourism in the Arctic and Antarctic Regions.* Wiley, Chichester, pp. 277-296.

Wright, J.P. and Schaal, D. 1988. "Groupthink: The trap of consensus investing." *Journal of Financial Planning,* Vol. 1, No. 1, pp. 41-44.

WTO 1997. *Yearbook of Tourism Statistics.* Vol. I, 49 Edition. World Tourism Organization, Madrid, p. 2.

WTO 2000. *News from the WTO.* World Tourism Organization. <www.world-tourism.org>.

WWF 1995. "Arctic Tourism Guidelines." *WWF Arctic Bulletin* No. 3. pp. 8-17. WWF Arctic program, Oslo, Norway.

Wylie, J. 1994. *Journey Through a Sea of Islands: A Review of Forest Tourism in Micronesia.* Institute of Pacific Islands Forestry, U.S.D.A. Forest Service, Ogden, Utah.

Yong, Y.W., Keng, K.A., and Leng, T.L. 1989. "A Delphi forecast for the Singapore tourism industry: Future scenario and marketing implications." *International Marketing Review (UK),* Vol. 6, No. 3, pp. 35-46.

Young, M. 1992. "Ecotourism—Profitable Conservation?" In Hay, J.E. (Ed.), *Ecotourism Business in the Pacific: Promoting a Sustainable Experience* (p. 55). Conference proceedings, Environmental Science Department, University of Auckland, New Zealand.

Index

Page numbers followed by the letter "t" indicate tables.

Svalbard *(continued)*
  Norway sovereignty, 29
  types of tourism in, 32
Swithinbank, Charles, 213
Syowa Station (Japan), 75

Tasmanian Department of Primary
    Industry, Water and
    Environment (DPINE), 34
Teniente Rodolfo Marsh Base (Chile),
    83, 98, 101, 129, 192, 213, 216
This Accursed Land, 50, 51
Tooluka, private yacht, 83
Torgersen Island, 134
Total Penguin, The, 45
Tour operators. *See also* International
    Association of Antarctica Tour
    Operators (IAATO)
  brochure accuracy, 166
  Delphi panel participants, 186, 187t
  Delphi panel responses, 189
  future Antarctic tourism, 207-208
  guides responsibilities in Galapagos
    Islands, 22
  guide-to-visitor ratio, 223
  IAATO regulations for, 115
  Madrid Protocol impact assessments,
    60
  number of passengers carried 2000,
    93
  ranking by passengers, 92t
  regulations in Svalbard, 30
  self-regulation, 114-117
  suggested code for in Arctic region,
    25
*Tour Operators' Initiative for
    Sustainable Tourism
    Development,* 11
Tourism. *See also* Antarctic tourism;
    Overflights; Ship-based tourism
  air-supported, 98-100, 204
  air-supported seaborne, 216-218
  beach, 181
  "carrying capacity," 5
  culturally aware, 7, 8
  definitions, 6, 15
  detrimental effects data, 5
  and the environment, 4-11
  environmental impact, 10, 11, 121

Tourism *(continued)*
  future trend study, 181
  global expansion, 3
  industry development, 2
  mass, 3, 4, 8
  "overnight" definition, 10
  socially conscious, 3, 5
  socioeconomic impact, 121
  special interest, 7
  types in Svalbard, 32
  wilderness, 19
  yacht-based, 89, 205, 219
"Tourism and Conservation: Conflict,
    Coexistence or Symbiosis," 6
Tourism Board of Tierra del Fuego
    (INFUETUR), visitor profiles,
    142
Tourists, types of, 69. *See also*
    Antarctic tourists, Visitor,
    characteristics
Turret Point, 212

"Undiscovered," destinations, 3
UNESCO
  Galapagos Islands World Heritage
    site, 22
  tourism seminar, 4-5
United Nations
  Department of Economic and Social
    Affairs, 70
  Environment Program, 11
  Rome Conference on International
    Travel and Tourism, 69
United States Antarctic Program
    (USAP), 186
Ushuaia, Argentina, 84, 118, 221

Vernadsky Station, 129
Victorian Tourism Award for
    Environmental Tourism, 108
"Virtual reality," flying above
    Antarctica, 101
"Visitor," definition, 69
Visitor characteristics
  overflights, 171t, 172t
  ship-based, 151t, 160t
Visitor motivation, 73
  overflights, 171, 173t

HAWORTH HOSPITALITY PRESS
Hospitality, Travel, and Tourism
K. S. Chon, PhD, Editor-in-Chief

TOURISM IN THE ANTARCTIC: OPPORTUNITIES, CONSTRAINTS, AND FUTURE PROSPECTS by Thomas G. Bauer. (2001). "Thomas Bauer presents a wealth of detailed information on the challenges and opportunities facing tourism operators in this last great tourism frontier." *David Mercer, PhD, Associate Professor, School of Geography & Environmental Science, Monash University, Melbourne, Australia*

SERVICE QUALITY MANAGEMENT IN HOSPITALITY, TOURISM, AND LEISURE edited by Jay Kandampully, Connie Mok, and Beverley Sparks. (2001). "A must read. . . . a treasure. . . . pulls together the work of scholars across the globe, giving you access to new ideas, international research, and industry examples from around the world." *John Bowen, Professor and Director of Graduate Studies, William F. Harrah College of Hotel Administration, University of Nevada, Las Vegas*

TOURISM IN SOUTHEAST ASIA: A NEW DIRECTION edited by K. S. (Kaye) Chon. (2000). "Presents a wide array of very topical discussions on the specific challenges facing the tourism industry in Southeast Asia. A great resource for both scholars and practitioners." *Dr. Hubert B. Van Hoof, Assistant Dean/Associate Professor, School of Hotel and Restaurant Management, Northern Arizona University*

THE PRACTICE OF GRADUATE RESEARCH IN HOSPITALITY AND TOURISM edited by K. S. Chon. (1999). "An excellent reference source for students pursuing graduate degrees in hospitality and tourism." *Connie Mok, PhD, CHE, Associate Professor, Conrad N. Hilton College of Hotel and Restaurant Management, University of Houston, Texas*

THE INTERNATIONAL HOSPITALITY MANAGEMENT BUSINESS: MANAGEMENT AND OPERATIONS by Larry Yu. (1999). "The abundant real-world examples and cases provided in the text enable readers to understand the most up-to-date developments in international hospitality business." *Zheng Gu, PhD, Associate Professor, College of Hotel Administration, University of Nevada, Las Vegas*

CONSUMER BEHAVIOR IN TRAVEL AND TOURISM by Abraham Pizam and Yoel Mansfeld. (1999). "A must for anyone who wants to take advantage of new global opportunities in this growing industry." *Bonnie J. Knutson, PhD, School of Hospitality Business, Michigan State University*

LEGALIZED CASINO GAMING IN THE UNITED STATES: THE ECONOMIC AND SOCIAL IMPACT edited by Cathy H. C. Hsu. (1999). "Brings a fresh new look at one of the areas in tourism that has not yet received careful and serious consideration in the past." *Muzaffer Uysal, PhD, Professor of Tourism Research, Virginia Polytechnic Institute and State University, Blacksburg*

HOSPITALITY MANAGEMENT EDUCATION edited by Clayton W. Barrows and Robert H. Bosselman. (1999). "Takes the mystery out of how hospitality management education programs function and serves as an excellent resource for individuals interested in pursuing the field." *Joe Perdue, CCM, CHE, Director, Executive Masters Program, College of Hotel Administration, University of Nevada, Las Vegas*

MARKETING YOUR CITY, U.S.A.: A GUIDE TO DEVELOPING A STRATEGIC TOURISM MARKETING PLAN by Ronald A. Nykiel and Elizabeth Jascolt. (1998). "An excellent guide for anyone involved in the planning and marketing of cities and regions. . . . A terrific job of synthesizing an otherwise complex procedure." *James C. Maken, PhD, Associate Professor, Babcock Graduate School of Management, Wake Forest University, Winston-Salem, North Carolina*

TO ORDER: CALL: 1-800-429-6784 / FAX: 1-800-895-0582 (Outside US/Canada: + 607-771-0012) / E-MAIL: getinfo@haworthpressinc.com

☐ YES, please send me **Tourism in the Antarctic**

___ in hard at $79.95 ISBN: 0-7890-1103-4.
___ in soft at $39.95 ISBN: 0-7890-1104-2.

- Individual orders outside US, Canada, and Mexico must be prepaid by check or credit card.
- Postage & handling: In US: $4.00 for first book, $1.50 for each additional book.
  Outside US: $5.00 for first book; $2.00 for each additional book.
- Canadian residents: please add appropriate sales tax after postage & handling.
- 5+ text prices are not available for jobbers and wholesalers.
  Discounts are not available on 5+ text prices and not available in conjunction with any other discount. • Discount not applicable on books priced under $15.00.
- Canadian residents: please add 7% GST after postage & handling. Canadian residents of Newfoundland, Nova Scotia, and New Brunswick, also add 8% for province tax. • Payment in UNESCO coupons welcome.
- If paying in Canadian dollars, use current exchange rate to convert to US dollars.
- Please allow 3-4 weeks for delivery after publication.
- Prices and discounts subject to change without notice.

Signature _____

☐ BILL ME LATER ($5 service charge will be added).
(Not available for individuals outside US/Canada/Mexico. Service charge is waived for/jobbers/wholesalers/booksellers.)
☐ Check here if billing address is different from shipping address and attach purchase order and billing address information.

☐ PAYMENT ENCLOSED $ _____
(Payment must be in US or Canadian dollars by check or money order drawn on a US or Canadian bank.)

☐ PLEASE BILL MY CREDIT CARD:

☐ AmEx ☐ Diners Club ☐ Discover ☐ Eurocard ☐ JCB ☐ Master Card ☐ Visa

Account Number _____

Expiration Date _____

Signature _____

THE HAWORTH PRESS, INC., 10 Alice Street, Binghamton, NY 13904-1580 USA

Please complete the information below or tape your business card in this area.

NAME _____

INSTITUTION _____

ADDRESS _____

CITY _____

STATE _____ ZIP _____

COUNTRY _____

COUNTY (NY residents only) _____

E-MAIL _____
(type or print clearly!)

May we use your e-mail address for confirmations and other types of information? ( ) Yes ( ) No We appreciate receiving your e-mail address and fax number. Haworth would like to e-mail or fax special discount offers to you, as a preferred customer. We will never share, rent, or exchange your e-mail address or fax number. We regard such actions as an invasion of your privacy.

☐ YES, please send me **Tourism in the Antarctic** (ISBN: 0-7890-1104-2) to consider on a 60-day **no risk** examination basis. I understand that I will receive an invoice payable within 60 days, or that **if I decide to adopt the book, my invoice will be cancelled**. I understand that I will be billed at the lowest price. (60-day offer available only to teaching faculty in US, Canada, and Mexico.) / Outside US/ Canada, a proforma invoice will be sent upon receipt of your request and must be paid in advance of shipping. A full refund will be issued with proof of adoption.

Signature _____

Course Title(s) _____

Current Text(s) _____

Enrollment _____

Semester _____ Decision Date _____

Office Tel _____ Hours _____

This information is needed to process your examination copy order.

FAX

② ㉘ 06/01   BIC01